TV BABYLON

Paul Donnelley is a professional journalist.
This is his third book.

PAUL DONNELLEY
TV BABYLON

VISTA

First published in Great Britain 1997
as a Vista paperback original

Vista is an imprint of the Cassell Group
Wellington House, 125 Strand, London WC2R 0BB

All photographs are reproduced by courtesy of
Dataday Productions Archives.

A catalogue record for this book is
available from the British Library.

ISBN 0 575 60167 1

Designed and typeset by Digital Artworks Partnership Ltd.

Printed and bound in Great Britain
by Cox & Wyman Ltd, Reading, Berks

97 98 99   10 9 8 7 6 5 4 3 2 1

For Sharon, with much love . . . always

'Television won't last. It's a flash in the pan.'

Mary Somerville,
radio presenter, 1948

In 1925 the editor of the *Daily Express* was told that John Logie Baird was in reception. He informed a reporter: 'For God's sake go down to reception and get rid of a lunatic who's down there. He says he's got a machine for seeing by wireless! Watch him – he may have a razor on him.'

CONTENTS

INTRODUCTION

F. Scott Fitzgerald said the rich are different. Yes, replied Ernest Hemingway, they have more money. The same could be said of the citizens of TV Babylon. That, however, is one of the few differences between them and you and me – the ordinary people who enter Babylon by switching on our television sets to see our favourite programmes and, sometimes, our favourite stars. Babylonians are, for the most part, the same as us. They eat, excrete and are on heat the same as us. Probably more than us in the last respect – they get more opportunities.

This country was the first in the world to have a regular television service when the BBC took to the air in 1936. Just under twenty years later, in September 1955, the Beeb was joined by ITV. The BBC split into two in April 1964 and Channel 4 joined the throng in November 1982. Channel 5 will be on air by the time this book is published. Satellite and cable stations provide us with further opportunities to watch the 'haunted goldfish bowl'. British television at its best outdoes programming from anywhere in the world. What other country could produce drama like *Brideshead Revisited* or comedy like *Fawlty Towers* and *Only Fools and Horses*? Sure, there is some appalling television but there are many jewels among the dross. Andy Warhol once opined that in the future everyone would be famous for fifteen minutes and television chatshows like *The Oprah Winfrey Show, Kilroy!* and *The Time The Place* seem to be proving Warhol's maxim. Does it take any special talent to *be* on television? No. Does it take any special talent to *stay* on television? Yes. However, talent does not excuse bad behaviour of any kind, be it criminal or sexual.

A few years ago the Canadian magician James Randi presented a series of shows on British television that sought to debunk myths. That is one of the aims of this book. An irate – not to mention stupid – female viewer wrote to the *Daily Mirror* lambasting Randi, saying that people needed something to believe in, whether it was fairies, UFOs or Uri Geller. Why? Why do people want to believe their idols are perfect? Why did it take the public forty years to believe Rock Hudson was gay? If it hadn't been for his tragic death many of his fans would still refuse to believe it.

I intend to show that our idols do have foibles, are possessed of feet of clay and in most cases are very far from perfect. I believe this is actually what makes them interesting. Can anyone say their enjoyment of *EastEnders* was lessened because, it seemed, half the cast had criminal records and one, Leslie Grantham, was a convicted murderer? No, of course not. Yet the press offices and agents of celebrities would deny us this knowledge, insisting their clients lead and have led a blameless life. People will refuse to believe facts about stars that portray them in a less than flattering light. As Michael Barrymore said of his audience when he came out in a London gay pub, 'The old dears won't believe it anyway.' One of the most ridiculous statements to emanate from someone's lips is the refusal to believe their favourite star could be homosexual because 'they are married'. Rock Hudson was married. Liberace was engaged – twice! What difference does it make if the idol is gay? It's hardly likely that the fan will ever meet their hero and if they do the hero is most unlikely to rush them off to bed (unless it's *EastEnders'* Steve McFadden, of course).

I believe the majority of stories in this book are told sympathetically. The next time you see one of the people in this book on the telly, just remember – they may be famous, they may be rich, they may be attractive but they are human just like you and me. Well, me anyway.

BAD BOYS & GIRLS IN BABYLON

There are some inhabitants of Babylon who attract bad press wherever they go – usually because of their own bad behaviour. While some are featured in other chapters such as 'Soap in Babylon' and 'Sex in Babylon', here are a fistful that we thought should be the subject of in-depth investigation. Ladies and gentlemen, we give you five of the baddest boys and girls currently in Babylon . . .

Nick Nick – Jim Davidson

Although he was already well known in the pubs and clubs around South-East London, it was on the talent show *New Faces* that 5´ 10 ½˝ comedian Jim Davidson first came to public attention. Since then Davidson has probably become as well known for his right-wing political beliefs, his drinking and his numerous affairs as he is for hosting *Big Break* and *The Generation Game*.

Born at 118 Holburne Road, Kidbrooke, London on 13 December 1953, Davidson lost his virginity aged 15 with a younger girl called Jane. Davidson's youth was filled with drugs – he freely admits he indulged in more than his fair share of LSD and cocaine and he also sold drugs when he was 19. The previous year he had taken his first trip up the aisle when, on 6 November 1971, at Woolwich Town Hall Register Office he had married Sue Walpole who was pregnant with his first child. Sarah was born on 25 April 1972 at 5.20 a.m.

Unsurprisingly, the marriage wasn't to last and they divorced. Wife number two was former promotions girl Julie Gullick, four years younger than him, whom he wed at Poole Register Office on 23 July 1981. Their son, Cameron, was born on 12 August 1982. During a stag night at the Strand Palace Hotel when he was married to his second wife Davidson had sex with nine prostitutes, sniffed coke and then had three more. Jim Davidson is very much a male chauvinist and Julie annoyed him because she was as unfaithful as he was. At one stage he pulled a replica gun on her lover, record plugger Gary Farrow, now Jonathan Ross's manager. Davidson and Julie divorced.

Davidson has had his brushes with the law, despite or perhaps because of his 'Nick! Nick!' routine about policemen having their brains removed and replaced by a 'nickometer' when they join the job. He has twice lost his driving licence for speeding. On 7 May 1985 he was fined £250 for possessing an Argentinian officer's gun.

Davidson's third wife was TV presenter Alison Holloway, eight years his junior, whom he took unto him on 19 February 1987. Alison has a fiery temper and the match ended in violence seven months later. Jim was constantly unfaithful to Alison and so was her third husband. Alison has finally found happiness on her fourth marriage (in Las Vegas on 13 April 1996) to American TV producer Burt Kearns.

Davidson was alleged to have had an affair with Fiona Wright, yet 'I only met her once.' Among the other women he has dallied with are: 6´ Brummy page 3 girl Janine Andrews for three months, who labelled him 'Sick Sick' – he threw a bottle of Remy Martin through a double-glazed window at her flat; call girl Pamella Bordes; gymnast-turned-television-presenter Suzanne Dando; his blonde housekeeper Lesley Smith; singer Tricia Duskey whom he was with for nine months and actress Lesley Ash for a month.

In September 1987 he took former topless model and prostitute Sandy Ross to his twelfth floor £150-a-night room at the Holiday Inn, Marble Arch, where, after drinking champagne, he became abusive and punched her twice in the mouth. She said, 'I would have charged Jim £200 for sex – but he wanted it for half price. He kept saying I wasn't doing my job properly. He was treating me like some street corner slut.' (No! Surely not!)

Wife number four Tracy Hilton was another former topless model who had a rhinoplasty in March 1990, and refused to marry him until after their son was born. She once broke her big toe kicking a door during an argument. Davidson eventually married Hilton in Barbados on 2 February 1990. They have three children with the old-fashioned names Charlie, Fred and Elsie. The marriage was punctuated with Davidson's alcoholism. In an interview in January 1995 Tracy revealed, 'A lot of the time I didn't like him. It had just become a relentless tirade of abuse. If he wasn't working he'd be up the pub drinking. Finally, twelve months ago, I decided that I just wanted our marriage to be ended. And it would have been because if Jim had carried on drinking, he'd be dead by now. Jim is a male chauvinist and is exasperating – that I can live with. But when he was a drunk, he was just impossible.' Although the Davidsons tried to make a go of their marriage they separated in early January 1996. Davidson described Tracy as 'a great mum, a good cook and fabulous at ironing but she doesn't understand how to be a wife'. Davidson was linked with 29-year-old estate agent Lisa Hyams, elder sister of actress Simone who had an affair with Michael Winner in 1992. Lisa Hyams admitted that Davidson had spent 'a couple of nights' at her rented semi-detached house in North London but said they were just friends. Later that year Jim was reconciled again with Tracy and their three children, but in March 1997 the marriage was reported to be finally over.

The Chris Evans Story

Born appropriately enough on April Fool's Day (1966) in Warrington, Cheshire, carrot-topped Chris Evans has two elder siblings – a brother David, twelve years his senior, and a sister Diane, three years older, from both of whom he is estranged. Chris left school at 16 and went through a remarkable twenty-one jobs in under four years. Probably his most bizarre was when he set up his own kissagram business, Kinky Kissagrams: The Skinniest Tarzans in Town. He began his career in showbiz in 1987 answering the fan mail for Timmy Mallett on Piccadilly Radio! That same year his girlfriend Alison Ward gave birth to his illegitimate daughter, Jade. Two years later, in 1989, he began to present *Round at Chris's* on London radio station GLR. His TV break came working for a satellite station but it was as the zany host of Channel 4's *The Big Breakfast* which he co-presented with Gaby Roslin that Chris first came to public notice. Always close to Gaby Roslin, Evans gave her his BAFTA award. In 1991 he married radio producer Carol McGiffin who used to be his landlady but the couple separated in August 1993 by mutual consent as Chris's star soared. While he was married Chris became friendly with a South African-born schoolteacher Brenda Kozen after meeting her at the Lingfield Health Club in Belsize Park, North London. A former aide to Chris believes that Brenda thought Chris would contact her when he left his wife. He didn't and instead began dating pop star Kim Wilde when she guest hosted *The Big Breakfast*, a highly publicized romance that came to nothing. Brenda died aged 31 of heart disease. Chris donated £1,000 to the school where she worked. The money went on a music system and tree planted in her memory.

Away from the safety of the studio at Lock Keeper's Cottages, Chris presented the Golden Rose of Montreux-winning *Don't Forget Your Toothbrush* also for Channel 4. It was said that the pilot did not go down well and when they filmed a second show Evans threatened to publicly humiliate anyone who did not seem to be enjoying themselves. Once the show was on air it was a miasma of laughs, games, celebrity pop guests (such as Roy Wood of Wizzard) and mess – 'Can you play golf with chicken curry?' A couple stood a chance to win a holiday in some romantic foreign location or a humble British seaside resort. The hostess on the show was Chris's model girlfriend Rachel Tatton-Brown, 25. Rachel had been a telephonist at the company that made the show until Chris made her production assistant and then promoted her to the hostess slot.

When the show returned for a second series Tatton-Brown's services had been dispensed with. She and Evans had gone their separate ways in October 1994 but that didn't surprise Carol McGiffin. 'She's a numbskull. She wouldn't have looked at him twice if he was a dustman. Women who wouldn't have given him a second glance before he appeared on the telly approach him because he's got fame and money.' Perhaps, but at least Rachel has not spoken out about her relationship with Chris, something that his estranged wife seems unable to stop herself doing. In December 1996 Carol was at it again. Apparently, she is still 'addicted to him. I can't get him out from under my skin. I annoy him and he annoys me.'

The glamour was now provided by Jadene Doran, on the show as 'Miss Let Your Hair Down'. The second series, which began on 26 November 1994, was as successful as the first. Evans had left *The Big Breakfast* at the beginning of October 1994. The format for *Toothbrush*, which was owned by Chris's production company, Ginger, was sold all around the world making Chris and John Revell, his producer, very wealthy men. Evans has always known when to get out on top and refused to make a third series of *Toothbrush*.

On 24 April 1995 he took over presenting the Radio 1 breakfast show and hosted a new show for Channel 4, *TFI Friday*. (As Evans was quick to point out, the 'F' did not stand for Four.) Although his professional career looked to be without parallel his personal life seemed to be suffering. He missed a breakfast show because he was too tired and emotional to turn up and was fined £7,000. He started another show with the words, 'At 2 a.m. last night I was lying on the cold tiles of a pub toilet floor, so drunk I couldn't even raise my head to puke.'

His relationships seemed to be going nowhere. His current friendship with researcher Suzi Aplin appears strained at best. According to two reports, he upset her when they attended a wedding in Ireland and he insisted that she wore a see-through outfit that clearly showed her underwear.

Evans has a reputation for being a perfectionist that often spills over into temper tantrums. One former colleague calls him 'the rudest, most objectionable bastard I've ever worked with'. An unconfirmed report has it that he would hold meetings in the nude to intimidate underlings. 'I earn £5,000 a week and I'm right,' he is said to have boasted. Not for Chris the usual showbiz sycophancy. He called Andi Peters 'talentless', David Mellor 'a joke' and said Anthea Turner's show was 'total shit'. He also lambasted a local DJ in Scotland when he took his Radio 1 show to the Highlands. Evans said his lowliest researcher earned £12,500 a year more than the DJ: 'We are successful. You're not. If you were any good, you wouldn't be on Moray Firth radio.' Despite earning a not inconsiderable amount of money, Chris has always been careful with it. 'He could peel an orange in his pocket,' is how one former girlfriend explained it. By his own admission he drove a hire car seventeen times around a car park to use up the petrol he had paid for in advance.

In November 1996 Chris turned up at the black tie Comedy Awards wearing a blue tracksuit top and was booed by the celebrity audience when he went up to collect his two prizes which he later gave to a surprised waitress. Three months later, on 15 January 1997, Chris resigned his Radio 1 slot after controller Matthew Bannister refused to let him work a four-day week. Rumours abounded that Chris's company Ginger was about to bid for the Channel 4 breakfast show. If he succeeds in becoming a TV mogul it will be a long way from the angry boy in Warrington.

Bad Grammer

Kelsey Grammer's character in *Cheers*, neurotic psychiatrist Dr Frasier Crane, was so popular that he was given his own spin-off series, *Frasier*. Grammer has led a checkered life and hasn't always managed to stay on the right side of the law.

Allen Kelsey Grammer was born on 21 February 1955 on St Thomas, one of the Virgin Islands. His parents divorced when he was just two. On 25 April 1968 Grammer's 38-year-old father was murdered by an insane taxi driver. When he was 18 Grammer claims he was offered a job bonking two women for $10,000 in a porn film called *The Bermuda Triangle*. He turned it down. Having been accepted to study acting at the prestigious Julliard School he was thrown out in 1975. That same summer saw one of the worst moments in Grammer's life when, on 30 June, his 18-year-old sister Karen was raped and murdered by three men. Dragged from the pavement outside the restaurant where she worked in Colorado Springs, she was taken to a nearby block of flats where at least one of the men raped her. Karen was then driven to a dark alley where she was thrown out of the car. When one of the men told her to look up, she did so, thinking her dreadful ordeal was almost over. Instead he pulled a knife and slit her throat and stabbed her. Karen dragged herself to a nearby caravan park where she bled to death. Her body would not be found until the next morning. Karen was the sixth victim in a seven-murder killing spree. Kelsey Grammer admits that was when he lost his faith. 'Before Karen's death I had an almost blind, naïve faith in God and the universe. I could see goodness and joy almost everywhere I looked. Karen's death changed that.' Death was again to visit the Grammer family. On 1 June 1980 his two half-brothers – Stephen and Billy – died in a freak diving accident. Stephen suffered an embolism in the sea and choked on his own vomit while Billy was eaten by sharks.

On 30 May 1982 Grammer married for the first time. His

wife was a pretty dancer called Doreen Alderman and he had met her at a party in New York. Marital bliss turned to wedded disharmony despite the birth of a daughter, Spencer Karen, in 1983 and the Grammers separated in 1984. The divorce wasn't finalised until 1990. Following the split Grammer was ordered to pay $52,000 a year in child support, more than he actually earned. Failure to comply with the maintenance order earned him ten days in the slammer, although the sentence was suspended. He still speaks with bitterness of the first Mrs Grammer.

The year of his separation saw Grammer win his first rôle in a major television series. He was cast as Dr Canard in the long-running daytime soap *Another World*. That year he auditioned for the rôle of Frasier Crane in *Cheers*. The character was due to appear in just six or seven episodes. Like many actors Grammer's heart was in the theatre but he was sensible enough to realize that half a dozen episodes of prime-time television would earn him more than a year treading the boards. Grammer claimed he had never seen *Cheers* and so had no idea what he was auditioning for. Whatever, he got the part. *Cheers* allowed Grammer to indulge in some of his favourite pastimes – drink and drugs. He had started using cocaine in 1979 and had also developed a liking for gin and tonic. Although a hit with the viewers, Grammer did not create a favourable impression with his co-stars, particularly Shelley Long. According to sources on the set, Long did her best to undermine Grammer's character by insisting some of his best, i.e. funniest lines were cut. The producers gave in to Long's demands because they believed she was one of the reasons the show was a hit. They were proved wrong when she eventually left to seek movie stardom, which has so far eluded her, and *Cheers* and Frasier continued to be successful.

Bizarrely for a TV star on a top-rated show Grammer lived in squalor. His house reeked of the Camel cigarettes he smoked and his ten dogs did nothing to freshen the ambience of the place. Most of his money either went to his ex-wife or up his nose. His then girlfriend, 27-year-old Cerlette Lamme, a

5′ 3″ former professional ice skater, left him because of his drugtaking although her replacement in his affections, model Teri McJessey, fared no better and Lamme was soon back on the scene.

In July 1987 he was arrested in Los Angeles for drunk driving and driving without a licence. As it was his first offence he pleaded no contest on 13 July and was given probation, ten days of community service and ordered to attend a rehabilitation programme. He was ordered to return to the court with proof he had carried out his punishment.

On 14 April 1988 Grammer was again arrested. This time he was charged with driving without a valid licence and not paying a speeding ticket. When he was hauled off to the station he admitted to the police he had approximately $25-worth of cocaine in his pocket. He avoided jail by asking to go on a 90-day rehabilitation programme. As on the first occasion, he did not complete the course.

On 6 February 1990 Grammer failed to report to court to provide evidence of his rehab programme following his 1987 arrest. Three months later, on 2 May, he again failed to show at Van Nuys Municipal Court for the April 1988 arrest. The night before he had been visiting bars. On that day a warrant was issued by Judge Aviva Bobb to bring Grammer into custody. Grammer surrendered to the police on 10 May 1990. On 24 May Kelsey Grammer went to prison to begin his 30-day sentence. However, due to jail overcrowding he was released after just ten days. On 6 August 1990 Grammer pleaded no contest to the possession of cocaine rap and threw himself on the judge's mercy saying he had been drinking alcohol since he was nine years old and admitted to using dope, marijuana and Ecstasy. Grammer was fined $500, put on probation for three years and sentenced to nine days' house arrest.

Being a TV star did nothing to harm Grammer's pulling power. As well as seeing the loyal Cerlette Lamme, Grammer was sowing his oats in many fields. In the autumn of 1991 his playing away came home to him when he discovered he was to become a father for the second time. The mother was not

Lamme but her best friend Barrie Buckner, a 29-year-old make-up artist, with whom he had been carrying on a secret two-year affair. Amazingly, Lamme stood by her man despite his drinking, drugtaking and rampant infidelities. Grammer insisted Buckner sign a confidentiality clause agreeing never to speak about him or their child or he would refuse to support her financially. (Buckner gave birth to a daughter she named Greer in summer 1992.)

In April 1992 Grammer met in a San Fernando Valley restaurant the woman who would become his second wife. Leigh-Ann Csuhany, 22, a 5′ 3″ Canadian, was working as an exotic dancer or, not to put too fine a point on it, a stripper. It was about this time that he and Lamme eventually split up after seven years. It is to Lamme's immense credit that she remained silent about her time with Grammer, never selling her story to a tabloid or seeking palimony. With Lamme out of the picture Grammer turned his attention full-time to romancing Csuhany. In May she left the Gotham City strip club in Canoga Park, Los Angeles where she had been working. Not all of Grammer's friends were enamoured with his new love. One described her as 'tacky and slutty', while another called her 'a typical gold-digger' – and they were among the kinder comments. On the night of 21/22 August 1992 the police were called to Grammer's home in Agoura Hills where there had been an altercation with Csuhany. They had argued over a feature in *Star* and she had smacked him in the left eye, giving him an impressive shiner. Csuhany was arrested for spousal abuse and taken to the police station where she was placed in handcuffs and leg irons because the police were worried she would injure herself. Five days later, Grammer told the police he did not want them to prosecute.

On 11 September 1992 Grammer secretly married the fiery ex-stripper in Lovelock, Nevada. It would be a tempestuous match fuelled by substance abuse and almighty rows and an underlying sexual passion that saw them join the 'Mile High Club'. When they were not bonking they were arguing and the arguments often became physical as Mrs Grammer regularly whacked her husband. He never struck her despite great provocation. In April 1993 on the top-rated *Arsenio Hall Show* Grammer announced that his wife was pregnant. The quarrels continued and during one she caused an almighty scene. The next day, 3 June 1993, Grammer served divorce papers on his wife and asked for the marriage to be annulled. The actor also claimed the ex-stripper was guilty of fraud and was of 'unsound mind'. He also asked for custody of his yet-to-be-born baby and hired bodyguards fearing an attempt by his estranged spouse on his life.

On 8 June 1993 Leigh-Ann attempted suicide at the Malibu Beach Inn by swallowing fifty Tylenol pills after drinking red wine and snorting cocaine. She was found by Los Angeles County Sheriff's deputies and rushed to Santa Monica Hospital where doctors saved her life and that of the baby. Two days later, Leigh-Ann underwent the abortion that Grammer had wanted. She blamed Grammer for breaking her heart. The couple were divorced on 13 September 1993 although Csuhany went on the tabloid TV show *Inside Edition* three days later tearfully begging Grammer to take her back. His response was to call the immigration department to have his ex-wife deported, claiming she was mentally unstable and a threat to his safety. Grammer went so far as to hire round-the-clock security. Leigh-Ann Csuhany-Grammer returned to stripping and billing herself as 'the wife of the *Cheers* star'.

Grammer's troubles were far, far from over. He was to be accused of having sex with a 15-year-old girl. In July 1993 he had been staying at the Somerset Hills Hotel in Watchung, New Jersey, while visiting some friends. These friends had a 5′ 9″ brunette teenage daughter and she went to Grammer's suite ostensibly to babysit his own daughter on 7 July 1993. That night Grammer allegedly had sex with her. The following month sex again allegedly took place, this time in Arizona. The teen's parents became suspicious and searched her belongings for clues. They were horrified to discover sexually explicit messages left for the girl on a phone line plus possibly incriminating letters that might suggest sexual intimacy. The parents called the police on 24 September 1993 but the girl refused to co-operate in the investigation. In November 1993 the *National Enquirer* and the TV show *A Current Affair* ran with stories that Grammer had had sex with a 15-year-old.

With a track record like his, most people would have stayed away from the gentle sex. Not Kelsey Grammer. Even as his life was being investigated once again he began dating a stunning blonde named Tammi Baliszewski who for simplicity's sake uses the surname Alexander. He even proposed to her and things seemed, for once, to be going Grammer's way on the romance front. However, 37-22-34 Tammi Jo Baliszewski from Kansas had a little secret of her own. She was a former nude model whose pictures had been used to advertise escort services in Las Vegas. Grammer promised his fiancée that he would give her a church wedding and set about getting his previous weddings annulled by the Catholic Church. Grammer didn't completely give up his old life. The night before he was due to host *Saturday Night Live* he visited Billy's, a Manhattan stripclub where he paid several of the dancers to disrobe for him.

A year after the allegations first surfaced, the teenage girl admitted that she had, indeed, slept with the TV star and had previously denied it because she was in love with him and didn't want to cause him any harm. She also admitted to using drugs including speed and marijuana. The jury heard 21 taped voice-mail messages Grammer had left the girl plus testimony from the girl. Prosecutor Nicholas Bissell, Jr, urged the jury to indict. On 24 February 1995 the grand jury of Somerset County voted not to indict Kelsey Grammer for statutory rape. His criminal ordeal was over.

In December 1995 Tammi Baliszewski Alexander, 33, decided she had had enough of Grammer and walked out on him. He pleaded with her to give him one more chance but in the summer of 1996 the devoutly Catholic Tammi finished with Grammer for good after discovering he had been constantly unfaithful to her. She found underwear belonging to other women in their bed. To get her revenge Tammi plans to write a kiss'n'tell book that reveals all Grammer's secrets. She will write about his obsession with strippers, how he went back to the bottle again and again, how he's the best lover she's ever had and his rages over what he considers to be sub-standard episodes of *Frasier*. There wasn't a problem in the bedroom. Tammi described Grammer as being 'like a lion. As a lover he's very passionate. We had quite a sex life at first. We made love every night.' Later she added, 'One night while we were making love, things got stranger than I ever imagined. All of a sudden he began to cry. He told me, "Leigh-Ann used to call me a fag. I'm not a fag. But I do want to know what it feels like to be a woman." Then he got up, put on my panties and reached for my bra. He really had a need to dress up in my underwear. Kelsey longed to be demeaned and dominated sexually. One night I found a note. He had written that because I wouldn't do certain things with him sexually, I should hire a surrogate female who would humiliate him ver-bally and physically. I also found out that Kelsey had had sex with one of my best friends.' Her final condemnatory words on her former fiancée were, 'Kelsey Grammer is an emotional vampire who sucked out all that was good in me and ended up throwing me away like an old handbag.'

On the evening of 21 September 1996 Grammer crashed his $75,000 red Dodge Viper sports car and the following month entered the Betty Ford Clinic in Palm Springs in a last-ditch attempt to fight his addiction. Meanwhile, Paramount stopped production of *Frasier*. His new girlfriend, blonde *Playboy* lin-gerie model Camille Donatacci, 28, has so far stood by him.

Where is Kelsey Grammer heading? Prison? Rehab? A pine box? No one, and that includes the man himself, knows but it will be one heck of a ride.

Rascally Ross

Paul Ross is the big brother of smooth-talking chat show host Jonathan. Unlike Jonathan who has been happily married for years to journalist Jane Goldman, author of a best-selling book on *The X Files*, Paul's marital track record is anything but smooth.

In 1977, aged just 20, Paul married his first wife, Anita. Both had been working in Sainsbury's when they met and they had a son in 1980. The marriage was destined not to last and Ross left his wife to move in with Kerry Bunce whom he had met one New Year's Eve. In 1988 he began an affair with blonde beauty Clare Staples, 23, and moved into a flat with her. Ross regularly showered Clare with love notes. In one he wrote, 'You were tall, solid, sad and funny, giggly, giving and sensational in bed.' The following year, Clare was out and Kerry was back in favour. Remarkably, Ross moved Kerry into the flat he had shared with Clare.

In an amazing twist Clare moved in with Anita Ross, Paul's ex-wife. That did not last long and Clare married but left her husband after a few months. Anita's divorce from Ross came through in 1990 by which time Kerry had given birth to their daughter, Dolly. Clare, the sister of Gladiator Zodiac, met TV hypnotist Paul McKenna when she saw his stage show. She later became his manager and fiancée but that relationship, too, was destined not to last. They separated in August 1995.

In 1991 with their second daughter, Violet, on the way Ross and Kerry were married with Danny Baker doing the honours as the best man. Two years later, Kerry gave birth to their third daughter, Bebe, while Ross was working on *The Big Breakfast*.

In October 1994 Ross began seeing chubby TV researcher Pippa Healy, 24, who worked with him on the LWT show *Big City*. Ross denied he was playing away from home despite a published picture of him kissing Healy and walking down the street holding hands. A blazing row ensued when Kerry Ross found out about her husband's infidelities but she agreed to take him back. The reconciliation worked because their fourth daughter, Hermione, was born early in 1996. Said Ross, 'That's the family complete – so I've had a vasectomy.'

The Pop Star and the Groupie

For many years singer Bob Geldof and TV presenter Paula Yates seemed showbiz's most golden, if unlikely, couple. He was the lead singer of punk band Boomtown Rats while she was the daughter of television's 'Bishop' Jess Yates and had made her name writing books about blondes and rock stars in their underwear and co-presenting television pop shows like *The Tube*.

Pouting Paula Yates preens for the camera

Paula Yates was born in Deganwy Castle, near Conwy, North Wales on 24 April 1960. Paula claims she was unable to speak or use the toilet until she was five. Her mother, former Bluebell girl Elaine who wrote sexy stories under the nom de plume Heller Toren, walked out on her when she was eight at which time Paula became anorexic. Her father locked her into an orange box while he played with his Wurlitzer. When she fell and cut her leg he wrapped a pair of his Y-fronts around the wound and left it. The garment grew into her leg and had to be surgically removed. By the age of 12 Paula was snorting heroin with an ex-jailbird. Fortunately, she didn't get hooked. She was sexually precocious: 'By the time I was about to hit 13, I thought I'd discovered the secret of success with men. You just dazzled them with your witty repartee and then gave them a blowjob while they were still wheezing from your last hilarious anecdote' – although Paula didn't have full sex until she was 17. At least that's the story she told in her autobiography. A family friend of the time has a different recollection. Mary Doylerush's daughter, Linda, was Paula's best friend from the age of five to 14. Far from being unable to speak Mrs Doylerush remembers that Paula 'always spoke beautifully and certainly knew how to use the toilet'. The desertion by her mother could not have happened when Paula was eight because cinefilm exists of a family gathering when Paula was 10. Her father is remembered as a popular figure and far from wrapping his underpants around Paula's injured leg, he took her straight to hospital. The anorexia claim is also refuted as Mrs Doylerush remembers Paula scoffing plates of baked beans with Dairylea triangles melted on top. Finally, neither Paula nor Linda appeared to have time for boys which makes her claims of teenage fellatio seem suspect.

Geldof and Yates got together in late 1977 and Yates gave the nine years older Geldof a blowjob in the back of his limo because she assumed that's what groupies did. In his autobiography *Is That It?* Geldof reveals that he thought Paula 'had been around'. He didn't take much notice of her until she followed him to Paris. She stuck so closely to him the rest of the group nicknamed her 'The Limpet'. The couple moved in together but did not marry until 1986 when they went through two ceremonies – one on 21 June in Las Vegas, the tackiness capital of the world, the other, two months later, on 24 August in Davington, Kent, where they owned a cottage. The couple had three children, one before the marriages and two after, and saddled them with typically silly showbiz names – Fifi Trixiebell, Peaches and Pixie.

Geldof was the major player in the partnership for many years with hit records like *I Don't Like Mondays* and *Rat Trap* but as the Boomtown Rats faded from the public view it was

Yates who became more prominent. Yet in July 1985 Geldof returned to the world stage when he organized the charity rock concert that became known as Live Aid.

Perhaps not wanting to be overshadowed, Yates was linked with a number of high-profile music biz figures including Terence Trent D'Arby, Ben Volpeliere-Pierrot from Curiosity Killed the Cat and Dr Robert out of the Blow Monkeys.

In September 1992 Geldof's company, Planet 24, launched *The Big Breakfast* on Channel 4. The company bought a house at 4 Lock Keeper's Cottages, Old Ford Lock, East London and broadcast from there. A bed was placed in one of the upstairs rooms and Yates was given her own slot interviewing celebrities on it. Geldof did interviews with major world figures such as Nelson Mandela in the early editions but these were soon dropped. When she and Geldof parted she was replaced by transvestite comedian Lily Savage.

The Geldofs split early in February 1995 after Paula's three-month affair with INXS rocker Michael Hutchence was revealed. 'The first time I went to bed with Michael he did about six things within the first hour that I'd never heard of but was firmly convinced were illegal,' remembered Paula. He said, 'I hope this isn't a bit much for a first date.' In an interview Paula claimed she 'didn't leave Bob for Michael and I'm tired of saying it'. (A former girlfriend of Hutchence claimed that he first bedded Paula in 1988 when she interviewed him for *Time Out* magazine.) Apparently Paula was jealous of Hutchence's girlfriend, supermodel Helena Christensen, and ripped up pictures of her whenever they appeared in newspapers or magazines. She determined to split them up and had an aide ring a newspaper claiming that she was having an affair with Robbie Williams, then of Take That, so that a paparazzo would follow her and snap her with Hutchence. Whatever, the Geldofs faxed a note to the *News of the World* saying they had 'decided to take a break from each other for a while. They both love each other fantastically . . . and . . . will . . . continue to love one another. They are each other's best friend.' Chauffeur David Collins revealed that Paula and

Hutchence had had sex in the back of his BMW 750i as he drove them to Heathrow where Hutchence was due to catch a flight to Paris. 'The first thing I heard was Michael's trouser zip. I've never seen anything like it. Then she obviously decided to take things further and climbed on top of him. He pulled her breasts out of her dress and started kissing them. The next thing I saw was her sitting astride him making love. Neither of them got undressed – they just pulled their clothes out of the way. The pair of them had no shame – and it was clear Paula was leading the way.'

For two months the couple continued to deny what was obvious to everyone in Babylon. On 20 March the couple were spotted sneaking out of the posh £170-a-night Chilston Park Hotel in Lenham, Kent, at 5 a.m. That was the day that Helena Christensen finally gave Hutchence the elbow. Apparently the couple had had an open relationship providing both were discreet about any flings. Discretion was not Paula Yates's strong suit.

In April 1995 at Browns nightclub in London's Covent Garden the couple publicly kissed and groped each other revealing once and for all the depth of their lust. Later the same year Paula had her breasts enlarged from 34B to 34C at a reputed cost of £2,000 and spent a further £6,000 on her teeth. In September 1995 GQ magazine ran a feature decrying Hutchence's actions, printing a picture of his former girlfriend and asking, 'Helena Christensen – Seriously, would you trade her in for Paula Yates?' Hutchence was soon on the phone to the editor, the late Michael VerMeulen, screaming obscenities at him. Even Helena was outraged. 'It was such a horrible thing to write. I was hurt by the feeling of how Paula would feel so I called her up to give her my support.'

In November 1995 Paula was sued for over £45,000 by the owners of a Mayfair flat she had rented following her split from Geldof. Rama Foundation of Zurich claimed that the flat was uninhabitable after Yates moved out.

The following month Paula was in financial trouble. British Telecom cut off her phone line after she failed to pay her bill of

£189.03 and American Express Europe Ltd issued a High Court writ against her for an outstanding debt of £22,238.

In June 1996, a month after they divorced, the Geldofs went to court to sort out their messy domestic situation. Bob had moved his new girlfriend, French actress Jeanne Marine, into what was the family home in Redburn Street, Chelsea, much to Paula's annoyance. She threw a stone through one of the windows in March 1996. On 12 June 'after three days of complete bloody nightmare in the High Court of Justice' the couple reached 'a half-decent solution' to their domestic troubles. Yates and the three children would move into the family home while Geldof and Jeanne Marine, who appeared nude in the French soft porn film *Paulette* in 1985, moved into a house supposedly owned by Yates's lover Michael Hutchence. Just to get in a final dig at her ex-husband, Paula said she would need to have the place fumigated before she could move in: 'I am not going to bring up a new baby in a house with nits.'

On 22 July 1996 Paula gave birth to Hutchence's 6lb 14oz daughter who, like her other offspring, was given a stupid name – Heavenly Hiraani Tiger Lily.

In September that year while Paula and Hutchence were in Sydney, Australia, their home was raided by police drug squad officers who took away opium found under their bed in a Smarties tube. A stash of pornography – pictures of Paula and Hutchence having sex – was also discovered.

Where next for Paula Yates? Your guess will be as good as hers.

BOOZE & DRUGS IN BABYLON

Many, many celebrities have problems with drugs and alcohol. Perhaps this is one area where being famous does not help you – where money can't buy happiness. It is obviously not just celebrities who fall foul when it comes to drink and drugs. Many people from all walks of life regularly get drunk, smoke a joint or do a line of charlie now and again. Why do we get on our moral high horses when a celebrity does the same? Perhaps it is because celebrities who drink heavily or take drugs constantly deny that they do. It is irritating in the extreme when they finally admit their problem, go to an expensive clinic and then sell their story for more money than most people see in years.

Here is a brief look at those inhabitants of Babylon who drank and more . . .

Uncle Frank & the Cocaine Orgies

For many years Merton College, Oxford-educated Frank Bough was the face of BBC sport. Saturday afternoons were not complete without his steady hand at the rudder of *Grandstand*. Deciding to forsake sport, Frank moved into current affairs as the host of the daily magazine show *Nationwide*, then on to *Holiday* and finally became the man in the nice sweaters who sat next to Selina Scott on *Breakfast Time*. His stint in the mornings earned him the nickname 'Uncle Frank'.

That image was rudely shattered in May 1988 when sensational revelations were made about Bough's private life. On 25 July 1959 Bough had married Nesta Howells and they had three sons, David, Stephen and Andrew. Seemingly the Boughs had a happy, if not idyllic, home life in Maidenhead, Berkshire. Yet away from home and the television screen Bough indulged in drug-taking and kinky behaviour. It all began to emerge when two reporters from the *News of the World* were discussing something completely different with the errant son of a wealthy family. He mentioned in passing that he had seen Bough freebasing cocaine with two hookers while dressed in women's lingerie. The two journalists were stung by the tale but knew it would never stand up in court without a confession from the man himself which obviously would never come – or so they thought. The newspaper dug around in the seedy world inhabited by pimps, junkies and toms and discovered more detail about Bough's behaviour. Without a confession all the info was useless. A meeting was arranged at which Bough denied everything. The newspaper hacks knew the TV star was lying and he knew they knew but without the necessary confession it would all come to nought. Then Bough lost his nerve. He confided in his business partner and *Nationwide* colleague Bernard Falk who explained there was a chance that the *News of the World* might never run the story but a frank (no pun intended) confession would get them off Bough's back and allow him to limit the damage the full story could do.

That was how Bough decided to act. He told his side of the story with certain parts held back. The editor of the *News of the World*, Wendy Henry, agreed to this but said that if other newspapers ran with the story so would the *NoW*. Bough explained that at a dinner party he had met a woman, Marie France Demolis a.k.a. Marie France Dupré, who offered him cocaine as a way of relaxing after a hard day under the Klieg lights. He did not know she was a madam but he attended parties where people bonked. Bough admitted snorting cocaine with prostitutes, watching couples have sex and needing psychiatric help to overcome his cocaine problem but he denied having sex. His story was refuted by prostitute Gillian Jex who revealed, 'He squeezed into a red camisole, stockings and suspenders – then we made love in every direction . . . He had to squeeze into the gear and it barely covered him. I then applied make-up to his face . . . We continued making love until our cocaine supply ran out.' The following day, Bough called this allegation a 'complete fabrication' saying he would issue High Court writs for libel but he never did.

The sad thing – for Bough – is that after he had denied the story the *News of the World* were in no position to publish. If he had kept his mouth shut his indiscretions might well have remained a secret between him and his hooker friends.

In a 1992 postscript, the *News of the World* was approached by a freelance journalist who told them Bough was up to his old tricks again. The star was tipped off by the paper but he assured them he had nothing to worry about as he was clean. The *Sunday Mirror* published pictures of Bough visiting 8B, Welbeck Street, London where the speciality was sado-masochistic sessions. Bough paid brunette, rubber-clad Penny White, known as 'Mistress Charlotte', £80 each time to humiliate him in the 'best-equipped' torture chamber in London.

Cheggers Drinks Pop

In the 1970s children were divided into two categories: those who watched *Magpie* and, therefore, *Tiswas* and those whose preferences ran to *Blue Peter* and *Multi-Coloured Swap Shop*. If you were in the latter category you tuned in every Saturday to see whatever location the producers had deigned to send Keith Chegwin to.

Yes, every week Cheggers would be in some local park where hundreds if not thousands of children were gathered eager to swap unwanted toys. To them Cheggers was the cheery ex-star of Children's Film Foundation movies and the high-pitched oppo of the studio-bound Noel Edmonds. With the third member of the triumvirate, Maggie Philbin, Cheggers and Noel under the name Brown Sauce had even had a song, *I Wanna Be a Winner*, in the Top Twenty.

Brown was about the only colour of sauce that would not later be a problem for Keith Chegwin as he battled alcoholism. As well as *Multi-Coloured Swap Shop* and the later *Saturday Superstore*, Chegwin also presented the seminal *Cheggers Plays Pop*. His big sister is former Radio 1 disc jockette Janice Long. In 1982 he married his co-presenter Maggie Philbin. Five years later Keith Chegwin began drinking in earnest. 'I was a home drinker, all that Special Brew stuff, four or five cans of that. It was a gradual process but the more I drank the more I got into it. The lagers changed to lager and whisky and then the lagers disappeared.'

Cheggers admits it was only in the latter stages of his drinking that it became a problem, when he tried to give up. He hid bottles of booze in suits, in the guttering of settees and even cut a hole in the bottom of a double bed and stashed his booty there.

When he bought a mountain bike his family thought that Chegwin had taken up a keep-fit programme. Nothing of the sort. 'I'd cycle fucking miles to off licences to get booze and distribute it around the countryside. I'd never come back though, that was the problem. They used to find me in country lanes.' When he was working Chegwin couldn't drink alcohol so he substituted Night Nurse and Plax!

In 1991 Chegwin finally admitted he had a problem and went on *Good Morning with Richard and Judy* to talk about it. It was the beginning of a painful journey back to sobriety and his current status as a cult figure.

Out of the Shadows of
Gladiators

Imported like many shows from America, *Gladiators* quickly became a smash hit among children of all ages. The show was not quite as squeaky clean as producers London Weekend Television would have liked. Elsewhere in this book you can read the sexy story of blonde *Gladiators* presenter Ulrika Jonsson. On his investigative programme *The Cook Report* Roger Cook alleged that two Gladiators were taking steroids to boost their performances. Former *Gladiators* opponent Kym Dalton was revealed as the star of pornographic films and had also appeared in the triple x-rated *Lover's Guide*.

Each Gladiator was given a name to make them seem super-human – Jet, Panther, Hunter, Warrior, Rhino, Wolf, Amazon and so on. Former nightclub bouncer Michael Jefferson King, 32, 6′ 3″ and 19 stone, was given the name Shadow because he was so tall he 'blocked out the Sun'. Born in America, King grew up in Southall, London, where he was remembered as being something of a wimp. After his parents went their separate ways King was taken by his mother to America where he became interested in body-building in the Bronx. When he returned to England in 1986, *Gladiators* was his chance for the big time and he blew it – big time. In June 1992 he had been given a conditional discharge over possession of cocaine and marijuana. He was also given a 12-month suspended sentence for stealing a girlfriend's £20,000 bracelet.

In January 1995 the *Sunday Mirror* revealed that the chain-smoking athlete who was on a reputed salary of £90,000 per annum was addicted to cocaine. He regularly visited a bar below Le Renoir restaurant on the Fulham Road where he was twice observed snorting the drug and downing bottle after bottle of beer. His third wife, Olivia, 30, whom he married in October 1992 was an escort who worked for the Chelsea Girl agency under the name Vivien. She left him because of his violence and womanizing. She said, 'He had several affairs during our marriage . . . He basically had no sex life for much of our marriage. He just couldn't perform when he took all those drugs.' She also claimed that he regularly beat her up including when she was pregnant with their twins. He was sacked on 30 January 1995 after admitting taking anabolic steroids. The following day he lied on GMTV, denying he had ever taken drugs, and then tried to sell the story of his drug-taking and that of other Gladiators to the *Sunday Mirror* for £100,000. Bisexual £500-a-night Hereford-born prostitute Claire Marsden, 26, revealed that Shadow had been one of her regular punters. 'I've slept with two Chippendales and a Dream Boy but he puts them totally in the shade.' She also said that she had snorted cocaine with him and indulged in three-in-a-bed romps. 'I like sleeping with women as much as men. And my girlfriend [Miranda] is very busty and very beautiful. That night was hilarious. Shadow fancied both of us and just didn't know where to start. We had an amazing session. And afterwards I was so shattered I fell asleep straight away. But then he woke me later and was ready for more. He's got incredible stamina.' Oddly, in an interview published on the same day, Olivia King said her husband had no appetite for sex because he was on crack cocaine.

In April 1995 King was signing on the dole, his career in tatters. By January 1996 he was reduced to working as a male stripper with two girls who had worked in a table-dancing club. On 29 October 1996 a warrant was issued for King's arrest after he failed to turn up in court to answer charges of motoring offences.

Awight? No!
The Story of a Tormented Genius

To the outside world it seemed that Michael Barrymore had everything. Riches. (He was reputed to be on a £2,500,000-a-year contract.) Fame. A loving wife who doubled as his manager. (Barrymore's wife, the two years older Cheryl, whom he married on 10 June 1976, is an equal partner in his company Michael Barrymore Ltd.) A mega-successful career. But the outside world could not have been more wrong. Michael Barrymore was a mass of contradictions. First, he was estranged from his own family. He has not seen his mother for many years, although he was close to his parents-in-law Eddie and Kitty Cocklin and was devastated by their deaths in 1990 and 1995 respectively. Secondly, Barrymore was a homosexual who did not feel he could come out because it would wreck his career. Thirdly, to drown his problems he took to drinking heavily. It was a vicious circle that saw Barrymore fall deeper and deeper into the twilight world of the alcoholic as he sought to hide from his problems.

Awight?! My kind of comic – Michael Barrymore

Michael Barrymore was born Michael Keiron Parker in Bermondsey on 4 May 1952. His father, George, was a drunk who terrorized his family. In his autobiography Barrymore describes his childhood as 'loveless'.

He worked as a junior hairdresser numbering Shirley Bassey and Lulu among his clientele before he entered showbusiness. One of his first jobs was as warm-up man on *Are You Being Served?* It was his performances on *Russ Abbot's Madhouse* that first got him noticed by an appreciative public. In 1992 he began presenting *Barrymore*, a variety show which featured Michael mucking about with various guests and members of the public. The show *My Kind of People* was a spin-off. In January 1997 his *Strike It Lucky* quiz show returned with a £10,000 jackpot as *Michael Barrymore's Strike It Rich*. Two years earlier it had been revealed that not all was as it seemed on *Strike It Lucky*. On several occasions the contestants were friends of Barrymore or his wife, Cheryl. One show featured Cheryl's uncle while another included Barrymore's personal assistant and his sister. Thames TV who made the show blamed 'a misjudgment'. When the show became *Michael Barrymore's Strike It Rich* it was a joint production between London Weekend Television and Fremantle (UK) Ltd.

Despite the success on-screen all was not well off-screen and in 1990 Michael's brother and mother sold a story to a Sunday newspaper about their famous relative, portraying him as a selfish, thoughtless man who had turned his back on his own family. Unsurprisingly, it caused a massive rift in the family which has never been healed. In March 1993 Michael had his first nervous breakdown. In April 1995 Michael's big sister, Ann, called on her warring family to end their feud. Three months later, on 24 July 1995, Barrymore entered the £350-a-day Priory Clinic to beat his alcoholism.

For many years it had been rumoured that Michael was homosexual and, in August 1995, two of his gay lovers revealed his secret to a tabloid. On 19 August the star finally confirmed it himself when he came out during a 'Hot Bums Contest' at a gay pub, the White Swan in the East End of London. Barrymore took off his wedding ring and launched into a version of the hit *New York, New York*, changing the words to 'Start spreadin' the news, I'm gay today.' As he left the pub the entertainer was approached by a reporter and a photographer from the *Sun* and he lost it with them. 'You fucking cunts are trying to ruin my life,' he yelled before grabbing hold of the cameraman and continuing his tirade. Barrymore went on Spectrum Radio's *G.A.Y.* show (it stands for Good As You) and confirmed his gayness to host Jeremy Joseph. Then Barrymore moved out of his marital home. The entertainer was seen in a relaxed mood around London's gay haunts and his constant companion was 22-year-old Paul Wincott. In January 1996 he moved back in with Cheryl. In May of the same year he spent time in a clinic in Southampton suffering from stress brought on by depression, exhaustion and a drinking binge. The next month he serenaded his wife outside a Soho eaterie. Two days later he was at a gay pub. In December 1996 he entered another clinic to stave off further stress.

Michael Barrymore has the love and support of the public in his battles to overcome his demons but does he have the necessary 'self-love'? Only time will tell . . .

Making an Impression – Mike Yarwood

Impressionist Mike Yarwood was rarely off the telly in the 1970s. His show *Mike Yarwood in Persons* was compulsive viewing for millions on a Saturday night. His repertoire of 200 voices kept the audience laughing. Yet behind the seemingly happy façade lay a tormented man replete with insecurities. Like many before him and like many no doubt in the future, Yarwood used alcohol to numb his pain.

Yarwood left school at 15 with no qualifications and, after various menial tasks, became a salesman for the Stone-Dri

Raincoat Company. When he was at school he wanted to be a footballer or a football writer. He actually had a trial with Oldham but was turned down and the local paper refused to give him a job.

Yarwood began entering talent contests. Although he never won once, he gradually began working the club circuit. He was hired as the warm-up for the TV show *Comedy Band Box* and eventually won a place on the show himself. The year was 1963 and Harold Wilson had just become leader of the Labour Party following Hugh Gaitskell's untimely death. Yarwood spent ages perfecting his impersonation of Wilson – 'my hit record' as he called it. (When Wilson left office as Prime Minister in April 1976 he awarded Yarwood the OBE in his Resignation Honours List.) At the time Edward Heath also became leader of the Conservatives and the Grocer too became a Yarwood staple. Throughout his career Yarwood has always maintained a benign attitude to his 'subjects' which meant that many of them became if not friends then certainly acquaintances of his.

Alcohol proved to be Mike Yarwood's downfall. It cost him his marriage and his career. He married Young Generation dancer Sandra Jean Burville in 1969 (he supposedly proposed using someone else's voice and did a show at the Savoy on his wedding night) and fathered two beautiful daughters, Charlotte, born on 19 October 1970, and Clare two years later, on 29 November 1972. The Yarwoods seemed to be the ideal family. He had it all: a successful BBC show, pretty wife and children and a Surrey mansion with a swimming pool. However, Yarwood was not a happy man. One moment he was charming and generous, the next morose and intolerable. Numerous times Sandra declared she would leave him but each time as she was packing her bags he cajoled her into staying.

Finally she could take no more and, in January 1985, she left him. Yarwood was bereft. He would call his estranged wife up to nine times a day and beg his daughters to sit with him. A few brief affairs could not console him and he admits he was celibate for five years. One of his girlfriends, manic depressive showgirl Suzie Jerome, killed herself aged 26 on 23 October 1986. The tragedy did nothing to lift his spirits.

Like Morecambe and Wise before him, Mike Yarwood had deserted the BBC for the money offered by ITV and signed a £250,000 contract with Thames TV in 1982. Without his wife but with the ever constant battle against the booze Yarwood found it more and more difficult to concentrate on his career. Thames TV cancelled his contract. In November 1988 Yarwood collapsed on stage while touring in the farce *One for the Pot*. Although he claimed he had forsaken the bottle, he was still a binge drinker. That Christmas Yarwood was due to appear in pantomime but felt unable to do so.

It was his lowest period. Yarwood blamed himself for not working and fell into a deeper pit of depression. He sought psychiatric help. By 1990 he felt he would never work again. He underwent hypnosis to cure his stage fright. In July that year he suffered a heart attack. He has not had a drink since 1 July 1991. Yarwood battled and battled and, in November 1993, appeared at the Royal Variety Performance where some critics acclaimed him as a sensation. It wasn't a way back for Mike Yarwood as now, nearly four years later, he is still in the showbiz wilderness.

And Finally . . .
the Newsreader & the Bottle

Reginald Bosanquet is a much-loved memory in television history. Unfortunately, he is probably best remembered for his supposed drinking and his ill-fitting toupee (which he claimed he wore for medical reasons) rather than his abilities as a newsreader. (In later life he received a letter from a woman enquiring about the origin of his surname. He wrote back informing her, 'My name is Huguenot.' She replied thanking him for telling her his real name but said she was actually interested in his assumed name of Bosanquet.)

Bosanquet was born on 9 August 1932 in Surrey, the son of B.J.T. Bosanquet, the man who invented the googly in cricket (known in Australia as the Bosie) and who died when his son was four. Reggie was born paralysed down the left side of his body, much to the annoyance of his father who muttered, 'It would have been better if he hadn't lived.' Although he recovered, the left side of his body was always weaker in adult life. Orphaned at the age of seven, young Reggie was evacuated to Canada in 1940. Upon his arrival in Montreal he had the ignominy of being deloused and when it was time for the Canadian families to pick the children Reggie was the last one to be chosen. Returning to England in 1944, he was educated at Winchester and New College, Oxford, where he obtained a Second in History. Bosanquet won scholarships to both Winchester and Oxford and this entitled him to certain privileges. At Winchester he was allowed to grow a beard and keep a badger while at Oxford he was entitled to wear a special gown but not get married. This was a problem because Reggie had fallen in love with Karin Lund and despite the rule they did get married. (They separated after five years.) Four months later, he joined ITN at its inception.

In May 1976 Reggie was suspended from *News at Ten* for four weeks after his ex-wife, Felicity Fearnley-Whittingstall, gave a series of interviews to newspapers.

A little known fact was that Reggie suffered from epilepsy. It was this and the drugs he took to control it which caused his slurred speech.

In 1978 Reggie was accused by a nurse of being the father of her newborn son, a claim which he vigorously denied. When the *Daily Star* ran the story he successfully sued the newspaper for libel. *Private Eye* lampooned him as Reggie Beaujolais for whom fellow newsreader Anna Ford supposedly carried a torch.

He resigned from ITN in 1979 after nearly twenty-five years. The satirical programme *Not the Nine O'Clock News* composed a paean to Reggie which was sung by Pamela Stephenson. 'I see you every night in my dreams . . . Oh-oh Bosanquet why did you go away?'

News at Ten finishes each bulletin with an amusing or lightweight story. One such story resulted in Reggie being deluged with letters from thousands of irate animal lovers. During the firemen's strike the army took over firefighting duties using the antiquated Green Goddess engines. One day an old woman whose cat had become stuck up a tree called them for assistance. The army duly arrived and rescued the moggy. In gratitude the woman invited them in for refreshments. Sated, they drove off and ran over the cat, killing it. A flicker of a smile appeared on Reggie's lips, much to the annoyance of those who prefer felines to humans.

He died on 27 May 1984. A much-missed talent.

Oprah's Drug Confession

The most successful chat show host in the world, Oprah Winfrey earns over £60,000,000 per year. She has always been very open on her show, talking at length about her childhood rape, her spinster status and more. On *The Oprah Winfrey Show* in January 1995 she was interviewing mothers who had given birth to crack-addicted babies. Amazingly, Oprah empathized with one of the women who said she was still smoking crack and admitted, 'I did your drug. This is probably one of the hardest things I have ever said. I have done this drug. I know exactly what you are talking about.' Then she broke down. Taping was stopped and it was twenty minutes before she was able to resume. Later, Oprah added that the drug use had been 'a great big secret that has always been held over my head'.

Oprah claimed she had used the drug to impress a boyfriend when she was a newsreader in Baltimore, Maryland. 'I had always thought I was more addicted to the man than the drug but I could never say it out loud. I was ashamed. I would never admit I had handed over my power to a man, to the point he could influence me to do anything for him.' Oprah's half-sister Pat (a former drug addict) and long-term boyfriend, Stedman Graham, co-founded the help organization Athletes Against Drugs.

Oliver Reed, Drink & the Lesbian

The drinking of actor Oliver Reed is legendary in showbusiness folklore. In January 1991 Reed was booked to appear on the Channel 4 chat show *After Dark*, an open-ended discussion that went out late on Saturday nights and ended when the participants or producer got fed up and went home. The subject under discussion was feminism and before and during the show Reed had imbibed too deeply and too often. He took umbrage at the views expressed by feminist lesbian Kate Millett. Reed grabbed Miss Millett and planted an unwanted kiss on her cheek before walking off the set.

Gay Gilbert in Drunken Rumpus

Irascible Gilbert Harding, one of the stalwarts of the original *What's My Line?*, was a lonely homosexual and heavy drinker. Interviewed by John Freeman on *Face to Face* Harding burst into tears while talking about the death of his mother. October 1953 was not a good month for Harding. On the 6th he was invited to a dinner by Hounslow Magistrates. When it came time for Harding to give an after-dinner speech, he stood up and said, 'I have been dragged along to this third-rate place for a third-rate dinner by third-rate people.' Not surprisingly, Harding was asked to leave. The next day he apologized: 'I behaved abominably.' The day after, Harding attended the première of *The King and I* and promptly fell asleep, missing the whole performance. He again grovelled: 'I'm sorry. I had a tiring day.'

Worst of the Best

For years George Best was a hero on the football field, winning rave reviews for his skills playing for Manchester United and Northern Ireland, but he ruined his career over-indulging in women and drink. In an effort to combat his alcoholism Best even had a pellet implanted in his stomach which would make him ill if he drank. He did. On 19 September 1990 Best appeared on the popular BBC-1 chat show *Wogan*. Unfortunately, he had partaken of too much hospitality beforehand and spoke loudly and in graphic terms of his drinking and sex life. The usually genial host Terry Wogan was not amused. He said later that if he had tried to have Best thrown off the show the results might have been worse.

Devine Intervention

Magenta Devine came by her unusual name because one day she turned up for work at her office with her hair dyed magenta. After working for publicist Tony Brainsby she broke into television interviewing celebrities on the cult show *Network 7* on Channel 4, thanks to her friend and mentor Janet Street-Porter. Rarely seen without her trademark dark glasses, Magenta looks rather like Miss Jones from *Rising Damp* when she removes her shades. When Street-Porter became Head of Youth Programming at the BBC Magenta followed her friend to present the travel show *Rough Guide*. As her career took off Magenta took cocaine, heroin and speed. She became a heroin addict because 'I needed calming down rather than speeding up and heroin did that. In the beginning it's great. It's not until you get into them more that they . . . affect your life and the problem begins. It becomes more important than anything.' Magenta first began taking drugs around 1983. 'In the beginning I really did it a lot then I stopped for years.' Eventually, Magenta began taking the heroin substitute methadone which is equally addictive. In early 1993 Magenta went to her BBC bosses and asked for a £12,000 advance on her salary so she could enter a private psychiatric clinic to beat her addiction. The money was agreed by Janet Street-Porter. Magenta's TV career continues . . .

CRIME IN BABYLON

Babylon isn't immune to crime. In fact, for many years crime and showbiz went hand-in-hand in Babylon. For some strange reason many celebrities thought it glamorous to associate with criminals. Barbara Windsor, Mike Reid, Roger Daltrey and the Americans George Raft, Judy Garland and Debbie Harry have all been associated with the thuggish Kray twins. Nowadays, celebrities seem at least to keep their distance from organized crime so they get involved elsewhere instead . . .

'Allo, 'Allo, 'Allo – Good Morning with Richard and Judy

Richard Madeley and his eight years older wife Judy Finnigan are the undisputed king and queen of morning television. Their *This Morning with Richard and Judy* show, first broadcast on 3 October 1988, is watched by countless housewives. The show was broadcast live from Liverpool's Albert Dock before it moved to London in September 1996.

On 13 May 1996 the couple tried for a prime time slot with their evening chat show *Tonight with Richard Madeley and Judy Finnigan*. Their first guest really set the tone for the whole series. It was former American football hero O. J. Simpson who had been acquitted, many believe wrongly, of the double murder of his ex-wife Nicole and her friend Ronald Lyle Goldman. Whether the pair had not done their homework on the case properly or felt intimidated by Simpson is unclear. What is certain is that he ran rings round them. The couple looked nervous and agitated. Critics slated the programme. Roy Hattersley writing in the *Daily Express* called it 'squalid and absurd . . . The brief interview would have been nauseous enough if it had been conducted with anything like competence.' The audience for the show was a disappointing seven million and after that ratings began to drop. The difference between daytime TV and prime time is immense. Very few presenters successfully make the transition between the two. From the evidence of their first *Tonight* it began to look as if Richard and Judy are not cut out for prime time television. Of the two it is believed that Madeley is the more ambitious. He sees himself as a hard news journalist and wants to be accepted in the same group as Jeremy Paxman, John Humphrys and his personal hero Robin Day.

It could have been very different when on 24 August 1990 Richard Madeley was arrested for shoplifting two bottles of champagne, a bottle of gin and five bottles of wine from Tesco's in Didsbury. According to the store detective, Angela Orme, Richard had visited the checkout with a full trolley of shopping but had made no attempt to pay for the booze. She stopped the TV star who said he had forgotten to pay for the merchandise but was happy to do so. She asked him to accompany her to the manager's office which he was quite prepared to do. The police were called and Richard, still protesting his innocence, was arrested and taken to Platt Lane police station. According to the store Madeley had stolen similar items plus soap powder six days earlier when he was seen by a cashier but not challenged. The value of the goods both times was approximately £60. Richard was charged with the second offence first and the 18 August offence later.

Richard Madeley denied all charges and Granada TV announced he would not be replaced on *This Morning*. The new series was due to start on 3 September and Madeley's familiar face was again at the helm with his blonde wife. He decided to be open about what had happened. Richard elected to go to Crown Court and it was decided that his ordeal should form part of the show until his trial.

The trial opened in court number five at Manchester Crown Court on 1 July 1991. Anthony Gee, QC, prosecuted. On the second day of the trial the security video from 24 August was played in court allowing Judge Michael Sachs to murmur, 'It's certainly not going to win a BAFTA, is it?' On day three of the case Madeley went into the dock and explained that he had simply forgotten both times to pay for the goods. His forgetfulness was, he said, a standing family joke and he remembered the time when on holiday in Devon he had left two bags of paid-for shopping with the cashier. 'It meant the family did not have much for dinner that night. I was not flavour of the month.'

The judge began his seventy-minute summation on 4 July at 2 p.m. A little under three and a half hours later at 5.24 p.m. the jury returned to the crowded courtroom to deliver their verdict. On count one of theft they acquitted Madeley but they admitted they could not reach a decision on count two. Once again they retired and once more they failed to reach a verdict on which they were all agreed. The judge dismissed them with the thanks of the court. Inside the court was bewilderment. The confusion was cleared up by Anthony Gee who told the judge that he did not believe that a second trial would be in the public interest or that Madeley was likely to get a fair trial. The judge directed a not guilty verdict be entered on the second indictment. Richard Madeley's eleven-month ordeal was over – almost.

Three weeks after his acquittal Manchester was flyposted with hundreds of posters advertising the 'Richard Madeley Trolley Dash'. In 1994 Bob Geldof, recently bankrupted for a day, was a guest on *This Morning* and Richard expressed surprise at the order. Geldof shot back, 'It's like shoplifting, Richard. I couldn't believe that either.'

It wasn't just celebrities who felt the need for a pop at Madeley. Presenting *This Morning* on 10 February 1995

Richard was shocked when a caller, Elizabeth from York, rang in to ask him to 'steal me a bottle of wine from Safeway's, please Richard'. Madeley blew his top. 'I knew we'd get one of these calls one day. These are sad people. These are anoraks. I mean, it's so easy to get a hoax phone call on radio or television. It's like a train thing to do. Go and spot some trains or buy yourself an anorak, love.'

The Fear of Stalkers

In recent years many celebrities have felt the need to hire bodyguards to protect them from over-enthusiastic fans who are often mentally deranged. In December 1980 the mad Mark Chapman believed his hero John Lennon had 'sold out' so he murdered him in cold blood. Three months later, the equally troubled John Hinckley tried to prove his love for actress Jodie Foster by shooting President Ronald Reagan.

●◆ Beautiful *Coronation Street* star Tracy Shaw (Maxine Heavey) was the unwilling object of a stalker's attention. 'I get letters sent by people of all ages. Unfortunately, some of them are from dirty old men who tell me what they are doing while they are watching me on TV. It's not nice to have to deal with that.' One night after she went out for a drink a man followed

'Our Maxine'

Tracy back to the flat she sometimes shares with another *Street* actress. The incident repeated itself on more than one occasion and, not surprisingly, Tracy began to get scared. A detour on the way home didn't work and she worried that if she delayed her journey the man might try something. She locked herself in and did not put on the lights lest the man find out which flat she was in. He began shouting and the neighbours called the police. The next night the stalker returned and began pressing the intercom. By a process of elimination he discovered the flat. 'I felt really scared. I have never felt that scared before. It made me realize that because of who or what I was playing, my life was going to change and I had to be much more careful.' As in all these cases the police told Tracy they were powerless unless the man actually did something. Thankfully, boredom set in and he gave up. It wasn't just a weirdo who made Tracy's life a misery. Jealous girls in her home town of Belper, Derbyshire, have made it almost impossible for her to socialize. 'Builders wolf-whistle, which I don't mind – and in Manchester everyone is lovely. They see me as "Our Maxine". But I get a lot of bitching from girls where I live. They want to fight me – I have no idea why. Maybe I have that look that says: "Come on, attack me." I really hate trouble so it stops me going out at the moment. I don't want to be hassled and have nasty comments thrown at me. I just want to go out and have a nice evening.'

●◆ Actress Samantha Janus is best known on television as the tarty Mandy in *Game On* but she also has a thriving theatre career. When she was appearing as Sandy in the hit musical *Grease* at the Dominion Theatre in London's Tottenham Court Road she became the unwilling object of a stalker. He would follow her to the theatre and wait outside. If he was spotted by the staff they would telephone her at home and she would enter the theatre by a different entrance. He would write rambling letters.

One said, 'I saw this bird flying in my garden the other day, which reminded me of you. So I chopped its leg off.' Mercifully he, too, got bored.

● Martine McCutcheon plays maneater Tiffany Mitchell in *EastEnders*. She received obscene rambling letters from a 43-year-old bisexual man who called himself Reece and was into bondage. One missive ran to thirty pages begging Martine to marry him. Another written in red ink on A4 paper has a 'script' with lines for Martine in which she dumped her then fiancé Gareth Cooke, 26. 'Reece' also writes about the bondage sessions he longs to enact with Martine: 'I could really love you, and ever so pleasurably for us both, tie you up. Ever so nicely and politely and gently, but strongly. Does Gareth do that?' The madman had first written to Martine's fellow *EastEnder* Letitia Dean (Sharon Watts Mitchell) but soon turned his attention to actress Susan Tully (Michelle Fowler Holloway) before his sick fantasies moved on to Martine. The brunette actress and her DJ fiancé were so worried by the nutter's ravings that the police were called and the couple went into hiding.

● A celebrity who was himself a stalker was James Farentino who played Dr Nick Toscanni on *Dynasty*. He was charged with stalking Tina Sinatra, his girlfriend for five years. In March 1994 Farentino pleaded no contest and was placed on probation for three years, ordered to seek counselling and keep at least 100 yards away from Miss Sinatra at all times.

☎ TV presenter Philippa Forrester combines beauty with brains presenting science programme *Tomorrow's World*. Yet it was in 1992 while presenting Children's BBC that she became the unwitting object of a weirdo's desires. Having just finished her stint she received a phone call from a man demanding to know why she had stood him

up for their date. The man's conversation became more
sinister as he told the star that she should not smile at
him like that if she didn't mean it. Fearing for her safety
she began to take taxis to work or, if she drove to the
BBC, she went via a circuitous route. Eventually,
Philippa was warned not to answer her telephone in case
her deluded fan was on the line. One day she forgetfully
picked up the receiver and was horrified when she heard
his voice. Straining to keep her cool, she managed to
continue a conversation long enough for BT to trace the
call. The man was warned off and, thankfully, has kept
his distance. 'I love working in television and would
never be put off by the odd aggressive fan or someone
who's a bit unbalanced or lonely,' said Philippa.

●◆ The beautiful Helena Bonham Carter was stalked by
Andrew Farquharson, a mad Scottish 27-year-old fan,
for five years. In that time he wrote to her, telephoned
her and even turned up on the doorstep of the house she
shared with her parents. At first Helena regarded the
intrusion as nothing more than a nuisance but then the
letters began to get more sinister and sexual in nature. In
February 1993 enough was finally enough and Helena
and her parents took out a restraining order on the nutter.

●◆ In December 1996 it was revealed that a lone pervert was
writing abusive and sexually explicit letters to twelve
middle-aged celebrity women. The man, who was
obviously deranged, included Heritage Secretary
Virginia Bottomley among his targets. Dame Diana Rigg
said, 'He is a very sick man. I've had so many letters I've
lost count.' *Forsyte Saga* star Nyree Dawn Porter has even
had letters sent to her children and was given a 24-hour
police guard when she appeared in a West End play. All
her mail is now intercepted before it reaches her.
Amazingly, one of the letters, addressed to Radio 4
presenter Sue MacGregor, bore the legend, 'If

undelivered please forward to Miss Susan Hampshire'.
Police believe the writer is a single man in his 40s or 50s
living in the Manchester area.

☎ *Grange Hill* starlet Paula Ann Bland found herself the
unwanted object of a nutcase's desires. Paula, a devout
Catholic, moved from *Grange Hill* to the men's magazine
Mayfair where she posed topless in 1988. 'I want to be as
famous as Samantha Fox. Showing your boobs is just
part of the job. Everyone does it – even top film stars. I
don't mind men looking at me at all. I think I attracted
more weirdos when I was in *Grange Hill*. I'd get letters
from dirty old men who were turned on by my school
uniform,' she said at the time. Unemployed chef David
Sturdy, 34, became obsessed by Paula when he saw her
on the telly and persuaded her he worked in the press
office at TV-am and arranged to meet her at the Ritz.
Paula sat on her own in the lobby for an hour when no
one turned up – nutter Sturdy's train was late. Sturdy
denied making nuisance phone calls but on 20 May 1988
he was fined £250 at Bow Street Magistrates' Court and
ordered to pay £50 costs and £100 compensation to only
child Paula. On Friday 13 December 1985 Paula's cousin,
22-year-old Karen Robinson, was murdered by her
ex-boyfriend. Paula did not attend the funeral.

☎ It is not just women who find themselves at the mercy of
nutters. Newsreader Trevor McDonald found himself
the unwanted object of a mentally unstable woman's
desires. She bombarded the popular presenter with
letters and turned up at ITN's Gray's Inn Road offices six
times. Trevor wanted to talk to her because 'that is the
West Indian way of dealing with things' but was advised
against that by security. The woman was taken to a
hospital in the north of England.

The stalkers continue . . .

Fry's Porridge

A self-confessed intellectual snob but also a man who generates extreme loyalty in his friends, Stephen Fry is a deeply complex man. As a child he was a kleptomaniac who tended to bury the things he stole. He passed nine 'O' Levels aged 13 at his minor public school, Uppingham in Rutland, and was then expelled for bunking off for three days to go to London to watch films.

When he was 17, Fry stole a coat from a restaurant and went on a three-month spending spree with the owner's credit cards. He was collared in Swindon and earned himself three months in Pucklechurch, a remand home, where he was nicknamed 'The Professor'. One of the few times in his adult life that Stephen Fry has ever cried was when his mother visited him in prison with three months' worth of the *Times* crossword. On probation for two years, Fry more than redeemed himself by winning a scholarship to Queen's College, Cambridge.

Stephen later had another brush with the law when he lost his driving licence and 'decided to rationalize the fleet' by selling most of his ten cars.

In the Drink

In August 1994 telly presenter Sharron Davies and her husband Olympic sprinter Derek Redmond fell foul of the law when they attempted a motoring con. Redmond was driving his silver Mercedes even though he was banned for six months. A traffic cop saw them but by the time he caught up with the couple Davies was in the driving seat. The pair swore she had been driving all along but the bobby didn't believe them and they were arrested. In court in January 1995 Redmond admitted he had been driving and was given another six-month ban and fined £610. Davies was given a conditional discharge for a year after admitting a reduced charge of obstructing police.

One in the Hand for a Partridge

One of the most popular TV shows in the early 1970s was *The Partridge Family* starring Oscar-winning Shirley Jones, her real-life stepson David Cassidy and future *LA Lawyer* Susan Dey as the members of a singing family who toured America in a brightly decorated bus. Jones was married to Jack Cassidy, the bisexual former gay lover of Cole Porter, by whom she had another actor-singer son, Shaun Cassidy, who achieved a measure of fame as one of *The Hardy Boys*. *The Partridge Family* made a teen heart-throb out of David Cassidy, propelling him to international stardom and on to posters on the bedroom walls of millions of girls.

The cheeky kid of the series was played by 11-year-old Danny Bonaduce. When *The Partridge Family* was cancelled in 1974 after just under four years Bonaduce found himself in the awkward position in which many teen actors find themselves – too young for adult parts, too old to play kids.

Bonaduce embarked on a downward spiral of drink and drugs. While spaced out on drugs he learned to speak Japanese. One day, again stoned, he was in a Japanese restaurant when two of the waitresses began jabbering away in Japanese. One said she had run out of money and was about to be thrown out of the country. In perfect Japanese Bonaduce offered to marry her. She accepted, got her Green Card allowing her to stay in the States and left him six months later. His second marriage was equally bizarre. He asked Gretchen for a date and, at the end of the evening, she accompanied him back to his home. However, once there she refused to sleep with him because she didn't believe in pre-marital sex so Bonaduce looked in the *Yellow Pages* and called a minister to marry them then and there. The next morning he believed she would think she had made a dreadful mistake. He tried to explain, 'Listen, I don't even know your name . . . ' She looked at him and said, 'It's Mrs Bonaduce. Try not to forget it.'

Although he professed to be very happy with his marriage, it didn't stop Bonaduce from getting into trouble with the law. On 9 March 1990 he was arrested for cocaine possession for the second time (the first had been five years earlier). Bonaduce had gone to a housing project in Daytona Beach, Florida to buy $20 of crack cocaine. He was sentenced to fifteen months' probation and community service.

Just over a year later, on 31 March 1991, in Arizona he solicited a prostitute for oral sex for $20 in his blue Camaro car. He drove the hooker to the outskirts of town and once there decided he wanted more than a blowjob. The prostitute refused and Bonaduce grabbed under her dress and was amazed and probably distressed to find a penis. He punched the hooker, took his money back and drove off. Police arrested him naked and covered in blood, hiding under a pile of clothes in a cupboard in his bedroom in the St Croix Villas on East Fillmore Street in Arizona. In August 1991 Bonaduce pleaded guilty to endangerment, no contest to misdemeanour assault and was sentenced to three years' probation and 750 hours of community service. He was also ordered to pay $4,500 damages to his victim whose name was Darius Lee Barney.

Woody or Woodyn't He?

If children do take after their parents it is fortunate that Woody didn't emulate his father. Charles V. Harrelson was a professional card player who in 1968 was convicted of the murder of Texas grain dealer Sam Degelia while Woody was still a child. Harrelson senior was paid $2,000 for the hit and served ten years in Fort Leavenworth. He is now incarcerated on a double life term for the 29 May 1979 murder of Judge John H. Wood, Jr in San Antonio, Texas, the first ever murder of a federal judge in America. Judge Wood was known as 'Maximum John' because of his tough sentencing and Harrelson was reputedly paid $250,000 for carrying out the killing. The crime resulted in the biggest FBI manhunt since the assassination of President Kennedy. The judge at his trial, William Sessions, described Harrelson as 'the most vicious, heartless, cold-blooded killer I have ever come up against'.

At school Woody was a delinquent who smashed windows and kicked a teacher. That behaviour saw him sent to borstal where the headmistress described him as 'one of the most troubled children I've ever had in my care'.

On 10 October 1982 the future star of *Cheers* was observed dancing in the road in Columbus, Ohio. Since his behaviour was interfering with traffic the police were called. The patrol car pulled up and the officers shouted to Harrelson to get out of the road. He ignored them and fell to his knees whereupon the cops walked over to him and smelling alcohol on his breath, arrested him for drunk and disorderly behaviour.

Harrelson, 5´ 9˝ and aged 21, was put in the back of a police van but as the vehicle began to drive away the back doors swung open and Harrelson jumped out. The police gave chase and soon caught up with him. As they attempted to re-arrest him Harrelson thumped one of the coppers. Meanwhile, the other one handcuffed him. Harrelson was charged with assault, resisting arrest and disorderly conduct. The court took his good character into consideration and he was fined $390.

As the thick barman in *Cheers*, Woody was loved by millions. In real life Woody couldn't have been more different from the Woody he played on the small screen – he drank heavily, smoked pot and slept with over 600 women. It was only when he met Laura Louie that he began to calm down, found God and fathered a daughter, Deni Montana.

Dirtysomething

Mel Harris, *thirtysomething* star, has a secret past. She was once involved in one of New York's steamiest love-triangle murder cases. And the beauteous green-eyed actress also covered up two unaccounted-for husbands. One is a discredited former Green Beret and suspected explosives trafficker who had been imprisoned for fraud. The other is a highly regarded dog trainer.

The 5′ 9″ Harris was a 22-year-old fashion model with the prestigious Wilhelmina Agency in New York when she became linked with the so-called Penthouse Murder Case in 1978. The plot revolved around Mel's closest friend and fellow model from the Eileen Ford Agency, Melanie Cain, 21, and her live-in lover, Howard 'Buddy' Jacobson, 49, once America's number one trainer of thoroughbred horses.

The murder victim was 32-year-old John Tupper, a muscular restaurateur who was heavily involved in one of America's biggest international drug-smuggling rings. On the morning of 6 August 1978 Tupper was shot, stabbed and bludgeoned to death in the hallway outside his duplex penthouse on the seventh floor of a posh Manhattan townhouse at 155 East 84th Street, a building owned by Buddy Jacobson. The corpse was stuffed into an army gun crate that Mel Harris's then fiancé, 31-year-old David Silbergeld, had brought from Vietnam where he had served as a munitions expert. The crate was hauled from the murder scene in a van to the North-East Bronx where it was dumped in a junk-strewn wasteland and set alight. When Melanie Cain discovered her boyfriend was missing it was Mel Harris that she called first.

A family out on a Sunday drive spotted two men in a Cadillac leaving the site of the burning crate. The car was intercepted by police and Jacobson was arrested, prosecuted for murder, convicted and sentenced to 25-years-to-life imprisonment. (He escaped, was recaptured and died of bone cancer in Attica, New York State Prison early in 1990.) His co-defendant was found not guilty and deported to his native Sicily where he was bumped off in a Mafia feud in 1990.

Mel Harris was one of the State's chief witnesses at the trial in the Bronx County Courthouse, near Yankee Stadium and the setting for Tom Wolfe's book *The Bonfire of the Vanities*. Before she took the stand on the twenty-seventh day of proceedings, 29 February 1980, Mel made a courtroom entrance worthy of a Cecil B. DeMille spectacular. All eyes turned to stare at the dark-haired beauty with the heart-stopping figure.

At her side, protectively holding her arm, was 26-year-old Brian Kilclinic, who in the previous year had opened a dog training school on Long Island and would soon open a Manhattan branch. His appearance at the trial caused a murmur among the press because at the time of the pre-trial hearing Mel Harris was married to David Silbergeld.

Harris's marriage to Silbergeld was short-lived. She became fed up with him after he was arrested and jailed for signing on the dole while working for a credit rating agency. Harris met Silbergeld in 1977 while she was living in Garden Apartment 1-A of the 84th Street townhouse with Ronnie Stone, a well-heeled jeweller. Harris stayed with Stone until Silbergeld invited her to move upstairs and share his penthouse apartment, 7-C, just across the hall from Buddy Jacobson's flat, 7-D, where Melanie Cain was living with the former horse trainer. Silbergeld was not a man a nice girl would want to introduce to her mother. Prior to Mel, he had been involved in a number of shady deals.

Just before he left the army as a captain following his return from South-East Asia, Silbergeld took part in manoeuvres at West Point and came under a cloud of suspicion when he could not account for the disappearance of eleven Claymore mines, sophisticated explosives each capable of causing damage equivalent to a dozen hand grenades. After a time at 84th Street Silbergeld was taken in for questioning by the Nassau County District Attorney, Denis Dillon, about the wrecking of Long Island dustman Harvey Hochlerin's 1974 Peugeot. A thug named Carlo Carrera was trying to attach a Claymore mine to the car when it went off prematurely. Carrera survived the blast but never returned to the penthouse apartment where he had been shown all there was to know about Claymore mines. One previous experiment at the townhouse resulted in a bath being blown up.

About this time in 1978 Silbergeld and Harris were married and moved to a West Side flat. The penthouse was sub-leased to Jack Tupper. Meanwhile, after five years Melanie Cain was beginning to tire of Buddy Jacobson, especially after setting eyes on the handsome Jack Tupper. In no time at all she had dumped Jacobson and was keeping Tupper warm at night.

At his trial, authorities postulated that Jacobson and others had killed Tupper because he had run off with his girlfriend. More informed sources believe, as Jacobson claimed, that Tupper was slain by members of his drug gang after double-crossing them in a $250,000 deal.

Harris's marriage ended just short of a year and she was swept up in Brian Kilclinic's arms. Four months after she swore to tell the truth at the trial she took another oath on 14 June 1980 when she promised to love, honour and obey the dog trainer. By now Mel Harris was taking acting lessons and appearing in minor stage plays. The going was tough and the breaks did not come, except for one – the breakdown of her second marriage.

The rest of Mel Harris's story is an open book . . . In December 1982 she met the man all of her press releases identify as husband number one, David Hume Kennerly, the

Pulitzer prize-winning photographer who was President Gerald Ford's White House lensman. Mel and David moved to Los Angeles where she began appearing in films and on TV in programmes such as *Moonlighting*. After taking time off to have their son, Byron, now 11, Mel returned to acting and landed the plum rôle of Hope Murdoch Steadman in ABC's hit comedy drama *thirtysomething*.

Although playing a happily married young mother on screen the rôle was not repeated off screen. Divorce ended her 'first' marriage to Kennerly in May 1988 and if you don't count husbands David Silbergeld and Brian Kilclinic, Mel took on her 'second' husband in a 102-second ceremony in November 1988. It isn't known whether the groom, actor Cotter Smith of TV's *Equal Justice*, knew what number husband he really was or, for that matter, if David Kennerly knew what number husband of Mel's he had been.

In April 1990 Mel gave birth to a daughter, Madeline Michael Smith. *thirtysomething* ended on 3 September 1991 and, as yet, Mel has not been cast in another hit show.

Baywatch Babe's Secret Husband

In interviews, *Baywatch* beauty Gena Lee Nolin extols the virtues of her husband, Greg Fahlman. She rarely mentions the fact that he is her second husband. On 21 March 1991, aged 19, she married David

Peek-a-boo! Gena Lee Nolin shows her knicks

Alan Feiler in the Chapel of Love in Las Vegas. On their wedding night Feiler took pictures of his nude wife while she was bound head and foot and had a clothes peg attached to her nipple. A month and a day later the marriage was over. Feiler filed for divorce and went on the run. In 1994 Feiler was jailed for fraud. He stole millions of dollars from pensioners.

SIR JIMMY SAVILE, OBE, KCSG

Jimmy Savile is one of the more eccentric characters in Babylon. Known as 'The Godfather', he is renowned for his altruism on behalf of numerous charities. He comes across as a man of the people, which is obviously what he wants, yet beneath the surface he is really a hard-nosed Yorkshire businessman. He doesn't fit into any category so here he has his own chapter.

James Vincent Savile was born the youngest of seven in Leeds on 31 October 1926 (the day that escapologist Harry Houdini died). He is cagey about his age. 'I first did *Top of the Pops* in 1964. (In fact he was the very first host on New Year's Day that year.) 'I was about 40 and too old then. I lied about my age for commercial reasons.' During World War II Jimmy was a Bevin Boy working in the mines for seven years but a mining accident in 1945 put paid to that and very nearly cost him his life. Told he would never walk again, he was encased in a steel corset for three years. One day he saw an old man hobbling towards him and realized to his horror that he was looking at a reflection of himself. With a determination second to none he threw away his crutches and steel corset, stuck a picture of a Rolls-Royce on his wall and vowed to make his fortune. His childhood was hard. His mother, Agnes, whom he called 'the Duchess' had to feed nine people on £3.50 a week so food was scarce. It has left him with an odd regard to nosh. When he had his Scarborough flat done up Jimmy told the designer not to put in a kitchen.

He became a DJ and went to work for Mecca in the early

1950s. This was the start of Savile's travels that have raised over £30,000,000 for charity and a good wedge has been deposited in one of the no doubt numerous accounts of Mr J. V. Savile. He charges £10,000 for each personal appearance. In 1983 Jimmy gave a series of interviews to the *Sun* about his days as a nightclub manager. In the features he was quoted as saying that he was nicknamed 'the Godfather' and was incredibly ruthless. One night a man was lying on the floor looking up girls' dresses to see what colour their knickers were. A bouncer told Jimmy and he arranged for the man to continue lying there but with his eyes closed. When the police arrived they apparently condoned his actions. 'Inspector's compliments,' said the sergeant, 'you didn't give the bastard half enough.' Jimmy was also quoted as saying, 'Some of the hairy things I've done would get me ten years inside. I never get physical personally. Let's just say that while I'm in Edinburgh very dodgy things happen in London. I'm quite innocent.' The feature was accompanied by a picture of 'the Godfather' in a fur coat and sunglasses.

He also wrestled professionally 107 times: 'Top of the bill every bout, not because I was a good wrestler, but because I was a larger-than-life personality. My fights were fucking bloodbaths, fucking hell, not many, you don't think any self-respecting grappler is going to go and lie down to a bleeding fucking blond-haired fucking wise-cracking boy do you?'

Exceptionally close to his 4′ 11″ mother, Jimmy still keeps all her clothes in a wardrobe in his Scarborough flat even though she died aged 86 in 1973! Once a year his cleaning lady takes them to be cleaned and then they are replaced in the wardrobe. The foyer of the block contains a board stating whether residents are in or out. Mrs Savile is still listed as 'In'! When she wanted some money she did all her cleaning, then told her son she had employed a daily and paid her £12. He reimbursed her the funds. The Saviles never expressed affection. 'Saying "I love you" to someone is a load of modern nonsense.' Of the time following her death, he said: 'The best five days of my life were spent with the Duchess when she was dead. She looked marvellous. She belonged to me. It's wonderful, is death.'

Even now Jimmy has a kind of Mr Spock-like reaction to emotion. 'I'm always on an even keel. The fluctuations in my life are very shallow . . . I don't have friends in the accepted sense, though I have lots of pals. I don't really need a confidant. My mother was more a good pal than an intimate. Emotions are dangerous. They can cause trouble and screw you up. It's common sense, isn't it? To me, most people's thinking is clouded by emotions which are influenced by problems which are invited by worry. I couldn't tell you whether I am emotionally deprived because I don't know what it is to be emotional. I may be emotionally lacking. I'll stand for that.' Jimmy's love life consists of brief encounters with various women 'from Land's End to John O'Groats'. He never rings girls and never gets jealous.

In 1975 Jimmy began his popular *Jim'll Fix It* show making wishes come true. Oddly or perhaps not Jimmy never wears make-up on television and doesn't use a deodorant.

In August 1988 Jimmy was put in charge of Broadmoor, the hospital for the criminally insane. He has been on friendly terms with most of the recent prime ministers and can pick up the phone to Buckingham Palace. When he received his knighthood in the summer of 1990 he received congratulatory telegrams from both Charles and Diana. Diana mentions him in the notorious 'Squidgygate' tapes when she is talking to her lover James Gilbey.

DIANA: Jimmy Savile rang me up yesterday and he said: 'I'm just ringing up, my girl, to tell you that his nibs has asked me to come and sort out the redhead, and I'm just letting you know so that you don't find out through her or him. And I hope it's all right by you.' And I said: 'Jimmy, you do what you like.'

GILBEY: What do you mean, help out the redhead, darling?

DIANA: With her publicity.

GILBEY: Oh, has he?

DIANA: Sort her out. He said: 'You can't change a lame duck or something but I've got to talk to her cos that's the boss's orders and I've got to carry them out. But I want you to know you're my number one girl and . . .'

GILBEY: Oh, darling, that's not fair. You're *my* number one girl.

DIANA: Well, he's sort of heterosexual and everything.

GILBEY: Heterosexual?

DIANA: Yes.

GILBEY: Is he? What do you mean heterosexual?

DIANA: Everything.

GILBEY: Oh he's everything. That's not heterosexual, darling. Oh, Squidge, you're so . . . Do you know what heterosexual is?

DIANA: No.

GILBEY: You and me.

DIANA: Oh right.

GILBEY: That's hetero.

DIANA: Oh.

GILBEY: The other is sort of alternating current. I never know how you, what is it, bi? Is he bi?

There have been some bizarre rumours about Jimmy Savile over the years. One, that he likes corpses. 'Rubbish. It's like an undertaker . . . he spends hours with dead bodies. Of course he does, it's his job. I'm not fascinated with dead bodies. It is very simple. Last night at Stoke Mandeville I was hanging around the porter's lodge until about half past two this morning. I am a voluntary helper. Therefore one of my jobs is to take away the lately deceased and I personally consider that task to be a considerable honour. Some people are most dischuffed with cadavers that freak them out and put their hair on end. Some people get hold of the fact that Jim likes looking after cadavers and say, "Aha, Jim's a necrophiliac!" I'm not a necrophiliac.' Two, that he's gay. Again untrue although his elder brother, Johnny, does say that when Jimmy is chatting up a girl he comes across as camp in an effort to disarm her. Apparently, it usually works. Only once has he been close to marriage, with singer Polly Browne of the pop group Pickettywitch. She ended the relationship. He denies this, claiming never to have been in love, never to have had a live-in girlfriend and never to have been near getting married. Three, that he is into little girls. 'I'm not a lover of children. I don't like children. They have to earn my respect. My sisters and brothers all had children but all I could hear was moaning and groaning. I never had any paternal feeling. I don't like children. Never in a million years would I dream of letting a kid, or five kids, past my front door. Never, ever. I'd feel uncomfortable.'

'I've never been a do-gooder. My attitude to other people is "If you want to go and stone your brain out, then it's all the same to me. I don't care."' Asked to describe himself, Jimmy bluntly states, 'I'm a thief. I steal hearts and minds. I go through people like a knife goes through butter. I have fun, but there's total respect. I don't denigrate anyone and I don't put them down.'

DEATH IN BABYLON

It is an incongruity that in many respects no one dies in Babylon because no matter how long after their 'death' we can 'bring them back to life' again simply by watching a re-run or a video of their greatest or even worst performances. However, the reality is that people do die, even in Babylon. Many go peacefully in their sleep, while others have a less fortunate end . . .

Stone Me!

Tony Hancock was undoubtedly one of the most successful post-war comedians Britain has produced. Like many comedians, he was also a manic depressive. (Harry Secombe substituted for Hancock in three episodes because the star was in a mental hospital.) Hancock abhorred the physical act of parting with money. He rarely carried cash. Once, after writing a cheque for £5,000, Hancock had to drink whisky before he could carry on. Hancock was a violent husband to his two wives.

After a slow start on the radio on 2 November 1954 with his 'repertory' company of Hattie Jacques, Sid James, Bill Kerr and Kenneth Williams, *Hancock's Half Hour*, written by Ray Galton and Alan Simpson (who met when both were patients in a TB clinic) became required listening for virtually the whole country. Williams used many funny voices on the show and pioneered the catchphrase 'Stop messin' about!' which Hancock was later to dismiss as 'a cardboardian stereotype'.

On 6 July 1956 the show moved to television. Only Sid James made the transition as a regular from the wireless to the small screen. Kerr disappeared completely, Williams after six weeks and Jacques made rare appearances. It seemed Hancock could do no wrong. His programmes contained classic one-liners, such as 'A pint?! Have you gone mad – that's very nearly an armful!' (*The Blood Donor*) and 'Does Magna Carta mean nothing to you? Did she die in vain?' (*Twelve Angry Men*).

It was not enough for the Lad Himself. He yearned for international stardom and made a number of unsuccessful films such as *The Punch and Judy Man* (1962). Hancock abandoned Sid James but, more importantly, he jettisoned his writers Galton and Simpson (who went on to create *Steptoe and Son* in the time they had allocated for writing more *Hancocks*). Without financial remuneration Galton and Simpson had worked on three scripts tailor-made for Hancock. He rejected them all. It was the biggest blunder of his career. If ever there was a comedian who could not function without writers, that comedian was Tony Hancock. He made a series for independent television which began on 3 January 1963 and ran for thirteen weeks. It went down like the proverbial lead balloon. Another ITV series, called simply *Hancock* (in 1967), saw Hancock as the wholly unbelievable owner of a nightclub. It was a disaster. Hancock began drinking even more heavily and had difficulty remembering his lines. Gerald Thomas, director of the highly successful *Carry on . . .* films, proposed a film which would reunite Hancock with Sid James. James was enthusiastic but Hancock nixed the idea.

In March 1968 he went to Australia in an attempt to revive his flagging career. He was to film 13 shows. With three episodes in the can and after rehearsals for the fourth finished, Hancock returned to his Sydney hotel room. The next day, 25 June 1968, four days after his second divorce, Tony Hancock committed suicide with an overdose of barbiturates washed down with vodka. He was 44 years old. He left two suicide notes, one of which contained the poignant phrase, 'Things seemed to go wrong too many times.'

Alas Smith & Jones

To outsiders it seemed that Pete Duel had everything to live for – a loving girlfriend, a nice home, money and a hit TV series. Yet, shortly after 1.25 a.m. on 31 December 1971 this handsome and talented actor killed himself.

Peter Ellstrom Deuel was born in Rochester, New York, on 24 February 1940, the eldest child of Dr Elsworth Shault Deuel and Lillian Marcella Ellstrom, a Swedish-American. Brother Geoffrey, born in 1942, and sister Pamela, born three years later, completed the family. Peter Deuel grew up wanting to be a pilot but discovered he had 20/30 eyesight and changed his plans to medicine. During two years studying to be a doctor at St Lawrence University, Watertown, New York, the college attended by both his father and grandfather, Deuel appeared in every play staged by the drama department. Deciding a life of medicine was not after all for him, Deuel joined the American Theatre Wing where he spent a further two years studying Shakespeare, restoration comedy, elocution, fencing, dancing and body movement. In 1962 Deuel landed his first paid job as an actor, a small part in an off-Broadway production of Electra at the Players' Theater in Greenwich Village where he also served as assistant stage manager. Deuel made his TV début in a one-hour production from the Armstrong Theater and then went on tour with Tom Ewell in the Broadway hit *Take Her, She's Mine*. On his return he decided to find his fortune in Hollywood.

Arriving in the movie capital Pete Deuel was cast in mainly villainous rôles before landing a part in the TV series *Gidget* which premièred on 15 September 1965. This led to his casting in one of the lead parts in *Love on a Rooftop* the following year. This vehicle gave him the opportunity to show off his talents in both comic and tragic situations.

In 1967 Deuel made his film début in *The Hell with Heroes* and impressed so much he was signed to a seven-year contract by Universal. Appearing as a guest star in a number of shows including *The Fugitive*, *The Virginian* and *A Man Called Ironside*, 6´ Deuel was signed to play the rôle of Hannibal Heyes (alias Joshua Smith) in a new ABC TV series entitled *Alias Smith and Jones* about two train robbers who have been promised an amnesty if they can stay out of trouble for one year. The series débuted in Britain in April 1971 on BBC-2 and was an instant hit. For the sake of simplicity Pete had altered the spelling of his surname to Duel. However, filming a weekly series was a hard slog and Duel did not relish the demands put upon him. In August 1971 he collapsed on set with the flu and was sent home. A reputation for being difficult followed although Pete claimed he was not hard to work with, merely a perfectionist. It is thought he was hoping another less strenuous series would rescue him from *Alias Smith & Jones* and then allow him to return to 'proper' acting on Broadway. Of acting in a series Pete had said, 'The quantity of work is Herculean and the quality is often non-existent.' A salary increase quietened him temporarily. 'Contractually, I have to do this series,' he told a journalist friend, 'or some other trash.'

Duel, a politically active Democrat, was vocal in his support for Eugene McCarthy. In November 1971 Duel stood for election to an executive post in his union, the Screen Actors' Guild, and was bitterly disappointed when he lost. When the telegram arrived informing him of his defeat he tacked it to a wall and then, taking his revolver, blasted a hole through it.

A keen environmentalist and twenty years ahead of his time, Pete loved to picnic far from civilization but he always tried to leave the countryside tidier than when he had arrived. Pete refused to buy containers that could not be recycled and campaigned to persuade everyone else to do the same. When he signed an autograph more often than not he would preface his signature with the words 'Peace and Ecology Now'.

Pete Duel was a typical man of the 60s. However, he found his release in alcohol rather than drugs. Thrice arrested for drink driving, he lost his licence but escaped jail by promising the judge he would give up the bottle. Pete received a $1,000 fine and was sentenced to 180 days' jail suspended for two years. Just a week after his plea to the judge, Pete Duel would die by his own hand.

In December he volunteered to spend two weekends working for a charity telethon – Toys for Tots. A picture taken at the time shows Duel holding a toy gun to his head. Often while in the make-up chair for the show Duel would place his prop gun to his head.

On Thursday 30 December 1971 Pete worked, as usual, on *Alias Smith and Jones*. According to the crew, he was in high spirits. At his home at 2552 Glen Green Terrace, a two-bedroomed bungalow in the Hollywood Hills, Pete read through the script for the next day. He had one visitor that night. Pete's girlfriend, 29-year-old Diane Ray, was a secretary and aspiring actress. Together they watched the latest episode of *Alias Smith and Jones* (Duel was not happy with the edition) and a Lakers basketball game. Duel drank a lot that evening which led to an argument with Diane who went to bed. At 1.25 a.m. Pete walked into the bedroom and stared at her for a long moment before going to a dresser where he took out a package Diane thought was a forgotten Christmas present. Taking the box into the living room, Pete smiled at his girlfriend and said, 'I'll see you later.' A few moments afterwards, Diane heard a loud sound like a firecracker. Going to find out what had happened, she saw Duel lying nude in front of the Christmas tree, a .38 revolver by his side and blood oozing from his right temple. Gathering her wits about her Diane called the police. At first, the authorities did not want to write the death off as a suicide and cited Pete's open-house policy for aspiring and out-of-work actors as a possible factor. Perhaps one of the resting thespians, jealous of Pete's success, had killed him. There was no evidence, however, that anyone apart from Duel and Ray had been in the house. Pete's friends dismissed the suicide theory and claimed it was an accidental death. None of them came up with a satisfactory answer as to why ecologist Pete had bought a gun, if not to kill himself.

It is interesting that when he arrived in Hollywood Pete had given himself five years before returning to Broadway. At the time of his death, Pete had spent six years in Tinseltown and the success of *Alias Smith and Jones* threatened to extend that period by some years. A memorial service was held on 2 January 1972 at the Hindu-Christian Self Realization temple in Pacific Palisades, California. Pete was not a member but his manager was. Pete's funeral took place on 5 January 1972 at the Baptist Church in Penfield, New York. Even now, over 25 years after his death, Pete Duel and all that he stood for are remembered not just for what might have been but also for what he achieved in his ever so brief life. He once said, 'Fame in showbusiness is not in proportion to actual achievement.'

His business manager has an enduring memory of Pete Duel. John Napier writes, 'I shall never forget early one morning about 4 a.m. one summer when Pete stood in front of my home, barefoot in blue jeans, looking out over the vast valley stretching far in the distance and began in a loud, strong, beautiful voice, to recite *Hamlet*. Even in my sleepless stupor I was suddenly caught up in the beauty of the speech as his *Hamlet* reverberated around the hills. When he came near the end of the speech the sun began to peak its brilliant head over a nearby mountain as if to pay tribute to a fine performance. "I love you, sun," he yelled and we broke into gales of laughter. Neighbours, be damned. It was a happy time. There were many happy times like that.'

Slower Than a Speeding Bullet

Long before Christopher Reeves took to wearing his underpants on the outside the Man of Steel was played by George Reeves, a burly ex-boxer and wrestler who appeared in *Gone with the Wind*. *The Adventures of Superman* was one of the most popular programmes on television in 1950s America.

Reeves had been born as George Bessolo on 6 April 1914 in Ashland, Kentucky. His acting career was interrupted by World War II. At the cessation of hostilities he found that he had lost momentum. Major rôles were still going to the established stars like Clark Gable and Humphrey Bogart while the younger upstarts such as Gregory Peck and Burt Lancaster hogged the romantic leads. Reeves was reduced to appearing in children's serials and playing opposite starlets during their screen tests. Although his friends knew Reeves was bitterly disappointed at being passed over for stardom never once was he unprofessional and he always did his best to put the starlets at ease for *their* big chance. In 1951 the producers of the *Superman* TV series began casting around for a new actor to don the mantle. The current incumbent, Kirk Alyn, wanted to do serious work on the New York stage and also wanted more money than the producers were prepared to pay. In late 1951 6´ 2˝ Reeves was sent along to audition by his agent. He had been preceded by over 200 hopefuls but as soon as producer Robert Maxwell saw Reeves he knew his search was at an end. Not only did Reeves look the part but he was a good actor to boot. Although he already had a muscular physique it was necessary to pad Reeves's costume with foam muscles. Over the next five years, Reeves played the title rôle in 104 episodes of the serial. To keep costs down each episode was shot in just two-and-a-half days. To escape continuity problems the characters wore the same costume in every scene.

Off-set Reeves spent a lot of time helping children and children's charities. He was often challenged to fights by belligerent kids but Reeves used his charm to diffuse difficult situations. One incident required all of his tact. A boy pointed his father's pistol at Reeves threatening to see if 'Superman' really could dodge speeding bullets. Reeves told the boy that although he obviously would survive others nearby might be hurt by the ricocheting bullet.

Reeves had no illusions about his work but if he felt anger he relied upon his wide circle of friends to remind him of his good fortune. He knew he was lucky to have an audience of more people in a week than most actors have in a year. His financial remuneration from the series was a not inconsiderable $50,000 a year. He spent money whenever he felt like it and his home, 1579 Benedict Canyon Road, became a regular drop-in for all sorts of characters. Reeves was sensible enough to make sure his hell-raising lifestyle was kept a secret from the ladies and gentlemen of the fourth estate. His career depended upon it. An arrest would have seen the series cancelled quicker than a producer could say charge sheet. Not only that but Reeves's professionalism would not allow him to hold up shooting because he was hung over. He had seen that happen too often at Warner Brothers with Errol Flynn. During one off-season Reeves appeared in the hit movie *From Here to Eternity* (1953) which won Best Supporting Actor and Actress Academy Awards for Frank Sinatra and Donna Reed. However, Reeves's rôle was pared to virtually nothing when test audiences wondered aloud what Superman was doing in Hawaii. Following the cancellation of *The Adventures of Superman* Reeves turned down the opportunity to star in a series about the square-jawed all-American hero Dick Tracy. He also rejected the opportunity of a nationwide tour on which, dressed as Superman, he would have sparred with boxer Archie Moore. The tour would have garnered Reeves $20,000 for just six weeks' work. Like many actors Reeves wanted to direct and had been behind the camera for the last three episodes of *The Adventures of Superman*. He had also bought the rights to two scripts intending to direct and star in both himself.

In May 1959 he was offered a feature rôle in a film to be made in Spain. Despite stories to the contrary Reeves could not have been happier and to add to his pleasure the producers of *The Adventures of Superman* approached him about reprising his rôle, a job Reeves was happy to accept. Personally, he was engaged to Leonore Lemon and the happy couple were due to marry on 19 June 1959. Three days beforehand Reeves retired early, only for his front doorbell to ring.

His fiancée answered the door to two friends, Carol von Ronkel and William Bliss. Reeves got up and went downstairs where he shouted at his chums to go away. A short while afterwards, he apologized for his uncharacteristic outburst and invited them in. The pals sat and chatted for a while until Reeves went upstairs. The talk continued until Lemon suddenly said, 'He's going to shoot himself.' The other friends were puzzled especially when they heard a drawer slide open. 'He's opening it to get a gun,' explained Reeves's fiancée. Within seconds a shot rang out and William Bliss raced up the stairs to find a naked Reeves with blood oozing from his left temple. The official autopsy listed the cause of death as suicide although Reeves's mother discounted this, having received a telephone call from the actor three days before his death in which she described his mood as 'splendid'. His colleagues also refused to believe the coroner's verdict and two bullets found embedded in the bedroom wall were never satisfactorily explained. Reeves's mother hired the famous Hollywood lawyer Jerry Geisler to look into her son's death, refusing to allow his cremation for three years. Was George Reeves's death suicide? Was it a mistake, a dreadful blunder? Or was it something far more sinister?

In 1996 the truth was finally revealed. In 1949 Reeves had started an affair with Toni Mannix, the wife of MGM studio executive Eddie Mannix. The affair progressed until 1958 when Reeves met and fell for Leonore Lemon. Hell hath no fury like a woman scorned and Mannix did not take her rejection lying down. She began to call Reeves at all hours of the day and night and hang up whenever he answered. On 9 April 1959 Reeves was involved in a car crash that could have killed him. Mysteriously, the brake lines on his Jaguar had been cut. On 12 June 1959 Toni Mannix decided to kill what she loved and hired a hitman. She knew that Reeves kept a Luger next to his bed because she had given him the weapon. The gunman was to break in quietly and shoot Reeves using his own weapon. If the gun could not be found, then the mission was to be abandoned. In her befuddled state Mannix believed that the world would believe Reeves had killed himself if his own gun was the killing weapon. The hitman found Reeves's Luger and for nearly forty years the world believed that TV's Superman had killed himself.

Suicide Isn't Painless

✝ On 15 July 1974 29-year-old newsreader Christine Chubbock of Miami's WXLT-TV's *Sun Coast Digest Show* made headline news herself as she finished reading a bulletin. 'In keeping with Channel 40's policy of bringing you the latest in blood and guts,' she said, 'you're going to see a first, an attempted suicide.' She then produced a .38 revolver and blew her brains out. Viewers saw her slump forward across her desk before the screen went blank. She died fourteen hours later without regaining consciousness.

✝ Sheree Winton, 60s showgirl and mother of Dale, killed herself aged 40 on 28 May 1976 in her bedroom in Hampstead, London. Her son found the body.

✝ One of the most popular shows of the 70s was *Fantasy Island* starring Ricardo Montalban and the dwarf Herve Villechaize. After the pilot, TV executives wanted to ditch 3´ 10˝ Villechaize in favour of a sexy girl but producer Aaron Spelling fought for the little actor and the network honchos relented. However, Villechaize was not one for gratitude. He believed he was the star of the show because he said, 'The plane! The plane!' His behaviour became increasingly bizarre. He brought a gun to the set and carried it everywhere. Outside his trailer he hung a sign that said 'The Doctor of Sex'.

When the trailer was occupied he turned the sign over and it read 'The Doctor Is In'. Eventually, it became too much and Paris-born Villechaize was sacked. He committed suicide on 4 September 1993 aged 50.

✝ Farmer Ted Moult was as well known for advertising Everest double glazing on television as for his appearances on panel games like *What's My Line?* A genial character and a devout Roman Catholic, Ted shocked his friends when he shot himself on 3 September 1986 aged 60. It is thought he had financial worries that affected his state of mind.

✝ Bisexual black actress Eva Mottley played Bella O'Reilly in the original *Widows* (1983). At the age of 22 she had a two-year affair with David Bowie. 'David and I share the same sexual tastes,' she said. Not long after she went to prison for possessing LSD. Inside she had gay affairs which continued on the outside. She killed herself on Valentine's Day 1985 aged 31.

✝ Imogen Hassall was beautiful, brunette and busty. She was also deeply unhappy. Her first husband, actor Kenneth Ives, best known to TV viewers for playing Hawkeye in *The Last of the Mohicans*, later married comedienne Marti Caine. Their daughter died at only four days old. Imogen's second marriage on 15 January 1979 to actor Andrew Knox, star of *Doctor on the Go*, was extremely brief. They separated after just four months. On 23 June 1975 she was fined £10 with £11 doctors' fees for being drunk in charge of a bicycle. An affair with tennis player Buster Mottram went nowhere. She attempted suicide a number of times before her naked body was discovered at her home in Wimbledon on 16 November 1980 when friends turned up to take her on holiday. She had her right hand on the telephone dial and an empty bottle of Tuinal barbiturates beside her. She was 38.

The Hex

It was said that handsome 6′ 1″ actor Jon-Erik Hexum had a guaranteed golden future ahead of him in Hollywood. He starred as macho time-traveller Phineas Bogg in the sci-fi show *Voyagers* and then he appeared with Joan Collins in the TV movie *The Making of a Male Model* (US 1983). The pair reputedly became a couple off-screen. Collins tried and failed to use her influence to get Hexum cast as her lover, Dex, on *Dynasty*. (The part went to Michael Nader.) Instead, Hexum was cast as Mac Harper, the lead in the series *Cover Up*. Mac Harper was a fashion photographer, a former Green Beret and, ironically, a weapons expert, who doubled as a secret agent. Off-screen Hexum was a practical joker forever fooling around. It was his sense of fun and jolly japes that cost him his life. At about 5.15 p.m. on 12 October 1984 26-year-old Hexum jokingly placed a gun against his temple, smiled and said, 'Let's see if I've got one for me' and pulled the trigger. Although the weapon was loaded with blanks (a wad of cotton and a small charge) it was still enough to shatter his skull. He immediately collapsed into a coma and was rushed to Beverly Hills Medical Center where his condition was described as extremely critical. Six days later, he was pronounced brain dead. His organs were transplanted and his death was ruled 'accidental'.

Other Deaths

The following also died untimely deaths in Babylon.

✝ Bob Crane, the star of the sitcom *Hogan's Heroes*, was murdered on 29 June 1978. He was 49. The killing remains unsolved.

✝ Roger Delgado was the original Master in *Dr Who*. He was killed in a car crash in Turkey on 18 June 1973. He was 55.

✝ Roy Kinnear fell off his horse while making a film in Spain on 20 September 1988. He was 54.

✝ Ross McWhirter, co-editor of *The Guinness Book of Records* and co-host of BBC's *Record Breakers*, was murdered on his front doorstep at 50 Village Road, Enfield, on 27 November 1975. He was 50.

✝ Singer Dickie Valentine perished in a car crash on 6 May 1971 aged 41.

✝ Stephen Watson played in the BBC sitcom *No Place Like Home*. He was killed on holiday in a car crash on 19 September 1986. He was 26.

✝ Mark Frankel, star of *Leon the Pig Farmer* and TV mini series, died in a car crash in September 1996 aged 34.

✝ Rock star Marc Bolan hosted his own TV show *Marc* in August 1977. A month later, on 16 September, Bolan was killed when the Mini driven by his girlfriend Gloria Jones ploughed into a tree on Barnes Common. He was 29 years old.

FEUDS IN BABYLON

The people who are in charge of Babylon would have us believe that it is all sweetness and light, that everyone really does love one another and no one argues – ever. This is, of course, utter balderdash. I am sure there are people you work with or went to school with or are related to who you cannot abide. Why should the stars of TV Babylon be any different? They aren't . . .

Holmes *v.* Turner

Throughout showbiz history there have always been famous double acts – Laurel and Hardy, Morecambe and Wise, Hinge and Brackett, Robson and Jerome, Little and Large. To that list will never be added the names of Eamonn Holmes and Anthea Turner.

The two were brought together to host GMTV and, from the start, they loathed each other. Rumours of a feud between the two occasionally surfaced but were always denied. On 27 March 1996 Holmes told guest Noel Edmonds that Turner's interviews sent him to sleep. Anthea claimed she left the set in tears. The two presenters were spoken to by the Director of Programmes and peace seemed to reign – until December 1996. That was when, after Anthea Turner had left the GMTV sofa for the last time, Eamonn Holmes vented his spleen on his former co-anchor. He told a journalist that he found Turner 'unbearable'.

'Anthea really talks down to people and leaves them fuming. She didn't seem to have any sense of how to treat people. I was the only one who had the guts to stand up to her – I was the only one with any power or clout to voice the concerns. I was a bit of a hero. I'm the one who stood up and said, "Eh, now, Princess Tippy Toes – behave yourself."'

Eamonn claimed that Anthea was obsessed with how she looked and would throw a tantrum if things did not go exactly the way she wanted. 'She would fight in the mornings to sit on a particular side of the sofa because she thought the lighting was better there.'

Holmes also said that when he did complain, Turner would go to programme bosses 'doing her little Miss Tiny Tears act . . . I've been an anchor man on TV for sixteen years. I've anchored live programmes five days a week – compare that to Anthea's record.'

TV bosses were not impressed and it was reported that Eamonn was ticked off by GMTV managing director Christopher Stoddart although no public comment was made.

An unnamed producer was quoted by a newspaper as saying that he found Holmes's attitude and behaviour towards Turner spiteful. The producer alleged that Holmes slagged off Turner to other presenters, leaked unfavourable stories to journalists about her and put her off by laughing when she was trying to interview someone.

Whatever the truth of the matter Eamonn Holmes is still on the GMTV sofa and Anthea Turner isn't and Holmes, 'for one, is delirious' about that situation.

Motormouth v. the Mancunian

Since its inception on Channel 4 on 24 August 1989 *The Word* had come in for far more than its fair share of criticism. The two hosts, Mancunian Terry Christian and wild child Amanda de Cadenet, were seen as amateurish and often overawed by their surroundings. Interviews were poorly conducted, guests embarrassed and it was rumoured that off-set the working-class Christian and the posh de Cadenet did not see eye to eye.

The word is sex – spelt Amanda de Cadenet

The situation resolved itself when de Cadenet left and was replaced by pop singer Dani Behr who had been one-third of the aspiring pop group Faith Hope and Charity. F, H and C were managed by Tom Watkins who had found fame for Bros and East 17. All went well on *The Word* until the producers decided the show needed livening up and brought in Mark Lamarr at Christian's recommendation. Although he speaks with a Cockney accent, Lamarr actually comes from Swindon, a fact that Terry Christian seemed to devour with some relish.

Dani Behr in a previous incarnation

In time, the two presenters, friends at first, developed a mutual hatred that made de Cadenet and Christian seem the best of mates. After one show Lamarr grabbed Christian around the throat, took a swing at him and tried to drag him outside to duff him up properly.

Things would have been worse had not security guards, there to keep an eye on the audience, separated the two hotheads. Christian's lawyers demanded an apology from Lamarr but none was forthcoming. 'I really shot myself in the foot. Before it happened the producer was saying, "We're grooming Mark to take over." But once I hit Christian, obviously it wasn't a good move. So I messed that up, but I don't regret it. I've had too many people come up and thank me for what I did,' said Lamarr.

The pair still had a series to get through, although Lamarr asked to be let out of his contract. Not surprisingly, tensions ran high that year. Two years later, Lamarr had had a chance to calm down. 'Terry and I are very different. We worked together and we didn't like each other, so tensions arose. But I don't want to slag Terry off and I certainly don't want to advocate violence. There was a time when I might have said, "I hit him but he deserved it." The thing with Terry is not something I'm proud of,' says Lamarr.

The Word made headlines as much for its vulgar stunts as its feuding co-hosts. Others joined the programme – the shaven-headed lesbian Geordie Hufty, Cambridge-educated Alan Connor (on 10 February 1995 Connor was filming a live link from a German sex club when some irate perverts pulled a gun on him and demanded £500) and another girl no one can remember, all of whom have quickly returned to the obscurity they so richly deserve. Eventually, it all became too much for Channel 4 and *The Word* ended with a whimper although Christian and Behr returned in the autumn of 1996 to present a 60-second version of the show masquerading as an advertisement for a soft drink. At the time Christian admitted, 'I hated all these daft events *The Word* used to feature. We had a lot of big names on the show but we only ever got a few minutes with them because the producers thought setting up some stupid pig race in the studio was more important.' The opinionated Mancunian went on to add, 'I never thought I was the right man for the job. I never felt particularly comfortable on TV but I made a lot of money doing *The Word*.' (Reputedly

£80,000 a series.) Christian and Lamarr may not have got on but the two of them also upset various guests during the show. Lamarr offended Zsa Zsa Gabor by constantly asking about her sex life. When she complained and told him to ask a serious question he asked what she was doing during the Los Angeles earthquake and then, before she could answer, quipped that she probably couldn't remember as she 'was too busy shagging at the time'. He also irritated Dannii Minogue by suggesting she was fat. She poured a pitcher of water over him live on air. Christian was interviewing the actress Joanne Whalley-Kilmer who originally came from Stockport and not so innocently enquired why her then husband Val Kilmer had never visited her home town. 'Is it because you're worried what people in Stockport might say about you being married to a bloke called Val?' Whalley-Kilmer walked out.

Lamarr went on to host the pop quiz *Never Mind the Buzzcocks* and was a team captain on the bizarre *Shooting Stars*. Christian presented a radio show for a while on Talk Radio UK.

TV-Mayhem

'We are absolutely on the edge of great television history,' said David Frost in January 1983 about the impending launch (on 1 February 1983) of ITV breakfast station TV-am. History did not go according to plan. Beaten to the off by two weeks by BBC's *Breakfast Time*, TV-am's 'Famous Five' of Anna Ford, David Frost, Robert Kee, Michael Parkinson and Angela Rippon were expected rapidly to win over audiences. (Esther Rantzen was originally part of the team but had to leave when she discovered she was pregnant.) Boss Peter Jay said the station had a 'mission to explain' – whatever that meant – while David Frost spoke of 'sexual chemistry' between the presenters.

Reporter Tom Holdin said, 'We've taken six weeks to do what the BBC has taken fifty years to do. We're all hacks, but they're *real* hacks. We know what's going to happen before it happens, we won't just react to news.' It was not to be. In an effort to rally the troops, Peter Jay announced in March, 'Don't panic, we're here to stay,' adding, 'We have the better talent. David Frost is the most successful and gifted presenter in the world today. Anna Ford is the most beautiful woman in England. Ours is the better team. It can't fail.' In the same month Frost said, 'There is going to be no axing from TV-am. No one is going to be kicked out, and no one is going to walk the plank.' Jay soon departed, to be replaced by Jonathan and Timothy Aitken.

Jonathan Aitken said, 'All the presenters are staying at TV-am. I think the Famous Five are a tremendous asset to the company.' Then he sacked Anna Ford and Angela Rippon. In June, at a reception held by Lady Melchett, Ford showed her former boss what she thought of him by throwing a glass of wine in Jonathan Aitken's face. Parkinson and Kee also departed, leaving Frost as the only surviving member of the Famous Five. Among those brought in was the puppet Roland Rat, said to be the only instance in history when a rat joined a sinking ship. In the end it wasn't falling audience figures that killed off TV-am, it was the broadcasting franchise system of Margaret Thatcher's Tory Government when the station was outbid by GMTV.

The Big Brek-feud

Channel 4's *The Big Breakfast* was, in the safe hands of Chris Evans and Gaby Roslin, the jewel in the station's crown. The zaniness of Evans and the nice-girl-next-door charm of Roslin, combined with the alien puppets Zig and Zag, newsreader

Peter Smith and Paula Yates's boudoir interviews, made the programme compulsive viewing for millions. But all good things must come to an end and Evans decided he was bigger than *The Big Breakfast* and decided to leave for prime time television and *Don't Forget Your Toothbrush*. Roslin, although great as one half of a double act, could not compete on her own – as was evident from her woeful Saturday night chat show. She, too, packed her bags and left the house for good.

Australian actor (he was Joe Mangel in *Neighbours*) and stand-up comedian Mark Little had stood in for Chris at various times and he was made permanent host. But who was to be his female partner? Various names were bandied about. Dannii Minogue. Julia Carling (or was it Julia Smith or Jules Carling?) Gillian Taylforth. Dani Behr. Mandy Smith. The vote eventually went to Zoë Ball, the 5' 10" daughter of veteran children's TV presenter Johnny Ball of *Playschool* and the excellent *Think of a Number*. Oddly enough, Zoë was working as a researcher on *The Big Breakfast* when it started and was trying to get in front of the cameras. After a couple of auditions with children's telly programmes she asked Chris Evans for his advice. He told her not to get into kids' TV because it was impossible to leave. 'Thankfully, I completely ignored him,' laughed Zoë.

In an interview three months before she joined *The Big Breakfast* Zoë confessed, 'It would be a nightmare if the show started losing viewers because of me.' Things did not begin well. On her first morning in January 1996 Zoë was due to make a spectacular entrance smashing through a stunt door. However, at the last moment she tripped and crashed through the bottom of the door. Mark Little looked on with a bemused expression on his face. It was not an auspicious start for the couple the producers hoped would make viewers forget Chris and Gaby. No chance. From the beginning the mould was set. 'I got a lot of stick for not being Gaby Roslin, for not looking like Gaby Roslin, for not talking like Gaby Roslin, for being about as far removed as anyone could be from Gaby Roslin. I wish I hadn't had this nagging feeling from day one that everyone expected me to be Gaby Roslin II,' explained Zoë. Mark Little did not regard Zoë Ball as his intellectual or professional equal and many times squabbles broke out on the set. On 12 March at the TV and Radio Industries Awards at the Grosvenor House Hotel the show won an award for Best ITV Programme. The two hosts picked up the gong and Mark said, 'This is a team award – let's not forget our Gaby Roslin.' According to insiders Zoë saw this as a dig at her and left. *The Big Breakfast* publicists did their best to paper over the cracks, denying there was any friction between the two hosts. Others, including the watching public, knew better. There was no chemistry between them and viewers showed their feelings the only way they knew how. They turned off in droves. Zoë tried to explain the situation with Little: 'With a co-presenter, it's almost like being married. You do have disagreements. Things like that happen all the time. There was this huge story going round the building that we hated each other.' Again *The Big Breakfast* bosses dismissed the new audience figures, claiming they were happy with the show and were not interested in ratings. No one believed that last one for a second. Something had to give.

One day Mark Little went on holiday . . . and never came back. It was a great relief to Zoë Ball when the BBC announced she was to spearhead their flagship Saturday children's programme, replacing Emma Forbes on *Live and Kicking* at a reputed salary of £200,000 a year. After seven months, she was able to bid farewell to *The Big Breakfast*. On her last day Zoë cried, 'but I think my tears were tears of relief'.

Since the end of the feud *The Big Breakfast* has been presented by ex-Gladiator Sharron Davies and Rick Prosser who uses the screen name Rick Adams – can't think why. They were replaced by Denise Van Outen and Richard Orford. Ratings are still dropping.

Kelvin MacFrenzy *v.* Jahnet Street-Pawta

Kelvin Calder MacKenzie was appointed editor of the *Sun* on 19 April 1981 and under his stewardship the paper rose to dizzying heights both in circulation and in the amazement of readers by some of the stories in its pages. Regularly the *Sun* was criticized and censured by the Press Council and regularly MacKenzie ignored the adjudications. It was reputedly MacKenzie who, while working on the *New York Post*, came up with the headline 'HEADLESS MAN FOUND IN TOPLESS BAR'. In fact, the *Sun* became known for its in-yer-face headlines: 'GOTCHA!' and 'STICK IT UP YOUR JUNTA' both at the time of the Falklands War, 'FROM TOE JOB TO NO JOB' about Tory MP David Mellor's resignation following an affair with an unemployed actress and the all-time classic 'FREDDIE STARR ATE MY HAMSTER' which was made into a T-shirt. MacKenzie's *Sun* had to 'shock and amaze on every page' and occasionally the editor went too far. One such incident was the allegation that pop star Elton John was cavorting with rent boys. That cost the *Sun* an enormous libel settlement said to be £1 million. Also under MacKenzie's editorship the paper carried a completely fabricated interview with the wife of a Falklands War hero and totally miscalculated the mood of the city of Liverpool after the Hillsborough disaster when almost 100 fans died.

Despite all this the circulation of the *Sun* soared to over 4 million copies a day while its nearest rival, the Robert Maxwell-owned *Daily Mirror*, was around a million copies behind. MacKenzie's reputation was that of a brilliant newspaper man with an eye for crisp layout and snazzy headlines but he also would give vent to his anger if his fellow journalists did not meet his high standards. His 'bollockings' were ferocious bawlings out of colleagues for 'crap pages. Throw it in the bin and start again,' or any other misdemeanours as the editor saw it. It was this that earned him the nickname 'Kelvin MacFrenzy' as much as his seemingly inexhaustible energy. Often he would call a hack into his office: 'Come in. Don't speak. Take your bollocking. Then fuck off and we'll never talk about it again.' One female reporter turned in a piece of work that MacKenzie did not approve of and she asked for an 'E for effort'. The editor gave her an 'F for fuck off'. MacKenzie also despised anyone whose views he disagreed with, a group that included beggars, most blacks, criminals, demonstrators, dossers, drug-takers, football hooligans, foreigners, graffiti artists, gypsies, hippies, homosexuals, militant trade unionists, muggers, peace campaigners, prisoners, prostitutes, Social Security scroungers, socialists, squatters, students, terrorists especially the IRA, tramps, vandals, winos and sex offenders.

Janet Street-Porter is a journalist and television executive well known for her liberal views and strangulated vowels. She is the complete antithesis of Kelvin MacKenzie. Born Janet Bull two months after MacKenzie, she began her career in newspapers (*Daily Mail* 1969-71, *Evening Standard* 1971-3) and magazines (*Queen, Vogue*) before moving into television in 1975 where she worked in front of the camera and behind the scenes on such programmes as *The Six O'Clock Show, Around Midnight, The London Weekend Show* and *Saturday Night People*. She won a BAFTA for her brilliantly innovative show *Network 7*. Poached to become Head of Youth (renamed Yoof because of the way Street-Porter speaks) Programmes at the BBC in 1988, she devised *Reportage* and *Rough Guide* among others. Incongruously, she is President of the Ramblers' Association. In 1988 in the *Sun* Kelvin MacKenzie had run a picture of a horse next to one of Street-Porter asking readers to vote which was the more attractive.

In 1993, after twelve years in charge, Kelvin MacKenzie stood down as editor of the *Sun*. He handed over the reins to Stuart Higgins, the man he once dubbed 'Higgy the Human Sponge'. MacKenzie moved within the Murdoch organization to become managing director of satellite TV station BSkyB in

January 1994. He did not enjoy his stint at BSkyB and resigned nine months later.

In October 1994 Street-Porter began work as managing director of L!VE TV, the Mirror Group's post-Maxwell foray into cable television. Her two-year contract was said to be worth in the region of £300,000. A month later Kelvin MacKenzie arrived as head of Mirror Group TV and de facto became her boss. The scene was set for a bitter feud that was captured in a fly-on-the-wall BBC documentary, *Nightmare at Canary Wharf*, which was shown on 11 December 1995.

Street-Porter had very definite ideas as to how L!VE TV should work and be run. She did away with offices and studios, making the entire 29th floor a studio-cum-office where shows would be broadcast while backroom staff worked around the cameras. She had the ceiling ripped away to reveal pipes and cable, causing one bemused visitor to ask – much to Street-Porter's annoyance – when the decorating would be completed.

Another Street-Porter innovation was to ask all members of staff to supply a photograph of themselves for the company noticeboard. This was so that everyone would get to know each other quickly. At the centre of this pictorial montage was a photo of Street-Porter and MacKenzie. Oddly, as time went by, some strange changes occurred. A moustache appeared on MacKenzie, followed by warts, then his face was covered by black ink. No one ever knew who had defaced the boss's pic but rumours strongly suggested the black biro of Janet Street-Porter.

The cable television industry is run by numerous individual companies around the country and they decide whether a broadcaster should be offered carriage or not. It was essential that L!VE TV was carried by as many cable companies as possible. A presentation had to be given by MacKenzie and Street-Porter to the various companies. This resulted in the farcical situation of two cars picking up MacKenzie and Street-Porter to deliver them to the same airport. They then sat as far away from each other on the plane as was humanly possible before taking two cars to their venue where they would arrive at the presentation as two old friends. As soon as the ceremonies were over the two-car travesty would begin again.

On 25 August 1995 Street-Porter gave the James McTaggart Memorial Lecture at the Edinburgh International Television Festival. In it she laid into the 'M people – middle class, middle brow, middle-aged and male, masonic in their tendencies and, not to put too fine a point on it, fairly mediocre' who run television.

Just three weeks later, on 11 September 1995, Street-Porter hastily left L!VE TV to join independent television company Chrysalis TV.

Without Street-Porter L!VE TV has not exactly flourished despite having a national newspaper's backing. Its most popular programme is the three-minute-long *Topless Darts*.

JR *v.* PC

Larry Hagman was the undoubted star of *Dallas*. It was his portrayal of the scheming J.R. Ewing that made the show a worldwide hit. When the series began in April 1978 there was not one major star in the cast. However, by the summer of 1980 Hagman had realized his worth to the show. Virtually the entire television world was asking 'Who shot JR?' and Hagman determined to make the most of this opportunity. He refused to sign his new contract, demanding more money. The producers hinted that perhaps the ambulance carrying JR to hospital might just crash necessitating plastic surgery on the face of Southfork's most infamous inhabitant. A stalemate ensued with Hagman and his agent on one side and Lorimar and executive producer Philip Capice on the other.

Eventually, the producers relented and Hagman got his pay rise, much to the annoyance of Capice who began a long-running feud with Hagman. Capice, who dated actress Barbara Bel Geddes, tried to control the set but was constantly undermined by Hagman who blamed the fall in ratings on the executive. Capice was also held responsible by Hagman for forcing the departure from the show in 1984 of writer and producer Leonard Katzman, the man credited by Hagman for making the show a hit.

The battle continued and Hagman even went to Capice's bosses insisting he be fired. The feud ended at the end of the 1986 season when Capice left *Dallas*. Capice did not deny or confirm that he was leaving because of Hagman. Leonard Katzman returned to the show as executive producer. 'The series had lost its way,' he said. 'JR had become Mr Nice Guy walking around with his hat in his hands. That was not what his character was founded on.' *Dallas* became a family affair for Katzman. His sons Frank and Mitchell both wrote and directed and his daughter, Sherril Lynn Retino (who died in 1995), played Jackie Dugan who was first Cliff Barnes's, then Bobby's secretary. *Dallas* ended in 1991 and Katzman wrote *The Dallas Reunion* shortly before his death from a heart attack on 5 September 1996, three days after his 69th birthday. Ironically, 5 September was the anniversary of the first showing of *Dallas* in the UK.

Les Grandes Dames de Soap

In the 1980s America and therefore the rest of the world was awash with night-time soaps – *Dallas*, *Dynasty*, *Knots Landing*, *The Colbys*, *Falcon Crest*, *Flamingo Road*, the list seemed to go on and on. Each programme tried to outdo the others with outrageous storylines, handsome men, beautiful women, glorious outfits, stunning locations. Then the producers hit on another selling point and began to hire stars from old Hollywood and recognized names, believing this would add to the viewing figures.

In *Dallas* Lorimar hired Oscar winner George Kennedy and Alexis Smith, while Aaron Spelling went for Ali McGraw, Oscar nominees Rock Hudson and Diahann Carroll, Kate O'Mara, George Hamilton, Christopher Cazenove and Stephanie Beacham on *Dynasty*. *The Colbys* had Oscar winner Charlton Heston, quadruple Oscar nominee Barbara Stanwyck, Oscar nominees Kevin McCarthy and Katherine Ross, Ricardo Montalban and, reprising her *Dynasty* rôle, Stephanie Beacham. *Knots Landing* usually relied on strong storylines but still hooked Julie Harris, Howard Duff, Oscar nominee Ava Gardner, Ruth Roman and Michael York. *Flamingo Road* also had Howard Duff and Kevin McCarthy.

Meanwhile, *Falcon Crest* went for Oscar winners Jane Wyman and Cliff Robertson, 40s glamour-puss Lana Turner, Bradford Dillman, Gina Lollobrigida, Cesar Romero, Kim Novak and Robert Stack for its quotient of old glamour.

Whenever big stars gather, they bring their equally big egos with them and the set of *Falcon Crest* was no different. Jane Wyman was the undoubted grande dame of Tuscany Valley and woe betide anyone who upset her. She was not best pleased when Lana Turner joined the show in 1982 after it had been a year or so on air. The two women did not get on and their feud dated back to the golden days of Hollywood when Wyman was critically acclaimed for her acting and won an Oscar for *Johnny Belinda*, while Turner was popularly acclaimed for her sex appeal. Turner had accompanied Ronald Reagan to the première of *Jezebel* before he became Wyman's second husband.

As soon as she arrived on set Lana Turner made her presence felt. She demanded no visitors be allowed when she was filming and insisted on having a limousine on stand-by should she want to go somewhere. This irked Wyman who told the crew to position her chair as far away from Turner's as possible. The producers did not want to lose Wyman and so decided to forgo the pleasure of Lana Turner's presence on the set. In the end things got so bad that they filmed their scenes on different days. If they appeared in a shot together, they filmed it separately and then the editors worked their magic to make it seem the two ladies were together.

Wyman also clashed with male lead Robert Foxworth. Somehow Foxworth discovered that Wyman's set caravan was six inches longer than his. He demanded equality on the trailer front. Like many actors, Foxworth harboured ambitions to direct and did so on a number of episodes. Wyman also demanded equality on the directing front. Although she never actually directed any episodes, every time Foxworth did so Wyman was paid a director's fee!

KIDS IN BABYLON

Here's One We Made Earlier

Blue Peter began on 16 October 1958 hosted by beauty queen Leila Williams and the late ex-soldier Christopher Trace. Created by Billy Bunteresque bachelor John Hunter Blair (he died of multiple sclerosis while watching the show) it was originally commissioned for just seven weeks and the items were clearly delineated – dolls for girls presented by Williams and model railways for boys by Trace. When Biddy Baxter joined the programme as editor in 1962 she decided that the show should have animals so that children who lived in flats or were unable to keep a pet were not excluded from the animal world. The first *Blue Peter* dog was Petra in the last programme before Christmas 1962. Unfortunately, the dog died of distemper two days after its first appearance and a substitute sought from a pet shop in Lewisham was passed off as the original. The second Petra was not the docile animal that millions of children believed her to be. She was virtually toothless and suffered from poor eyesight. Remembered Christopher Trace, 'She would gum you to death given half the chance.' When she died in September 1977 a bust was commissioned from the sculptor William Timym and placed in the *Blue Peter* Garden where it stands to this day.

The *Blue Peter* tortoise was called Fred until two years after its début when it was discovered that it was really Freda. As if the ignominy of being thought the wrong sex wasn't bad enough, presenter Mark Curry began his first performance on the show by treading on her.

In 1964 Valerie Singleton outraged cat lovers by telling them to wash their animal's eyes with 'boracic acid'. The Beeb was swamped with calls saying that would blind the feline. Just before the six o'clock news an announcer informed viewers that Val had made a mistake and meant to say boracic powder. The same year the programme fell foul of the Temperance Union. A recipe for ginger beer was, the teetotallers claimed, more than half as alcoholic as beer and a 'dangerously alcoholic beer'.

On Thinking Day (the annual Girl Guide celebration in honour of founder Lady Baden-Powell) the most popular *Blue Peter* team ever of Valerie Singleton, John Noakes and Peter Purves invited 200 Girl Guides and 100 Brownies into the studio to sing round the 'camp fire', a prop made of electric light bulbs, covered in gelatine surrounded by fireproof prop logs. As the rendition of *If You're Happy and You Know It, Clap Your Hands* echoed around the studio the 'fire' quickly went out of control and clouds of smoke billowed around, almost obliterating the girls and the presenters. They continued singing until two fire officers ran on to the set to extinguish the flames.

For another show Peter Purves was interviewing the owner of an evil-looking American eagle owl. Peter was told about the bird's unusual friend, a mouse. The owner put the mouse at the feet of the owl and it began to jump about between the bird's enormous talons.

Said Peter, 'How amazing! In the wild they would be natural enemies.'

'Oh yes,' said the other. 'In the wild the eagle owl lives on small mammals. But they've been friends now for . . . ' In a trice the owl flicked its head and the mouse was halfway down its gullet. There was stunned silence in the studio. Then a voice was heard saying, 'Quiet, quiet studio. Here we go. *Blue Peter* eagle owl insert take two.' Peter, the owner and the owl carried on as if nothing was amiss.

'An eagle owl is a very unusual pet, isn't it?'

'Oh yes, it is and he's got a very unusual friend too.'

'Really?'

'Yes, it's a mouse . . . but he can't be with us today.'

Another time chaos reigned in the *Blue Peter* studio was in 1969 just as our intrepid threesome was about to set out on their annual summer expedition. Since the destination was Ceylon, it was thought fun to have a baby elephant from Chessington Zoo in the studio. That's how Lulu came to be part of BBC children's television folklore. All went well until very near the end when Alec 'Smithy' Smith, the keeper, tried to lead Lulu off the set and was dragged back. Then Lulu disgraced herself by leaving two messes on the floor, headbutting Val in the stomach and standing on John Noakes's foot. As the presenters tried to say goodbye Lulu came back into view dragging her hapless keeper behind her right through the indescribable. Trying to avoid the elephant and not to laugh, John stepped straight into the present she had left on the floor. 'Oh dear,' he remarked with considerable restraint, 'I've trodden right in it.'

Diff'rent Strokes for Diff'rent Folks

One of the most popular programmes on American television from 1978 until 1986 was *Diff'rent Strokes*. It was the story of two orphaned black boys from Harlem who were adopted by a rich Park Avenue businessman, Philip Drummond. The boys, Arnold and Willis, were played by Gary Coleman and Todd Bridges respectively. The female of the series was Dana Plato who played Drummond's teenage daughter Kimberley.

Coleman was stunted in growth because of kidney trouble. It led to rumours that he was, in fact, a middle-aged midget rather than a precocious child. Born on 8 February 1968 Coleman now stands just 4′ 8″ and his life has been anything but plain sailing. He has undergone three kidney transplants since 1986 but it was in 1985 that the most traumatic incident of his young life occurred when his parents told him he was adopted. In 1981 a book had been written in which Coleman's mother lovingly described his birth. If that was a lie, reasoned Coleman, what else was false? Coleman stormed out of the house and fired his parents as his managers and trustees. In February 1989 he issued writs for financial mismanagement of his earnings. A year later, he issued further proceedings against his parents claiming they had 'tarnished' his reputation in showbusiness. Shortly afterwards, Coleman moved out to Arizona, shaved his head, put on weight and changed his name to Andy Shane. Coleman/Shane invited a young grocery store clerk to live with him and has followed a reclusive lifestyle ever since.

Todd Bridges fared even less well. He was arrested aged 16 in 1981 after police wondered if the $30,000 Porsche was his or was stolen. Bridges cried racism. In February 1983 Dana Plato accused him of giving her a black eye and breaking her wrist. Following the cancellation of the series Bridges found it difficult to get work and turned to cocaine to alleviate his problems. In March 1986 Bridges took his car to be serviced and told the mechanic that if the work was not completed by the next day he would return and shoot the owner. Unsurprisingly, the failed actor wasn't taken seriously. The next day the owner's Mercedes was blown up. Bridges narrowly avoided prison. Later, he became close to Kenneth Clay, a security guard, who spent his spare time in a crack house. When Bridges ran out of money he began stealing from the house which annoyed Clay. An argument ensued and Bridges pistol-whipped his former friend before shooting him six times. Miraculously, Clay survived although Bridges was charged with attempted murder. In jail awaiting trial Bridges attempted suicide and was placed in the psychiatric wing. Bridges was acquitted on a reduced charge of attempted involuntary manslaughter and released. In May 1990 he was arrested in possession of cocaine. In August of the same year

Bridges was tried for assault. He was defended by Johnnie Cochrane (later to achieve the acquittal of accused double murderer O.J. Simpson) who claimed that Bridges was 'too coked up' to have committed the crime. Bridges was acquitted.

The third member of the team, Dana Plato, left the show when she became pregnant. She also found it difficult to get acting work as an adult. Her marriage broke up and her ex-husband, Lanny Lambert, was awarded custody of their son, Tyler. In January 1988 Dana entered rehab at Cedars-Sinai Medical Center. In the hope of attracting some attention from producers 5´ 2˝ Plato posed for *Playboy* magazine in June 1989 but the only offers she received were for triple x-rated movies. Plato went through a series of jobs ending up working in a dry cleaners for $5.75 (£3) per hour. She was fired from that job following a dispute with a fellow employee. On 28 February 1991, she applied for a job clearing up the rubbish and cleaning toilets in the building where she lived. Plato didn't get it and, in desperation, she donned a black hat, coat and sunglasses and held up a video store with a starting pistol. She stole $164. After Plato left, the shop assistant, Heather Dailey, rang the police at 10.25 a.m. and said, 'I've just been robbed by the girl who played Kimberley on *Diff'rent Strokes*.' Plato was arrested because she went back to the shop fifteen minutes later to collect the glasses she had left there. 'Can you believe? Dana is some dumb chick,' said the arresting officer. She was taken to Clark County Detention Center and held for five days. She was allowed to leave only after singer Wayne Newton posted the $13,000 bail because he knew 'the trauma of being a child star'. After pleading guilty to a charge of attempted robbery, she was put on probation for five years and ordered to perform 400 hours of community service. In January 1992 Plato was again arrested for forging a prescription for 400 Valium tablets. She was charged with four counts of obtaining a controlled substance by fraud and four counts of burglary with intent to commit a crime. Plato, in jail for 31 days before she made bail, threw herself on the mercy of the court. The judge showed leniency, giving her a suspended sentence and another five years' probation. That same year, Plato confessed to a tabloid that she was an alcoholic. After getting breast implants Dana showed them to the world in the film *Compelling Evidence*.

Three young actors with the world at their feet all blundered into ruining their lives. Comedian Jay Leno joked that the cast were due to reunite on the crime show *America's Most Wanted*.

A Wilted Rose

One of the most popular quiz shows in the 50s and 60s was *Double Your Money*, hosted by the avuncular Hughie Green. The show was based on the American quiz *The $64,000 Question* which, when it finally made it to the UK, was called *The 64,000 Question* – which title made no sense at all. One night in February 1964 15-year-old Monica Rose appeared as a contestant on *Double Your Money*. She made such an impression with the audience that two months later, having celebrated her 16th birthday, she was invited back as a hostess.

The working-class girl from a second floor flat in the White City was soon earning £60 a week and travelling the world mixing with the great and the good. The cracks began to show quite quickly. On her 17th birthday Monica gave an interview to a journalist and bemoaned the fact that she never had the opportunity to see any of her old friends. In October 1966 she wore a dress that many felt too risqué for the times and received a sackful of letters of complaint. It was all too much for Monica and she disappeared for two days. She turned up when she heard her mother was worried. In March 1967, Monica announced she was giving up showbusiness and left *Double Your Money*. In April 1967 she took a drugs overdose and shortly afterwards she lent her car to a friend who discovered drugs in it. Within a year she was back on *Double Your*

Money and stayed with the show until it finished in July 1968.

At the time Monica was living in luxury but happiness was not to be hers. Rose wanted something money could not buy: a happy marriage with a nice husband. Her long-term boyfriend was Michael Evans who also doubled as her manager, but they never got as far as a church. For two years after *Double Your Money* ended Monica was mostly unemployed and moved to a less fashionable part of London.

In 1971 Hughie Green hosted a new show called *The Sky's the Limit* and offered Monica a job as the hostess which she gladly accepted. Her relationship with Evans ended. Two years later, Monica announced she wanted to be a pub entertainer, to prove to the world she could do more than be a television hostess.

In 1977 she put £2,000 of her own savings into *Our Kid* at the Winter Gardens, Morecambe, to keep it open but it was too little too late and the show closed. Three years later, Monica was rushed to hospital suffering from nervous exhaustion.

Shortly afterwards Monica met and married lay preacher Terry Dunnell, became a devout Christian and moved to Leicester where she worked as a check-out girl. The happiness that children would have brought eluded her and Monica underwent a hysterectomy. Ill-health was to dog her until the end of her brief life, which ended on 8 February 1994 when she committed suicide just three days short of her 46th birthday.

MONEY IN BABYLON

The love of money is the root of all evil, quoth St Paul. Dr Johnson and Oscar Wilde both disagreed. Said Johnson, 'There are few ways in which a man can be more innocently employed than in getting money,' while Wilde's view was, 'When I was young I thought money was the most important thing in life; now that I am old I know it is.' In Babylon money talks and boy, does it talk loudly. Telephone numbers are constantly bandied about as the figures supposedly paid as salaries to TV stars. In the vast majority of cases the figures are way, way out. Still, it makes for conversation down the pub . . .

Julie Goodyear and the Raffle

From the time she set foot in *Coronation Street* in 1966 as a machinist Bet Lynch seemed larger than life – indestructible. But Julie Goodyear was far from that. Just before Christmas 1978 cancerous cells were found on Julie's cervix and she underwent an operation to remove them. The op was not a success and in May 1979 Julie had a hysterectomy. This time the procedure was successful and Julie was given the all-clear.

Julie had been tested for cancer at Christie's Hospital in Manchester. As a way of repaying the debt she felt she owed the hospital, Julie launched the Julie Goodyear Trust to raise £500,000 to build a new testing facility. In November 1980, three months after the launch, the Trust had raised only £18,000 towards its massive target. Support for the Trust was disappointing. Julie arranged for a Datsun car to be raffled but the value of the car was £2,650. Raffle prizes then could only be worth a maximum of £2,000, which meant the raffle was illegal. It was then decided to overcome the legal obstacle by making the competition a game of skill. Raffle ticket buyers had to guess the number of miles the car could travel on a gallon of petrol. Not enough tickets were sold to cover the cost of the car. Julie handed over the running of the raffle to market traders William Clarke and Rodger Forster.

In March 1981 24-year-old Vicky Montague won the car. She announced she would sell it and hand the money to the charity. This magnanimous act caused untold trouble. Julie, her personal assistant Janet Ross, Vicky Montague, William Clarke and Rodger Forster were arrested on 12 November 1981 and charged with defrauding the public into buying raffle tickets in a bent competition.

Appearing in court the five were charged with 'conspiring together and with persons unknown to defraud people into buying tickets for a competition in aid of the Julie Goodyear Trust Fund, by falsely representing that the Trust was conducting a genuine and honest competition. The charge alleges that a false winner had been predetermined and that the car was destined for sale and the proceeds were to be given to the Fund.' The two men pleaded guilty and were given six-month sentences suspended for a year and a half.

In March 1982, just before her 40th birthday, Julie appeared in court. The prosecution alleged that Julie had known of the fraud beforehand and the plot had, in fact, been hatched in her home in Heywood, Lancashire. The enterprise began as a jolly jape, said Clarke, but it was formalized when Julie gave her assent. Julie claimed she had told him not to go ahead. Competition winner Vicky stated she had asked for her name not to be on the winning ticket but her mother had convinced her to allow it. After five days of testimony Judge Basil Gerrard instructed the jury to return verdicts of not guilty on the three women.

After all her efforts the Julie Goodyear Trust raised £80,000

– a worthy sum – but still massively short of the target. The money was donated to Christie's Hospital and the 'Julie Goodyear Laboratory' was opened on 29 September 1983. Julie's beloved mother, Alice, died of cancer on 11 May 1987.

Ken Dodd *v.* the Inland Revenue

Ken Dodd is without doubt one of Britain's best known and most beloved comedians. His tickling stick, buck teeth and wild hair make him an instantly recognizable figure wherever he goes. (At the Comedy Awards in late 1996 Chris Evans said the funniest sight he had seen all night was Dodd getting into a lift with straight hair and a set of rollers.)

Kenneth Arthur Dodd was born in Knotty Ash, Liverpool (yes, it really does exist) on 8 November 1927, 1928 or 1931 depending on which source you believe. He began entertaining aged 14 with a ventriloquist act for which he was paid half a crown (12½p). Like many comedians he worked the clubs (as Professor Yaffle Chuckabutty – Operatic Tenor and Sausage Knotter) before turning professional in 1954. His first gig was at the Nottingham Playhouse and since then, according to his friend John Martin, 'Doddy's life is one big tour.'

As well as telling jokes Ken Dodd is the consummate entertainer – he is listed in *The Guinness Book of British Hit Singles* as the 49th most successful singer of all time, with over 20 hits including a number one in 1965 with *Tears*. Dodd has even managed an entry in *The Guinness Book of Records* for telling jokes non-stop for three and a half hours. In the 1982 New Year's Honours List he was awarded the OBE.

Like many showbiz personalities from working-class backgrounds – Jimmy Tarbuck, Kenneth Williams, Cilla Black –

Dodd is a committed Tory and in the 1979 General Election which brought Margaret Thatcher to power he campaigned on behalf of the Conservatives in the North-West. In probably the most ironic statement he has ever made, Dodd said, 'Harold Wilson – I used to put him down on my tax forms as a dependant.'

On 8 June 1988 Dodd was charged at Liverpool Magistrates' Court with eighteen offences of being a 'common law cheat' in failing to pay the proper rates of income tax going back fifteen years. The case was the result of a three-year investigation by the Inland Revenue of claims amounting to nearly £1,000,000. Dodd did not attend the hearing and was not represented.

On 9 August Dodd placed £825,000 of bonds and certificates with the Inland Revenue. The next day, at a second hearing, Dodd's passport was seized to stop him fleeing the country and another nine charges were added to the sheet – three of tax fraud and six of theft. Dodd was released on £50,000 bail.

The criminal trial was adjourned for a fortnight in June 1989 after Dodd's lawyer, the eminent George Carman, QC, revealed that the comic had ventricular tachycardia – an irregular heartbeat – and the stress of a trial could kill him. The judge, Mr Justice Waterhouse, lambasted the comic's defence team for producing the medical evidence so late in the day. The trial proper opened at Liverpool Crown Court on 19 June 1989 with Dodd facing eight charges of cheating and false accounting and with a further three charges ordered to lie on the file. Prosecutor Brian Leveson, QC, told the packed room, 'He fed his own accountants absolute garbage. Not once did he lie but many, many times.' Mr Leveson said that Dodd hid £700,000 overseas to avoid paying tax. When investigated by the tax man Dodd failed to mention twenty accounts on the Isle of Man. When working he would be paid twice – once by cheque with VAT and a second fee in cash which was undeclared. In January 1986 Dodd and his accountants handed over a set of accounts that, said Mr Leveson, were 'not worth the paper [they were] written on'. Dodd again denied he had accounts overseas including in Jersey and the Isle of Man. He gave the Inland Revenue authorization to investigate banks on the Isle of Man and then withdrew his authority the same day.

On the second day of the trial Mr Leveson told the court that Dodd hid £336,000 in cash in three houses including his own at 76 Thomas Lane, Knotty Ash. (Dodd claimed he was worried the banks and the pound were collapsing.) The court was told that despite a fabulous income Dodd lived a frugal life. He spent £9 a week on clothes, £26 a week on groceries, £10 a week on gifts, another £10 on entertaining and £7 a week on booze.

On 4 July Dodd's former agent, Jack Oatley, took the witness stand and told the court that Dodd had insisted on cash payments for jobs. Three days later, Dodd himself was giving evidence and he explained that the cash in his house was his own identifiable means of his success. 'It made me feel very proud that I had generated this amount of cash. I didn't want a Rolls-Royce – you can't go for chips in a Roller. I didn't want a Ferrari, oil paintings, or a villa with a swimming pool in Spain. I've never been there.' Dodd told of the £26,000 country lovenest called The Mount that he had bought in Wirswall, Shropshire, for himself and his then fiancée Anita Boutin. Sadly, she had died of a brain tumour in 1977 aged 45 and they had never moved in. The house was now derelict. Dodd further explained his determination to have a child with his new fiancée Anne Jones, describing the fertility course she had endured – to no avail.

On the seventeenth day of his trial fellow comics Eric Sykes and Roy Hudd paid tribute to Dodd's talent and his humanity. Sykes said, 'He is now the king. You had Tommy Cooper and Eric Morecambe . . . and Ken Dodd. That was the order.' Dodd wiped away tears as Sykes spoke.

On 21 July 1989, after twenty-two days, Ken Dodd's ordeal was over. Doddy was rightly cleared of diddling the tax man.

Farewell Benny!

Very few British comedians have made the successful transition to America. One who did was Benny Hill, who lost favour in his homeland when it was decided that his shows were sexist and demeaning to women. Hill, who was not the avuncular character of legend but a lecherous man who offered work to young girls in return for sexual favours (see 'The Devil and the Angels', pp. 116-19), had been immensely popular at Thames TV for twenty years. In April 1989 the company invited Hill to attend a worldwide programme market at Cannes. Thames's publicity described the comic as 'a genius' and 'a world legend in his own lifetime'. On 25 May Thames announced pre-tax profits of £31 million. Sales to America of the *Benny Hill Show* alone had accounted for £1 million. Five days later, without warning, Hill and producer Dennis Kirkland were summoned to the office of John Howard Davies, head of light entertainment at Thames, and sacked. Although former child actor Davies was the executioner, no one to this day has admitted responsibility for the firing. Thames's action effectively killed Benny Hill's career as far as British television was concerned but it also put Thames on the slippery road to oblivion. (In the great licence auction fiasco of 1991 they lost their remit to broadcast in the London area to Carlton TV.)

In 1984 Hill and his show earned Thames TV International the Queen's Award for Export Achievement. The *Benny Hill Show* was sold to 127 countries. With only 142 nations in the world equipped with TV, that was a truly magnificent achievement.

JR v. BC

On 5 September 1978 the familiar strains of the theme tune to *Dallas* were first heard on BBC-1. Soon millions were tuning in to the dirty double dealings of Texas oil folk the mega-rich Ewings and their adventures among the beautiful people in downtown Dallas. The show, made by Lorimar, had begun five months earlier on CBS in the States where *Variety* had unwisely declared it 'A limited series with a limited future.' Soon the show was compulsive viewing for millions who wondered what villainy the evil J.R. Ewing would get up to next that would drive his long-suffering wife Sue Ellen back to the bottle. Even Radio 2 DJ Terry Wogan got in on the *Dallas* act, labelling the diminutive Charlene Tilton who played Lucy Ewing 'The Poison Dwarf' and gently taking the mickey out of the show. Some believe it was Wogan who made the show such a hit in Britain.

In fact, things could have been vastly different as *Dallas* started out as 'Untitled Linda Evans Project'. When the first episode was written it was decided that it was not suitable for Evans and she was dropped from the plans. (Later, when ABC was being slaughtered in the ratings by *Dallas* in the US, executives asked Aaron Spelling, creator of *The Love Boat* and *Charlie's Angels* among many others, to come up with a rival. Thus *Dynasty* was born and, ironically, Linda Evans became the star.) *Dallas* was originally conceived by its creator David Jacobs as a Romeo and Juliet story. The son and daughter of feuding families, one rich and the other poor, would fall in love and marry. He would bring her to live with his wealthy family but then die, leaving her to fend alone. As we all know, that did not happen – nevertheless *Dallas* was soon a runaway ratings success on both sides of the Atlantic. At its peak *Dallas* was watched by people in an incredible 98 countries. The episode broadcast on 21 November 1980 in which it was revealed who had shot JR was the highest rating show in

American TV history. Nearly 80 per cent of people who watched television tuned in that night. (It was eventually knocked off the pinnacle by the last-ever edition of *M*A*S*H**.) In Britain the episode was watched on 22 November (coincidentally, the anniversary of the day John F. Kennedy was shot in Dallas) by 27,300,000 viewers, over 3,000,000 more than had watched the show when JR was shot.

At the end of the 1984-5 season Patrick Duffy, who had played goody-goody Bobby Ewing from the start, decided he had had enough of *Dallas*. Bobby, Duffy opined, had become 'a dimensionless do-gooder' and he wanted out, vowing never to return. Lorimar offered Duffy an extra $10,000 a week but the actor stood firm. On 3 April 1985 his character was killed off in spectacular style – run over by his wife's evil half-sister Katherine Wentworth as he saved Pamela. The Ewings tearfully gathered round his bedside as Bobby begged them to, 'be a family' before going to the great soap factory in the sky. When the episode was broadcast on 17 May it was watched by 60,000,000 Americans.

At this time the off-screen drama almost took over from that on-screen. *Dallas* was a guaranteed ratings winner for the BBC. Whatever ITV put against it was always soundly thrashed and, after a while, this began to rankle with ITV executives. Although the series had finished its seasonal run in America it was still being shown in Britain when Bryan Cowgill, the managing director of Thames TV, decided to do something about it. He offered *Dallas*'s distributors £54,500 an episode, considerably more than the £29,000 the BBC paid. Michael Grade, controller of BBC-1, responded by yanking all the remaining episodes of *Dallas* from the screens. He threatened to show them at the same time as Thames were showing their new acquisition. Pressure was brought to bear on Cowgill from his superiors at Thames and *Dallas* returned to its rightful home on the BBC. In a masterstroke the Beeb continued to pay the same £29,000 but the shortfall had to be made up by Thames. Bryan Cowgill left Thames shortly afterwards.

Patrick Duffy returned to Southfork and *Dallas* ran until

1991 when falling ratings did what no one else could do – kill off JR.

In 1996 JR returned in a feature length TV movie that carried on where the series left off.

SEX IN BABYLON

Sex is probably the most talked about subject in Babylon. Who's had who? Who's gay? Who likes to be covered in whipped cream? The fascination with sex is neverending so without further ado, let's get stuck in . . .

The Devil and the Angels

In *Star Turns*, his dual biography of Benny Hill and Frankie Howerd, scriptwriter Barry Took investigates the sex lives of both comedians. One was a closet homosexual although very open about it in showbiz circles while the other was suspected of similar tendencies. Benny Hill's friends jumped to his defence, insisting any accusation of homosexuality was simply wrong and ill-informed. And they were right.

Benny Hill was born Alfred Hawthorne Hill in Southampton on 21 January 1924 (although for some reason in later life he knocked a year off and insisted he was born in 1925). He was the middle one of three children, all now dead. Hill was exceptionally close to his mother, Helen, but kept his distance from his father, Alfred, known as 'the Captain', by all accounts a stern man. In 1941, aged 17, young Alfred left Southampton and travelled to London to seek fame and fortune in the precarious world of showbusiness.

Not long after his arrival in the capital city Hill was propositioned by a gay comedian looking for a new partner (for his act). He plied the youngster with booze and edged closer on the settee. An arm around the shoulder, a hand on the knee. It was only when he leaned forward to kiss him that Hill jumped up and ran away. Later when asked by a group of gay dancers if he was queer, Hill is said to have replied that he felt very well. When the matter was pressed he said, 'Not really but I have my funny little ways.'

Hill was said to have had two great loves in his life which left him unable to give himself completely to any other woman. One of these was actress Annette André, star of *Randall and Hopkirk (Deceased)*. It was claimed that whenever she came on screen he had to leave the room. Although Hill would have wanted it otherwise, the relationship was always that of friends and never a romance. 'We used to laugh together and were good friends, but that was it,' she said many years later. 'I never had an affair with him, I didn't want to.' It came as a shock to her when Hill proposed one day in 1963. She declined and did not speak to him again until just two months before his death in 1992.

It was on the *Benny Hill Show*, broadcast on Thames TV from 1969 until 1989, that Hill began to attract massive audiences and three BAFTA awards (for Best Light Entertainment Programme [1971], Best Light Entertainment Production and Direction and Best Script [both 1972]).

However, the show also brought a great deal of criticism from feminists. The readers of a women's magazine voted the *Benny Hill Show* their least favourite programme. In 1987 Colin Shaw, director of the Broadcasting Standards Council, declared, 'It's not as funny as it was to have half-naked girls chased across the screen by a dirty old man. Attitudes have changed. The kind of behaviour that gets a stream of men sent to magistrates' courts each year isn't at all amusing.' Alternative comedian Ben Elton wondered aloud if in the days when it was unsafe for women to go for a walk in parks it was a good idea for a show to be broadcast showing Benny Hill chasing women in their underwear. Hill was outraged at Elton for breaking the unwritten rule that one comic does not pub-licly criticize another. Without specifically naming anyone he hit back. 'They criticize me for chasing girls through a park, when in real life it's not safe for a girl to walk through parks alone. If they watched the show properly, they would see it's always girls chasing me.'

The girls were nicknamed in the press 'Hill's Angels' after the gorgeous trio in the American cop show *Charlie's Angels*. Sue Upton, one of the original Angels and a close friend of Hill, came to his defence. She stated somewhat naïvely, 'Benny isn't the dirty old man people think . . . He is the perfect gentleman when he dates his glamour girls. They all say so. He always walks on the road side of the pavement. That's the height of good manners.'

But others told a different tale. One young and very attractive brunette actress tells of being invited for a Chinese meal by Hill and then back to his flat at 2 Queens Gate, London SW7, where Hill expected sexual favours. When she declined to service the fat comic he asked her to leave and she never got to appear on his show.

Beautiful model and actress Stefanie Marrian was just 16 when she went to see Hill about work on his TV show in 1966. According to a newspaper story Hill invited the teenager to his flat for an 'audition', whereupon he produced a bottle of champagne to help her relax. As he poured the drink, Hill told her there were three ways to become a success. 'Either you need talent which you don't have, or outstanding beauty which you don't have either. Or you scratch my back and I'll scratch yours.'

Stefanie Marrian then related how Hill showed her how to pleasure him. He took her into his bedroom where he stripped her before taking off his own clothes except his underpants. Stefanie grabbed her clothes and bolted for the door. A few days later, she went back. 'I'd never seen a man naked before and the sight of Benny was no laughing matter,' she said. 'He didn't want to make love, but enjoyed me masturbating him on his purple bed. I hated the sight of his naked body, but he loved me wanking him. It was like a holy ritual and I was his virginal creature.'

Stefanie, who with her 33½-22-34 figure went on to become the *Sun* page 3 Girl of the Year in 1976, related how Hill would strip off and lie on his bed with her between his legs stroking him. 'I always kept my knickers on and he would never touch me. He would constantly put me down and make me feel dirty. Each time we met I would masturbate him, no matter where we were.' According to the model she pleaded with the corpulent comic to make love to her not long after she had lost her virginity aged 17 (to Shakespearian actor Alan Tucker). She tried everything in her repertoire of tricks to turn Hill on, including wearing stockings and suspenders and bending over in front of him while wearing no knickers, but nothing seemed to work. 'He kept saying he was afraid of making me pregnant. But once when he did try to touch me up, he did it wearing rubber gloves. He would also invite his friends round and expect me to sleep with them, but I would always refuse.'

Blonde model Nikki Critcher told how one day in the studio Hill had grabbed her breasts and squeezed so hard she had to slap his face to make him let go. 'I'd been warned by other girls that Benny was always trying it on, but I'd never seen that side of him until one day he suddenly grabbed my breasts. I feel sorry for Benny. I think he was very lonely.'

In *Star Turns* Barry Took opines that Benny Hill's sex life was carried out with prostitutes in faraway places like Marseilles, Hamburg, Tokyo and Bangkok. It seems that Benny Hill didn't have to go far to get his kicks after all.

However, perhaps the most poignant statement is made by Hill himself. 'In relations between the sexes the male is always disappointed.'

Pammy & Tommy

She was every man's dream. He was every mother's nightmare. Canadian-born Pamela Denise Anderson was the
clean-cut blonde goddess of *Baywatch* with a figure to die for,
albeit surgically enhanced. (One unkind wag commented that
Pamela could never stand near a radiator in case she melted!)
A *Playboy* cover star a record-breaking six times, she was probably the world's most photographed woman after the Princess
of Wales. The world knew most of her 34D-24-34, 5´ 3˝ secrets,
including how she lost her virginity aged 15: 'It was pretty
awful. He was desperate to do it, and I agreed. We did it in the
car five or six times in four hours. Each time it lasted a few seconds and wasn't great. It hurt and I thought it was overrated.
But once we learned how to make love, I loved it. And I still
do'; how she has had two breast augmentation surgeries – one
in Vancouver in 1987 before she posed for *Playboy* (she was the
magazine's Miss February 1990 centrefold) and one in Beverly
Hills before *Baywatch*; how she wears a ring on the second toe
of her right foot; how she had had 19 boyfriends but had only
had sex with 15 of them. 'Compared to some of the girls I
know, I'm practically a saint! I have been sexually active since
I was 15. I'm not the sort of girl who jumps into bed with guys.
I need to be good friends with a man before I even consider
going to bed with him. I don't want sex – I want men to make
love to me. I love being in love, I'm a very sensual woman. I
love making love to men I'm deeply in love with.' One of
them, Scott Baio of *Happy Days* and *Charles in Charge* fame,
gave her a set of car mats for their first Valentine's Day and a
sewing machine for Christmas. He was the third man she'd
made love to, and after his gifts he was soon history. Another
was Dean Cain, star of *Lois and Clark*. Others included hair-
dresser-turned-movie-mogul Jon Peters whom she claimed
was just a friend because of the age difference; Poison rocker
Bret Michaels; and Vince Neil who ironically used to be in

Mötley Crüe. In an interview Neil said, '[Pamela] was exhausting. She wanted sex at least ten times on our first night. That time, she never took off the mini-dress she was wearing. She was insatiable. It was the best sex I've ever had.' *Baywatch* co-star David Charvet became her lover, as did Kelly Slater, another friend, and MTV host Eric Nies. (Charvet lost his virginity to her: 'He was very young and wet behind the ears. I taught him how to love. I created him as a lover. I showed him what I liked and what turned me on. He is still one of the best lovers I've had.')

Greek-born Tommy Lee was the hard-living, pierce-nosed, twice-divorced drummer for rock band Mötley Crüe, a man who took no prisoners in his search for endless fun. He had the word 'Mayhem' tattooed on his chest in six-inch-high letters and was known to party all night and most of the next day. His second wife was blonde actress Heather Locklear (now married to rocker Ritchie Sambora of Bon Jovi) whom he married on

Yuk! Mrs & Mr Lee being nice to each other

10 May 1986. He had her name tattooed on his left forearm. She finally left him over his womanizing and they were divorced in 1993. On 25 March 1990 Lee was arrested for mooning at the audience during a concert in Augusta, Georgia. He was charged with performing a sexually explicit act and indecent exposure. On 8 February 1994, when he walked through a metal detector at Los Angeles International Airport carrying a semi-automatic pistol, Lee was arrested and charged with possession of a concealed and loaded weapon. At his trial he was sentenced to one year's probation, a $200 fine and $340 costs. Seven months later, on 22 September, Lee got into trouble with the authorities again. This time he was

handcuffed and sprayed with Mace during a fight in a West Hollywood nightclub. On 21 December his then girlfriend, Bobbie Brown, 25, whose name is tattooed on his neck, informed police that Lee had beaten her up at his $4 million beach house. He was arrested for spousal abuse before being released on $50,000 bail. On 25 February 1995 Bobbie claimed Lee had proposed to her on a beach just two weeks before he met Pamela! 'Pamela Anderson tried to be me. She copied my looks, my hair, my body and my walk. Now she's stolen my guy. But my feeling is that they will both live to regret it.' Bobbie went on, 'It devastates me that a man I loved, who said he loved me, could have sex with me one Sunday, and two Sundays later, take marriage vows with a woman who could pass as my double. I could take the humiliation more if it was anyone other than her. When we were both struggling actresses years ago, she modelled herself on me. She had cosmetic surgery on her lips and breasts to look like me.' Bobbie also claimed that Lee 'can't control his moods. He once suggested he could have me killed if he wanted. He'd yank me across the room by my hair if I even spoke to another man. In clubs he even followed me into the ladies and into the cubicle. He relished humiliating me. I think of them in the beach house we shared, making love in the bed where Tommy and I made love, and it crucifies me.'

Pammy and Tommy seemed an ill-matched couple. On New Year's Eve 1994 they met and he asked for her telephone number. She gave it to him but had second thoughts and refused to go out with him because of his wild ways. Tommy Lee was not a man to give up that easily. Known as T-Bone because of the size of his penis, he was determined that Pam would be his. Oh, yes – she would be his. Learning that she was holidaying in Cancun, Mexico he flew out there and within four days, on 19 February 1995, they were standing on the beach – she in a white bikini, he in shorts – exchanging their wedding vows. 'Everything was so relaxed. Tommy and I stayed in bed making love until 2.30 p.m., then he put on his shorts and I put on my white bikini . . . It was so spontaneous and unconventional,' said Pam. The couple whispered sweet nothings in each other's ears ('It was our own affirmation of our love and how we will never leave each other – ever') before Tommy picked up his bride and raced into the sea. 'My bikini top slipped and a nipple popped out – but what's a nipple between friends?' Eschewing wedding rings the couple had their names tattooed on each other's ring fingers. Shortly afterwards pictures from their honeymoon began to circulate, showing the couple having sex, Anderson performing a blowjob on her husband and massaging his erect penis between her breasts.

On 18 March Lee got into a fight in a nightclub in Santa Monica after a man held Pamela's hand and stroked her hair. Just over three weeks later, Lee was in a fighting mood again when he clashed with another of Pam's admirers, Sean Michaels, the wrestler not the porn star. For months after the wedding the tabloids on both sides of the Atlantic were full of stories of how much the couple were in love and how they had sex at every opportunity often going into great detail. Lee said that each night they shared a bath filled with rose petals, before romping on more petals in bed! Pamela remembered, '[The] first time was incredible. Tommy satisfied me in a way no man has ever done before . . . We made love for hours . . . We made love morning, noon and night – and sometimes morning, mid-morning, noon, afternoon, evening and midnight. We couldn't keep our hands off each other.'

On 8 August 1995 the first cracks began to appear in the apparently idyllic match. Pamela denied reports that Lee had hit her. Less than a month later, on 1 September, Pamela again denied the couple were thinking of splitting. On 5 December Pamela announced she liked to do the housework in the nude to give Tommy a thrill. On the same day a video of the couple having sex mysteriously appeared. Six months later, a second porn video appeared.

Determined to start a family the couple had even picked out names for their children – Spirit for a boy and Patience for a girl. It would only be after three heartbreaking miscarriages that on 5 June 1996 Pamela gave birth to a 7lb 7oz baby boy whom they called . . . Brandon. (What happened to Spirit?) British celebrity magazine *OK! Weekly* paid a sum not unadjacent to £150,000 for the world rights to the first pictures of the newborn infant who, considering he has two good-looking parents, looked not too dissimilar to the creature that popped out of John Hurt's chest in *Alien*.

On 18 August 1996 Pamela reputedly threatened to leave Lee if the porn tapes became public. Exactly a month later, Pamela brought a multi-million-dollar lawsuit against *Penthouse* for publishing pictures of her and Tommy having sex.

On 15 November 1996, six months after the birth of baby Brandon, Pamela Anderson filed for divorce from Tommy Lee citing the usual 'irreconcilable differences' as the reason. According to tabloid reports Pamela had kept a diary of alleged abuse she had suffered at Tommy's hands, including details of how he beat her up when he couldn't perform in bed because he was suffering from brewer's droop, how he would come home smelling of cheap perfume and how girls would ring up for him late at night and then hang up. It seemed as though the match was over, as everyone had predicted. However, reports on 1 December 1996 stated that the couple were considering a reconciliation. Later reports said they weren't and then they were . . .

Women began coming forward claiming they had slept with Tommy while he was married to Pam and saying they were the reason the marriage ended – as if it was something to be proud of!

One of the first was hardcore porn star Debi Diamond who has appeared in over 400 skinflicks in a 'career' lasting over fifteen years. The authoritative *X-Rated Videotape Star Index* describes Debi as 'Very enthusiastic about sex but of the grungy kind. Too tall and too big a frame, small tits, lean mannish body, not ugly but not pretty facially.'

Another was former $1,000-a-night Heidi Fleiss hooker Suzie Sterling, 27, who confessed to a three-day sex and drugs binge with Tommy after they met in the House of Blues nightclub on Sunset Boulevard, Los Angeles. They went back to the home Tommy shares with Pam on Malibu's Heathercliff Road. Suzie remembers it stank of stale cigarette smoke. Once there he did some coke while Suzie drank tequila and smoked a joint. Suzie gave Tommy a blowjob because she didn't want unprotected sex 'because he'd already told me he'd used needles for drugs' before he went down on her on the piano on which Lee composed love songs for his wife. The next day they ate Chinese naked in bed before Tommy drove Suzie home. That night he took her back to his home and she stayed for two days. 'It was non-stop sex. We had wild sex and rough sex . . . once he even sucked my toes.' The couple even made out on a trampoline. Ever the gentleman, Tommy told Suzie that Pam's breasts were lopsided because of the silicone implants. Later, with Pam, he bumped into Suzie and her boyfriend Nick Savalas, son of Telly and former boyfriend of *Beverly Hills 90210*'s Tori Spelling. Tommy told Suzie to act as if nothing had happened. 'For me it was just a fling. For them it was their marriage.'

Ulrika, the Cameraman and the Gladiator

Ulrika Jonsson first hit the British television screens as a weathergirl on TV-am in May 1989, ten years all but one month after she first arrived on these shores. It was when her name was romantically linked to bachelor Prince Edward that Ulrika's name began to appear in the gossip columns. (Ulrika has never confirmed or denied any involvement with the prince except to say they were friends.)

Blonde. Attractive. Swedish. Daughter of a broken home. Eva Ulrika Jonsson was cannon fodder for the tabloids. While working at Scansat, a Swedish satellite channel, she met John

Turnbull in December 1988. He was a freelance cameraman while Ulrika was a humble secretary before she managed to get in front of the cameras. Ulrika was not the most popular of employees either at Scansat or at TV-am. Female colleagues refused to talk to a journalist preparing a profile on her. She and Turnbull began dating and soon the romance was serious. Three times Turnbull proposed and three times Ulrika turned him down. They moved in together in 1989 and he proposed once more. Ulrika accepted and they married in St Giles's Church in Stoke Poges, Buckinghamshire on 29 September 1990. On the night before her wedding, Ulrika was understandably suffering from the jitters and went to her mother for support. According to her, however, the meeting did not go well. 'I wanted a bit of parental comfort. I was pissed off. But you just tuck it under your belt and get on with

Ulrika Jonsson – not a leotard in sight

your day. But it didn't make me feel good.' She was given away by her stepfather, Michael Brodie, because her own father, Bo, could not be bothered to attend. (Bo Jonsson died of a heart attack on New Year's Eve 1995 aged 54.) In 1992 she was voted 'Rear of the Year'. (Gladiator Hunter would win the same award in 1996.) A year later, a former colleague alleged that Ulrika would regale technicians with all the details on what she had got up to the previous night. 'Ulrika has a very sexy voice and her sound checks soon became the highlight of the programme warm-up.'

Ulrika's career really took off in July 1992 when she was chosen to host TV's fitness competition *Gladiators*. One of the cameramen on *Gladiators* was Phil Piotrowski. He was the same age as the blonde. On 31 August 1993 a paparazzo walking down the King's Road in Chelsea saw the star being kissed by a man outside Peter Jones. He snapped a picture, little realizing the affectionate man was not husband John Turnbull but her *Gladiators* colleague. Their brief affair (it had begun in July 1993 shortly after the second series of *Gladiators* was in the can) was exposed to public glare on publication four days later.

Ulrika went to visit a psychotherapist. 'I'm not blaming the breakdown of my relationship with John on the way I was brought up. But it became pretty clear pretty quickly that I'd arrived at my marriage . . . carrying some fairly weighty emotional baggage.' After a lot of soul searching Ulrika decided to give it another try and was reunited with Turnbull. 'I think maybe one of the reasons I'd begun to begrudge my relationship with John was because, apart from anything else, it hadn't even brought me the baby I longed for.' That situation was resolved in March 1994 when the couple announced they were expecting a child and pals believed their happiness was complete. Cameron Oskar George Turnbull was born in Wycombe General Hospital on 18 October 1994 weighing in at a hefty 9lb 11½oz. In an interview three months after the birth Ulrika claimed, 'Our marriage is now stronger than ever. The bottom line is that, if you can get through something like this, you can get through most things. We're much more aware of each other's needs now. We know we're together because we want to be together.' She added, 'We waited until we'd been back together for three months before we decided to try for a baby. We both felt there was little point wasting any more time but I had no idea I would get pregnant at the first attempt.' However, as has happened in numerous cases of this kind, the baby could not paper over the obvious cracks in the relationship and on their son's first birthday in October 1995 Ulrika finally split from her husband. Turnbull later said, 'I have been deceived and disillusioned. I deserved better.' The couple were divorced in May 1996. In the petition Turnbull said it was 'intolerable' to live with Ulrika who did not contest the action.

Following the split Ulrika's name was linked to muscle-bound 6´ 3˝ Gladiator Hunter (real name James Crossley) whose previous girlfriend was fellow Gladiator Jet (real name Diane Youdale). In an interview the 38-25-35 brunette beauty had said, 'We are very attracted and making love is great, but I do think sex is overrated to a large degree. Generally our physical fitness in bed is a good thing when it comes down to sex, as deep down we're happy with our bodies and don't need constant reassurance from each other.' Some believe the affair began in July 1995 *before* Ulrika split from her husband. Jet said of her replacement in Hunter's bed: 'Ulrika, Hunter and I do the *Gladiators* live events together and there are no tensions. Uli and I don't sit there comparing notes on him. I really like Uli. She's a very funny lady and I've always admired her. She's very beautiful and always has time for people.' Ulrika confessed to 'the best sex I have ever had' with the Gladiator. The presenter, who has a tattoo of a red devil on her bum, is incredibly insecure about her looks. 'I don't wake up in the morning and think, cor, what a sex symbol I am. I think that I am very, very ordinary, and desperately plain. I've always had people around me who've said, "You've got a fat arse," or, "Your stomach looks revolting," or "Get a bigger bra for your breasts." So I've always felt quite reluctant to feel sexy and be naked in an unprivate moment . . . I've always felt my body isn't good enough.' Her criticisms of her appearance went on: 'I'm basically pear-shaped. I have a long body and short legs. I own a Wonderbra but I don't wear mine hardly hardly hardly at all. The trouble was getting one that fitted, because they don't do a big enough cup. Wonderbras are for women with smaller breasts, to hoist them up and make them look voluptuous. And frankly, my dear, I don't need that help.' The self-deprecating comments continued. In an interview in late 1996 she complained, 'I'm not extremely beautiful today. I would like to be younger, I feel a bit old at times now. Like many other women, I've dieted, got bigger, dieted again and, at the end of the day, I can see lines on my face. I am looking older, I know I am not going to be completely and utterly skinny or all the other things I might like to be.' An interesting comment was made by her mother, Gun, in an interview: 'I remember looking at her when she was about eight and thinking she wasn't so pretty. She had buck teeth.' With her mother absent for much of her childhood and publicly criticizing her now, it is no wonder Ulrika has feelings of insecurity. These must have been exacerbated by being surrounded by all the beautiful bodies on *Gladiators*. Still, her anxieties did not stop her getting romantically involved with one.

James Crossley, 18 stone, is six years Ulrika's junior. He was quoted as saying, 'Ulrika and I have slept together and all I can say is she's a passionate, beautiful woman.' For her part Ulrika said, 'It isn't just the size of his biceps, he has something between his ears. I couldn't last two minutes with somebody dim, it would kill me. I have to laugh as well. At the beginning of a relationship, when sparks are flying all over the place, the physical side is always very exciting. I'm a very physical and passionate person, but I need an all-encompassing relationship.'

While filming a *Gladiators* special in Mauritius in the summer of 1996 Ulrika and Crossley were forever hugging and showing their undoubted affection for each other. She even wrote him a note that read, 'Much, Much Warm & Tender Love To You From Me!'

Has Ulrika conquered her demons? Maybe not, but she's on the way.

The Truth Is Here – The Se-X File

Gillian Anderson is out there . . . and there fortunately

One of the most popular television programmes in the mid-1990s is Fox's *The X Files* starring David Duchovny and Gillian Anderson as FBI investigators Fox Mulder and Dana Scully. Numerous books and magazines sold as authors and journalists jumped on the sci-fi bandwagon. Investigative journalists began digging in the background of the show's two stars and it was soon revealed that Gillian Anderson had had anything but a regular upbringing.

Born in Chicago on 9 August 1968, Gillian came to Crouch End in North London aged two when her parents emigrated to England. Nine years later, she was uprooted again and went to Grand Rapids, Michigan where she was bullied because of her English accent. She soon got into trouble. A school prank of gluing all the school doors shut ended with Gillian being arrested because a police car drove by and she was wearing high heels and couldn't run fast enough to escape.

Still at school 5′ 3″ Gillian was voted 'Most Bizarre Girl', 'Class Clown' and 'Girl Most Likely to Go Bald' because she regularly teased her hair into bizarre styles. When she was 13 she returned briefly to London and became a punk, dyeing her blonde hair a vivid shade of purple. Back in the

ultra-conservative Grand Rapids she stood out like the proverbial sore thumb.

At the age of 14 Gillian lost her virginity to a musician.
Gillian admits she had a string of one-night stands when she
was a teen. At 15 she fell for 21-year-old Ralph Len Wallace,
the lead singer of a punk band. He said, 'Within minutes we
were making love on the freezing warehouse floor. It was
memorable. Gillian loved sex. She had a body as great then as
it looks now. I put a heart in my diary for every time we made
love. Flicking through there are too many to count.' They went
out together for three years during which time Gillian regularly appeared on stage with his band dressed either in a
wedding dress or a collection of bandages. Although Gillian
was still underage she was sexually very active but she
admits she didn't enjoy sex until she was 22. She recalls, 'For
ages I thought it was something I had to do.' The relationship
lasted three years until Gillian won a place at the Goodman
Theater School at DePaul University in Chicago.

Gillian appeared in a number of off-Broadway shows before
auditioning for the rôle of Dana Scully in 1993. The show also
helped her love life. She fell in love with the show's then production designer, pony-tailed Clyde Klotz, and married him
on the 17th hole of a Hawaiian golf course on New Year's Day
1994 after just three months of dating. The ceremony was carried out by a Buddhist priest. 'It was Clyde's smile that first
attracted me. He was very quiet, rugged and cool,' she remembers. 'I like switching back and forth between being in control
and being submissive.' In January 1997 it was reported that
Gillian had split from her husband and was dating
Yorkshireman Adrian Hughes although she insisted they were
just friends.

The Downfall of Jason King

Peter Wyngarde was born Cyril Goldbert in Marseilles, France, on 28 August 1925, the son of a diplomat. He first appeared on stage in a Japanese prisoner-of-war camp show (as featured in the movie *Empire of the Sun*) but spent two years after his release in a Swiss sanitarium. He came to England and studied to become a lawyer. Instead, he became a professional actor. In 1956 he played a brave Chinese pilot in Bertolt Brecht's *The Good Woman of Setzuan* at the Royal Court Theatre. To ready himself for his rôle Wyngarde would sit in a rubbish bin outside the theatre. In April 1958 he appeared with Vivien Leigh on the West End stage in *Duel of Angels*. He came to public acclaim playing Jason King in 1969 in the crime series *Department S*. Department S was a branch of Interpol devoted to solving seemingly insoluble mysteries. The show never quite took off because being made in England and trying to cover the American market, it constantly fell between two stools. The undoubted star of *Department S* was champagne-swilling crime novelist Jason King who graduated to his own show in 1971. Wyngarde was known on screen for his bouffant hair, loud shirts and outrageously bushy moustache. Women were devoted to him and he received innumerable fan letters including offers of matrimony and more besides. In a survey 30,000 Australian women voted him the man they would most like to be seduced by.

Wyngarde's world came crashing down in 1975 when he was arrested in a public toilet and accused of committing an act of gross indecency with Gloucester crane driver Richard Whalley, 24. On 17 October Wyngarde was fined £75. Following his conviction Wyngarde all but disappeared from the small screen, although he made the occasional appearance in films and more regular ones on the stage. In court his lawyer, Laurence Keen, denied his client was gay and blamed the incident on too much alcohol. Peter Wyngarde has never married.

The Weathergirl & the Cad

In the 1980s and 1990s independent television stations employed a series of attractive, bouncy blondes to present the weather. Among them were Ulrika Jonsson, Sally Meen, Trish Williamson, Tania Bryer, who was nicknamed Tracy Sunshine, and Sally Faber.

Sally Faber came from a privileged background. Born on 24 February 1965 as Sally Barr she had an affair with Earl Spencer, the brother of the Princess of Wales, before either of them was married. Christopher Barr, her father, told a journalist, 'She obviously takes after her old man. I've put it around in my time. She's an attractive girl with healthy appetites and obviously oversexed. She had a lot of boyfriends . . . I'm sure she slept with them too.' Sally married Eton and Balliol, Oxford-educated David Faber, 27, the grandson of former Tory Prime Minister Harold Macmillan, on 15 October 1988 at St Andrew's, Buckland Monachorum, Devon. Faber had once worked for disgraced Tory MP Keith Best and from 1985 to 1987 Faber was 'personal assistant' to best-selling novelist Jeffrey Archer who was then Deputy Chairman of the Conservative Party. While working for Archer, Faber was booked for speeding on the M5. He was driving his boss back to Wellington School to present the school prizes.

In April 1992 Faber, who is said to be worth £4 million, was elected Tory MP for Westbury with a majority of 12,618. The same year Sally gave birth to their son, Henry. The Fabers had bought a six-bedroomed house in Devon and crossword fanatic Sally decided to take up horse-riding, hiring James Hewitt as her teacher. In November she and Hewitt began an affair.

As the world now knows, in 1991 Hewitt had finished his five-year affair with the Princess of Wales, the details of which were recounted in Anna Pasternak's best-selling book *A Princess In Love*. An ex-girlfriend told *Tatler* magazine that

'God gave him piercing blue eyes, wavy russet hair and an enormous dick – but He didn't give him much of a brain.' Another added, 'The trouble with him is that, in finding his way through life, he keeps his compass in his trousers.'

In December 1993 Sally Faber left Carlton after her one-year contract was not renewed. That same month David Faber sued his wife for divorce, citing her adultery with Hewitt as the reason for the breakdown of the marriage. In January 1994 the name of the former Life Guards captain was dropped from the petition because, he intimated, he would fight it. However, on 16 May 1996 Faber, by then Parliamentary Private Secretary to Foreign Office Minister Baroness Chalker, was granted a decree nisi and Hewitt's name was cited in the divorce.

It was not the first time and would not be the last that the names of James Hewitt and the Princess of Wales were mentioned in Babylon. Another of Hewitt's inamoratas was the gorgeous 5´ 6˝ Maggie Moone, the resident singer on *Name That Tune*. Their relationship began in 1991 after she met him at a polo club lunch. And, of course, the Princess of Wales's name was romantically linked to England rugby captain Will Carling whose blonde wife Julia for a time co-presented *The Big Breakfast* and a pop show on satellite television. At first Julia Carling was defiant, saying the Princess had picked on the wrong couple, but still the Carlings split. Julia took her revenge publicly during an edition of *The Big Breakfast*. In April 1996, Diana had bizarrely attended, in full make-up and jewellery, an operation at Harefield Hospital performed by heart surgeon Magdi Yacoub. On 25 July Julia spoofed Diana, appearing on the show in hospital greens playing the children's game Operation with Gillian Taylforth and *Baywatch*'s Jaason Simmons and Alexandra Paul. She claimed the Princess had her highlights done especially for the operation. Three weeks earlier, on Diana's 35th birthday, she had suggested the Princess be given a copy of the book *How to Find Your Ideal Man*.

Gorden & the Rent Boys

Gorden Kaye is the quiet star of the hit sitcom *'Allo 'Allo*. He worked steadily, including an eight-month stint as Bernard Butler, Elsie Tanner's accident-prone nephew in *Coronation Street*, in a profession renowned for its long bouts of unemployment, but it wasn't until he was cast as the cowardly café owner René Artois in the BBC comedy that Gorden Kaye's face became known to the public at large.

Huddersfield-born Gorden Kaye is a homosexual. This is a fact that, like many gays in showbusiness, he has not sought to hide and has not made a song and dance about. It is simply the way he is. Although viewers can and do forgive their idols some strange peccadilloes, many actors and presenters choose not to allow the public to see a side of their character that they think they may find distasteful. This is patently absurd but we only have to look at the number of leading Hollywood men who are out of the closet – none – for us to realize that the public wants its heroes to be aggressively heterosexual.

Despite his closeted homosexuality Gorden found women chasing him. 'Look at me. I'm the wrong side of 40, I'm overweight, I'm going bald and I've got a dodgy eye. Someone once described me as TV's most unlikely sex symbol and I think they were right,' he said in a 1985 interview. 'I don't live the life of a monk exactly, but one has to acknowledge one's physical appearance.'

Gorden was forced out of the closet in January 1989 during another stage run of *'Allo 'Allo*. The *News of the World* planned to out him, so, in order to thwart their plans, he spoke at length to his journalist friend Hilary Bonner, the showbusiness editor of the *Daily Mirror* who would ghostwrite his autobiography for him. During a previous stage run of *'Allo 'Allo* in July 1987 Gorden ventured to Soho's Wardour Street where 'on three or four occasions' he picked up rent boys, 'which I realize now was very silly. But I have never done anything illegal. And I have certainly never knowingly been with anyone underage.' He became friendly with one of the male prostitutes and spent a weekend with him.

Gorden had once told a friend he would commit suicide if knowledge of his homosexuality ever became public. Thankfully, when his secret was revealed a weight was lifted from his mind and he announced he intended to weather the storm. 'I do not feel I have done anything wrong . . . I know some people will not agree, but . . . that is how I see it. I am not a bad person . . . I have never corrupted anybody. I have never forced my attention on anybody. I am not that kind of homosexual . . . I do not wander the streets picking men up. I am not even particularly highly sexed. I am not at it like a rabbit every night. Far from it. But yes, I am gay. And yes, I have been with male prostitutes. Often it has been for companionship as much as anything else . . . When I was younger I had serious relationships with women. I was once even engaged for two years [to Alice until I introduced her to the man she would marry]. But as I grew older I realized I had to accept where my true feelings were.'

On the afternoon of 21 January 1989 Gorden had his first test as to how the public would react to the exposure of his homosexuality when he had to face the audience at the matinée performance of 'Allo 'Allo. The 2,300-strong crowd at the London Palladium were united in their support for him, as were the overwhelming majority of the 'Allo 'Allo television audience.

Arthur Lowe – Obeying Orders

Known to one generation as Mr Swindley in Coronation Street, known to another as Captain Mainwaring in Dad's Army, known to a third as the voice of the Mr Men, Arthur Lowe was a truly talented actor. He was always in demand for films, television and theatre.

The pompous Captain Mainwaring, manager of the Swallow Bank in Walmington-on-Sea as well as leader of the Home Guard, was not too dissimilar to Arthur Lowe. Both believed things should be done just so and any deviation from this was wrong.

They had another disturbing connection. They both had overpowering wives. Elizabeth Mainwaring never appeared on screen. Her footsteps were heard and her backside was spotted bearing down heavily on a bunk in the Mainwarings' Anderson shelter in one episode.

Joan Cooper Lowe did appear in *Dad's Army*. She played Dolly, the sister of Private Godfrey. It was at Joan Cooper's insistence that she was cast in the rôle. She was determined that Arthur Lowe should not appear in any performance in which a part wasn't reserved for her. He was a brilliant character actor. She was a mediocre actress who should never have left rep. This was the reason why for the last ten years of his life, when he should have been reaping the benefits of his talent in Hollywood and earning a fortune, Arthur Lowe was touring minor theatres starring in plays that were hardly worthy of his talent. It was only in this way that Joan Cooper could be assured of a part in her husband's personal and professional life.

Joan Lowe had a voracious sexual appetite. Arthur Lowe had little or no desire to make love to his wife every night. It was not that he didn't find her attractive, it was simply that his sex drive was nowhere near as high as hers. 'If you're not fucking me, who are you fucking?' she would shout before indulging in her second vice – booze. She consumed copious amounts of gin which usually set her off on another rant. The drinking sessions would get heavier and heavier until she passed out and he would wearily put her to bed before sitting on the edge, his head in his hands, wondering what to do next. Why didn't he leave her? Because he loved her. Because he loved her he did work that was beneath him. Because he loved her he died in a Birmingham theatre an hour before the curtain went up. The show and his widow went on. She didn't attend his funeral because she was touring. Ultimately, Arthur Lowe did not achieve the acting greatness that could have been his because he loved a drunken nymphomaniac.

Mariella Frostrup – the Voice

Mariella Frostrup, dubbed the sexiest voice on television by male critics and 'that bimbo' by Janet Street-Porter, who has never met her, married pop star Richard Jobson when she was 18 but they divorced three years later and stayed friends. His picture of her is in her sitting room. As presenter of ITV's film review programme *The Little Picture Show* the blonde, attractive Mariella was known only to night owls and insomniacs. That all changed in 1993 when she began dating theatre producer Nick Allott, estranged husband of Anneka Rice who had gone off with TV mogul Tom Gutteridge. Newspapers in their usual euphemistic way reported that Mariella was 'comforting' Allott. She told a journalist, 'It makes me out to be some sort of Mother bloody Theresa. For God's sake, I'm shagging the man.'

A year later, the relationship was over and Mariella declared, 'One broken marriage and a couple of live-in relationships convinced me the most important thing money could buy was freedom. Gone are the days when I would go to three parties a night so as not to miss any potential of bumping into the man of my dreams. I am just one of an army of women who do not consider being single a misfortune but rather a desirable state of affairs.'

Blind Date, the Porn Star & the Vicar

London Weekend Television's *Blind Date* is one of TV's most popular programmes. Host Cilla Black (the original host in the pilot was camp comic Duncan Norvelle) asks a boy to pick a date from a choice of three girls who are hidden behind a screen. He makes his decision from the scripted answers they give to three questions he poses. A girl also gets the chance to pick from three unseen males. The remainder of the show consists of bringing back the two couples from the previous week and seeing how they got on.

The three questions 'posed' by each contestant usually give rise to a contrived double entendre answer from one of the hopeful daters. In 1995 some rudery was added to the show without the need to resort to the contestants' answers.

Beautiful 21-year-old blonde Jo Palmer from New Oscott, Birmingham, appeared on *Blind Date* as a girl picking a guy to go on a trip with. Although Jo was introduced as a drama student she already had some experience of appearing before the cameras in a drama LWT were unlikely ever to show. Shortly before her prime time début Jo had featured in a rather saucy video. Jo was seen fondling the bare breasts of busty blonde 'Tara' before they were joined by 'Lonny' who proceeded to have sex with the blonde. Jo didn't have sex with the man. Apart from her unwillingness to have sex on film, there was another very good reason why Jo wouldn't bonk the man. He was her uncle Reece Jackson and the woman in the video was her bisexual aunt, Denise.

Not surprisingly, the story hit the front page of the *Sunday Mirror* and Jo was invited to appear on a porn television station's chat show to discuss the film and *Blind Date*. She arrived at the studio with her aunt, uncle and two hardcore porn stars. Nervous at first, she thoroughly enjoyed her brief moment of fame. Jo also appeared naked in *Penthouse* magazine revealing all her charms, which included her pierced belly-button.

Jo declared there was nothing wrong with what she had done and that a girl had to do lots of things these days to become a success. Jo has since worked in a table dancing club and as a waitress as she waits for her second big break to materialize.

Jo wasn't the only contestant to inject some scandal into *Blind Date*. In 1993 three soldiers appeared and it was discovered that they were moonlighting for an escort agency. In November of the same year one of the contestants was revealed as a male stripper whose act involved him dressing up as a Nazi stormtrooper. In January 1995 a Church of England vicar appeared and was chosen by a busty 32-year-old blonde former convent girl who worked as a legal secretary in the West End and supplemented her income by delivering kissagrams. The Reverend Simon Gatenby, also 32, a bongo player with a pierced ear, went on the show to prove that not all vicars are fuddy-duddy types and he went like the proverbial lamb to the slaughter. It seems rather too pat that the kissagram, who boasted of a 34DD chest, just happened to pick a C of E vicar when the other two contestants were far more suitable. Contestants sign a confidentiality contract agreeing not to talk prior to their appearance. Despite this, the former kissagram – whose ambition is, surprise surprise (sorry, that's the other show), to be a TV presenter – appeared in a profile and fashion shoot in a tabloid newspaper for which she was paid £1,500.

While the vicar is too Christian to believe he was set up by the programme, when he and his date got back to the studio she described him as a vain man who took eleven sunbed treatments before their appearance, shaved the sides of his head to hide his thinning hair and kept dozens of pairs of silk boxer shorts in his room. She added, 'The first night I wanted to impress Simon. I wore a skintight, black PVC catsuit. Most men would have fallen back off their chairs. Simon didn't even bat an eyelid. I was stunned, but he never made any sort of move towards me. Over dinner I told him everything about myself – my past, my ex-boyfriends and why I'd been single for a year. Simon . . . dodged all my questions about his personal life.' The girl then said she went up to her room and sobbed her heart out. The pictures of her do not seem to suggest a girl who would be reduced to tears by rejection from a vicar.

The kissagram claims she rang LWT to complain her pictures looked awful and her comments had been taken out of context. She was told she looked lovely. LWT Press Officer Zoe McIntyre refuted allegations that the Reverend Simon had been set up. 'We are here to advise, project and protect.' People who had seen the show and the newspaper article might claim they failed on the last one at the very least.

Nudity

If there is one thing that differentiates many inhabitants of Babylon from the rest of us it is that they don't mind shucking their clothes at any opportunity. It gains notoriety and a fan base of slavering males plus it doesn't do the old bank balance any harm. Here are just some inhabitants who have given their all for art and the occasional buck!

 In the 1970s so-called sex comedies were very popular and we saw, if we were lucky, Joanna Lumley going nude in *Games Lovers Play* (1970), Lynda Bellingham baring a breast in *Confessions of a Taxi Driver* (1973), and Diane Keen showing her threepennies in *Sex Thief* (1973).

A number of women have appeared in various states of undress in magazines. Joan Collins bared all in *Playboy* when she was 50 and although she hasn't disrobed for the small screen she has got 'em off for *The Stud* and *The Bitch*. TV stars Pamela Anderson, Donna D'Errico, Erika Eleniak (all *Baywatch*), Samantha Fox (*The Six O'Clock Show*), Jane Seymour (*Dr Quinn, Medicine Woman*), Lysette Anthony (*Two Up, Three Down*), Shannen Doherty (*Beverly Hills 90210*), Amanda de Cadenet (*The Word*), Rachel Williams (*The Girlie Show*), Donna Mills (*Knots Landing*) (in a shower fully clothed) have also all appeared in *Playboy* pictorials. Aussie singer-actress and *Hello!* perennial Dannii Minogue posed nude in the October 1995 edition of Australian *Playboy*, went topless for *loaded* and wore see-through top and knickers for the November 1996 issue of *Sky Magazine*. Paula Yates got her kit off for *Penthouse*. Former *Brookside* babe Anna Friel appeared naked in the January 1997 edition of *Sky Magazine*. She also went nude in her film début *The Tribe* (1997). Volkswagen advertisement girl Paula Hamilton has bared her all in pictures that have appeared in pornographic magazines. Former *Wheel of Fortune* hostess Carol Smillie used to be a topless model. Apollonia Kotero used to date Prince, used to be in *Falcon Crest* (1985-6) and used to be a topless model. Blonde Susie Ann Watkins played Leonie Toft in the Channel 4 sitcom *Rude Health* (1987-8). Her charms were displayed in all their glory over seven pages of *Mayfair*. Another *Mayfair* babe was former *Grange Hill* starlet Paula-Ann Bland who played Claire Scott. Paula also went topless as a dolphin trainer in the film *The Fruit Machine* (1988). 'I saw the rôle as a real challenge. I got scared to death during training when the dolphin, taught at first to remove a ribbon tied round my boobs, took away half my shirt as well. I'd only done my first topless shots four weeks before, so I was a bit embarrassed during filming.' *Dr Who* assistant Jo Grant was played by Katy Manning. She posed naked next to a Dalek for a men's magazine after she left the series.

You Rang M'Lord actress and Prince Andrew's ex-girlfriend Catherine Rabett posed for nude photographs that were published in the *News of the World*. At first she denied they were of her but eventually came clean. *Friends* star Jennifer Aniston went topless but covered her nipples with her fingers in the 7 March 1996 edition of *Rolling Stone* magazine.

Louise Germaine and friends

 The Dennis Potter trilogy *Pennies From Heaven* (1978), *The Singing Detective* (1986) and *Lipstick on Your Collar* (1993) was awash with nudity. Gemma Craven bared her lipstick-covered nipples in *Pennies* while Alison Steadman took her clothes off for *The Singing Detective*. *Lipstick* star Louise Germaine posed nude in *Mayfair* under her real name Tina Reid when she was just 15 years old. The pictorial got the issue pulped. She bared her breasts in *Lipstick*. Carrie Leigh also appeared naked. For blonde beauty Carrie, 34-24-36, it was a tremendous ordeal as three times she had narrowly escaped being sexually assaulted. 'When viewers see me in *Lipstick on Your Collar* they won't understand what it took to appear naked in front of a studio full of men. The best piece of acting I did was actually pretending that I wasn't scared stiff.' In Potter's *Blackeyes* Gina Bellman stripped off and also appeared in a state of undress in the December 1995/January 1996 edition of *Arena*.

Some programmes use lesbianism as a way of getting actresses to get their clothes off. Charlotte Coleman and Cathryn Bradshaw played lesbian lovers who got naked in the controversial 1990 BBC series *Oranges Are Not the Only Fruit*. Kerry Fox and Sophie Ward played lesbian lovers in the 1995 play *A Village Affair* and both were seen topless. The story is of a woman who scandalizes a small village by having a gay affair. Art imitated life in 1996 when Ward left her husband for another woman. Amanda Redman, now best known as *Beck*, appeared topless in *Richard's Things*, a 1980 TV movie in which she had a lesbian affair with the widow (Liv Ullman) of her lover.

The 1992 film *The Pleasure Principle* featured four television actresses taking their clothes off. Haydn Gwynne, best known for *Drop the Dead Donkey*, *Two Up, Three Down*'s Lysette Anthony, *Chancer*'s Lynsey Baxter and Sara Mair Thomas. The lucky man to bed the four beauties was Peter Firth who co-starred with Amanda Donohoe in *Laughter of God*.

Serena Scott Thomas, who played the lead rôle in the movie *Diana: Her True Story* (1992), appeared in a full-frontal nude scene in the drama *Harnessing Peacocks* in 1993. She stands naked in front of a mirror trying on hats. She said, 'I was worried about what I would look like so I went to the gym three or four times a week before so I wouldn't look blobby. It's difficult the first time you take your dressing gown off – you think "Oh no". I thought all the cameramen would be looking at my bum. But they couldn't care less. They were more interested in their tea break.' Serena's sister, Kristin, has also appeared nude on television in the ITV drama *Body and Soul*.

Jemma Redgrave and Sarah Neville both appeared nude in *The Buddha of Suburbia* (1994). Debbie Watling went topless in the wartime serial *Danger UXB* (1979).

 Actress Sally Geeson played Sally Abbott in the 70s sitcom *Bless This House*. She appeared topless in the Norman Wisdom movie *What's Good for the Goose* (1969). *Bread* star Gilly Coman went topless in the ITV drama *Stay Lucky* (1990). *Peak Practice*'s Saskia Wickham went topless in the film *The Prince of Jutland* (1994).

 Gorgeous Arkie Whiteley stripped for a sex scene with Bob Peck in the thriller *Natural Lies* (1992). 'I was totally nude apart from my stockings and a tattoo I put on my bottom using a transfer. It was quite erotic and I was surprised at myself. It was a turn-on. I wished I had more to do. I thought the nudity was right for the part. This was my first full-frontal nude scene and it took two hours to shoot.' Arkie's previous experience was a shower scene with Adam Faith in *Love Hurts*. 'That was hilariously unsexy. I was wearing a body stocking and he had these huge white knickers on and stood on a box to look taller. The hot water from the shower kept steaming up the camera.'

 Greta Scacchi and Toyah Willcox made an old man very happy in 1983 when they appeared nude alongside Lord Olivier (he kept his clothes on) in *The Ebony Tower*.

 Dervla Kirwan is best-known as Phoebe in the BBC sitcom *Goodnight Sweetheart* and Assumpta Fitzgerald in *Ballykissangel*. She went topless in the TV adaptation of the Melvyn Bragg book *A Time to Dance* (1992).

 Used to playing a doctor in *Cardiac Arrest*, Helen Baxendale stripped off for the BBC thriller *Truth or Dare* (1996). 'I found it embarrassing to appear naked in front of strangers – let alone to make passionate love to some fellow I didn't know. It wouldn't be so bad if you didn't have the whole film crew watching and then you realize that half the bloody nation will watch you doing it anyway. I have it away with a couple of blokes but they're bare-arsed too for the sake of equality. I don't like nudity at all – I wouldn't even go topless on the beach.'

 The Camomile Lawn (1992) was awash with nudity as actresses Tara Fitzgerald and blonde Jennifer Ehle regularly got their kit off for nude romps. Tara, a chain-smoking brunette, also stripped for a nude scene in *Hear My Song* and the Hugh Grant film *Sirens*. 'I don't worry that film makers will pigeonhole me as an actress who's prepared to take her clothes off. I don't mind being filmed nude but I am not saying I will rip my clothes off for anything – it has to be the right fee.' Tara also went topless in *The Vacillations of Poppy Carew*. 'It's a very English thing to get freaked out by nudity but it doesn't embarrass me.'

Heavenly Helen Mirren shows what she is made of

Rachel Weisz had three days to get to know co-star Ewan Stewart before a nude scene in *The Advocates* (1992). 'The love scenes we did were quite difficult. We each had a glass of Cointreau beforehand, but it was still embarrassing making passionate make-believe love in front of a camera crew. The result isn't too explicit so I won't be worrying when my mother watches it.'

 Award-winning actress Helen Mirren regularly takes her clothes off for the big screen. She went nude in *Age of Consent* (1969), *Savage Messiah* (1972), *Hussy* (1980), *Cal* (1984) and *The Cook, The Thief, His Wife and Her Lover* (1989) and topless in *Caligula* (1980), *Excalibur* (1981) and *Pascali's Island* (1988). She also went topless on the small screen in the Anglia drama *Cause Célèbre* (1988) based on the true story of Alma Rattenbury, a songwriter of the 1930s who took a toyboy lover. The lover was convicted of murdering her husband and sentenced to death. Alma committed suicide before learning his sentence had been commuted to life. Cherie Lunghi also went topless in *Excalibur* and with Richard Gere in the flop *King David* (1985).

 Julie Graham and her partner have delighted millions with their Thelma and Louise-style ads for a brand of car. Julie also played Alice in the drama *Harry*. She appeared nude in the film *The Fruit Machine* in 1988. A crowd of passers-by gathered to watch and wouldn't leave even when the crew offered to pay them! 'It was really embarrassing. When I actually took my clothes off they were stunned into silence,' remembers Julie. In the Channel 4 film *Rosebud* (1995) Julie, who has a pierced belly-button, appeared naked with a man and another woman in sex scenes. Julie obviously feels comfortable with lesbianism because she shaved her head and stripped to play a lesbian sex slave in the film *Preaching to the Perverted* (1996).

 Not only did Alex Kingston bare her breasts in *Moll Flanders* (1996) but she also used to be a teenage nude model. This obviously helped as *Moll Flanders* contains a staggering seventeen sex scenes. 'I've had sex every day this week,' she told one interviewer. 'I don't know how I find the energy.'

Kids' TV presenter Zoë Ball wore nothing but bikini bottoms and a lot of body paint to promote a soft drink in 1996. Amazingly, the pictures were published in the teen magazine *Smash Hits*.

A number of TV hostesses have had previous careers as topless or nude models. These include Teri Clark (*Take Your Pick*), Sue Lee (*Winner Takes All*), Kathy Lloyd (*Bob's Your Uncle*), and Emma Noble and Kimberley Cowell (*Bruce's Price Is Right*).

Several of the secretaries/assistants/nurses on the hit sitcom *Are You Being Served?* have also been models. Penny Irving appeared nude in men's magazines and Candy Davis, the daughter of a NASA physicist, won the 'Miss Nude '82' beauty contest and £500. She worked as a stripper doing stag nights and then spent a year working at Paul Raymond's Revuebar before returning to stripping. Candy married actor Gary Olsen (PC Litten in *The Bill* and Ben in *2.4 Children*) and changed her name to Clare Grant in the hope of attracting serious rôles. They never came and she worked as a stripper once again to support them both when he was resting. The couple divorced.

Amanda Donohoe . . . with her clothes on for a change

The most popular of *Charlie's Angels* Farrah Fawcett inadvertently became the first woman to show a nipple on American prime time TV (nudity, unlike in Britain, is still virtually banned on the six networks – CBS, NBC, ABC, Fox, WB and UPN). In the episode 'Angels in Chains', first broadcast on 20 October 1976, she revealed all. Commented the beautiful Farrah, 'When the show was number three [in the ratings], I figured it was our acting. When it got to be number one, I decided it was because none of us wears a bra.' Farrah went on to bare a whole breast in the sci-fi flop *Saturn 3* (1980) and wasn't overly clad in the flop *Sunburn* (1979). American critic Rona Barrett wrote, 'The only thing tinier than the bikini Farrah Fawcett wore was La Farrah's talent.' Farrah bared all in the Christmas 1995 edition of *Playboy*.

 Amanda Donohoe, who went naked in her first film rôle in *Castaway* and caused a sensation playing the bisexual C. J. Lamb on *LA Law* (1990-2), appeared topless in the TV films *An Affair in Mind* and *Laughter of God*.

 Wonder Years sitcom star Olivia d'Abo, daughter of the Manfred Mann singer, appeared nude aged 15 in the Bo Derek film *Bolero* (1984). *Dallas*'s Victoria Principal (Pamela Barnes Ewing) appeared topless in the film *The Naked Ape* (1972) and Deborah Shelton (Mandy Winger) disrobed in *Nemesis* (1992), *Sins of the Night* (1993) and *Silk Degrees* (1994). *Moonlighting*'s Cybill Shepherd went topless in *The Last Picture Show* (1971). *Beauty and the Beast*'s Linda Hamilton went topless in *Separate Lives* (1994). *Baywatch*'s Alexandra Paul went topless in *Sunset Grill* (1992) and nude in *8 Million Ways to Die* (1986). *Twin Peaks*' Sherilyn Fenn showed her twin peaks and much more in *Two Moon Junction* (1988). Savannah star Jamie Luner appeared topless in the film *Tryst* (1994).

You may have noticed a distinct lack of men in this section. Strangely, men don't seem to like giving their all for their art. Jesse Birdsall, later to be seen in *Eldorado*, stripped off in *Annika*, the story of an English boy in love with a liberated Swedish girl. Christina Rigner, 17, did the honours as the Swedish girl and, yes, she did strip off completely. Jimmy Smits, David Caruso and Dennis Franz have all bared their buns in the cop show *NYPD Blue*. Former *Moonlighting* star Bruce Willis shows little Bruce in the raunchy film *Color of Night* (1994), Michael Douglas bares his bum in *Basic Instinct* (1992), *Kung Fu's* David Carradine in *Boxcar Bertha* (1972), and Monty Python's Graham Chapman appears nude in *Life of Brian* (1979) while John Cleese shows all in *A Fish Called Wanda* (1988). *Dallas's* Christopher Atkins appears nude in *Blue Lagoon* (1980), *Only Fools and Horses'* Paul Barber shows his arse in *The Long Good Friday* (1980) and if you look very carefully in slow motion you can see an actor's crown jewels for a brief second in *Moll Flanders*. The final words on the subject of nudity must go to Shelley Winters who memorably said, 'I think it's disgusting! Shameful! And damaging to all things American! But if I were 22 with a great body, it would be artistic, tasteful, patriotic and a progressive religious experience.'

A Fair Cop!

To millions of TV viewers Jeff Stewart plays the irritating but ultimately harmless PC Reg Hollis three times a week on *The Bill*. The actor, who also dated Joan Collins's youngest daughter, Katy Kass, for five years until September 1995, has another less savoury way of spending his time off from Sun Hill nick.

Stewart, who was born in Aberdeen, is a regular attender of domination fetish parties where people are whipped and voluntarily submit to all sorts of indignities. Approached at one of these by a journalist, Stewart was unwittingly more than willing to reveal all his sexual secrets. He was also smoking hashish, a Class B drug, as he chatted.

Stewart, who runs marathons for a hobby, revealed that at the parties he is into domination. 'I'm good at it. I love to tease my partner first – tickling her with the end of the whip for ages before I actually do any whipping. I think this anticipation is a big part of the whole thing. I've got a bed with metal bars at the top and [she can] hold on to those. It's only one step away from being handcuffed.' Stewart also showed the reporter his leather mask which has a zip across the mouth.

Stewart's sexual preferences, although out of the norm, are his own business, and smoking hashish, although illegal, is not outrageous drug abuse. Amazingly, he posed for pictures dressed in his bondage gear.

In February 1996 it was revealed that Katy Kass had attended some of the S&M parties with Stewart. According to a 'friend', this upset her mother, who was grateful the relationship was at an end.

Rock & the Kiss

It was Rock Hudson's looks rather than his talent that made him a movie star. As the world now knows, Rock Hudson's career was based on a sham. Rather than the ladykiller of celluloid fame, he was, in fact, a promiscuous homosexual who regularly trawled gay bars looking for pick-ups. It was said that during the filming of *Giant* Elizabeth Taylor fell in love with Hudson. Hudson fell in love with James Dean.

The glossy prime time soap *Dynasty* was created for ABC and Aaron Spelling by Esther Shapiro and her husband Richard as a rival to CBS's *Dallas*. In America the series gradually gained momentum and overtook *Dallas* in the ratings, something it never achieved in this country.

Dynasty relied as much on its big-name guest stars as it did on its outlandish plots to win over audiences. The character of Alexis was originally going to be played by Sophia Loren until her husband, Carlo Ponti, asked for $150,000 per episode – a figure way too high for Aaron Spelling. The rôle went, of course, to Joan Collins and re-established her on the world stage.

On 9 October 1984 it was announced that Rock Hudson had signed to play handsome horse breeder Daniel Reece for six episodes with an option for four more and a spin-off series the next year. When Hudson arrived on set at the end of October he looked ill, seriously ill. His previously muscular 6′ 6″ frame was nearly skeletal and his clothes hung from the bones. All sorts of rumours about the nature of Hudson's condition were doing the rounds. AIDS was still virtually unknown to the public at large. In an interview with *U.S.A. Today* Hudson claimed his weight loss was due to a stringent diet and he was more than happy with his appearance. It was not a convincing explanation.

One scene was to cause controversy not just on the *Dynasty* set but around the world. Millionaire Daniel Reece, who owned the Delta Rho Stables, was an old flame of Krystle Carrington (played by Linda Evans) and the script called for the two to kiss.

According to his authorized biography Hudson returned to his home, known as The Castle, and flung the script across the room. He discussed his dilemma with his close friend Mark Miller – admit he had AIDS and finish his career or kiss Linda Evans. At that time no one knew for certain how the virus was passed on and it was believed that casual contact – even touching – was enough. Hudson made a decision. Throughout his career Hudson had always put his career first. Career. Sex.

People. They were the three driving forces in his life. Dying from AIDS, there would be no exception to his rule.

Prior to the scene Hudson was sitting next to Joan Collins in the make-up room. He chain-smoked and small-talked as the technicians performed their wizardry – trying to make Hudson look human. After he left for the set Joan Collins's openly gay hairdresser speculated that Hudson had the deadly AIDS virus. Immediately prior to the kiss Hudson utilized every mouthwash and gargle he could find and then kissed Linda Evans. As soon as the director shouted 'Cut!' Evans rushed to her dressing room where she spent fifteen minutes cleaning her teeth, using antiseptic mouthwashes and harshly washing her face. The next day Evans told Joan Collins she had gone through with the kiss because she did not want to hurt Hudson's feelings!

Back home Hudson said to Mark Miller, 'The fucking kiss is over with. Thank God!' Miller said Hudson thought it was one of the worst days of his life. The episode was aired on 6 February 1985. Former actor George Nader is Mark Miller's boyfriend and the two men, together with Tom Clark, Hudson's former lover, were the closest friends Hudson had in the world. Nader taped the episode as he watched it. He said, 'I could see where Rock kept his lips closed and hit Linda on the side of the cheek for a brief, chaste kiss. He did not open his mouth, no saliva was exchanged.'

Hudson completed his contract with *Dynasty*, smoking forty cigarettes a day on the set and drinking vodka as if it was water. When it was announced in July 1985 that Hudson was suffering from AIDS the cast and crew of *Dynasty* were united in their sympathy for him. No one seemed bothered that Hudson might have exposed Linda Evans to a deadly disease. (Remember, at that time no one knew for certain just how contagious the disease was or exactly how it was passed on.) The reaction from the public was different and Hudson was widely criticized for his thoughtless actions. Even Mark Miller admitted he was worried about touching Hudson despite knowing he could not get the disease through touch alone.

His official biographer Sara Davidson wrote, 'Rock did not give the matter [of kissing Linda Evans] a second thought, once it was over. It was a lifelong pattern: he did not seem vulnerable to guilt.'

It's a Gay Old World

During his successful Channel 4 programme *An Audience with Kenneth Williams*, the gay actor, raconteur and diarist related the story of his hairdresser father's insistence on him learning a 'proper' trade. When Kenneth voiced the possibility of a career in the theatre his father, Charlie, snorted, 'All the women are tarts, all the men are poofs!' Fortunately, Kenny was not deterred and brought joy and laughter to millions before his suicide at his London flat in April 1988 aged 62. A reading of his diaries, published posthumously, reveals the often suicidal depths to which he regularly sank, depressed over his career and his sexuality. Kenneth Williams was a homosexual who did not want to be part of that often oppressed group.

Charlie Williams may not have been absolutely right in stating that 'all the men are poofs' but certainly the world of showbusiness attracts more than its fair share of gays, be they actors, producers, directors, make-up artists, dressers or publicists or even just hangers-on. Many of them are allowed to be open about their sexuality in a way that would not be possible in a straight vocation.

However, when they reach a certain level, many actors feel the only way to proceed is to contract marriages so the public will be unaware of the true nature of their sexuality. Many marry lesbians which allows both parties to sleep with whomsoever they wish while always having a partner on hand for public appearances at premières and the like. A large number of Hollywood film stars, including many heart-throbs, are closet homosexuals.

It was claimed that Rock Hudson, for many years a movie heart-throb and latterly the star of the television detective series *McMillan and Wife*, contracted just such a lavender marriage. He stayed married to Phyllis Gates, his gay agent's secretary, for two years until he could no longer live the lie. (Mrs Hudson never remarried and consistently denied she is a lesbian, claiming in her book that she and Rock led a full married life and she had no inkling where his true desires lay.) From the divorce until his death on 2 October 1985 Hudson was a promiscuous homosexual and a regular visitor to gay bars in California. It was a surprise to his many friends that his secret did not become public knowledge until just three months before his death when his publicist, Yannou Collart, announced in France that Hudson was suffering from the dread disease, AIDS.

Rock Hudson is, of course, not the only TV AIDS casualty. The American prime time soap *Dallas* has seen three of its cast die from the disease. The most prominent was probably Dack Rambo who played Jack Ewing, JR's good cousin. (Jack was brought on to the show during the year that Patrick Duffy took off from playing perennial good guy Bobby.) He succumbed on 21 March 1994 aged 52. Rambo claimed that the heterosexual Larry Hagman was a homophobe who regularly attempted to stir up trouble on the set. Young, handsome Timothy Patrick Murphy played Lucy's lover and Ray Krebbs's nephew Mickey Trotter who died in a car crash caused by Sue Ellen's drink driving. Murphy died from AIDS in December 1988 aged just 29. Tom Fuccello played Senator Dave Culver in *Dallas*. He died from AIDS aged 56 on 16 August 1993. He kept his illness secret from all but his family and closest friends. He was diagnosed as HIV+ in 1988 and kept working on the show until January 1991. Shortly before his death he lost his mind.

René Enriquez played the perpetually worried Lieutenant Ray Calletano on hit cop show *Hill Street Blues*. In biographies and interviews he told of a wife who had tragically died. It was untrue. Enriquez was a homosexual bachelor who contracted AIDS in 1987. As he became more and more ill he told his family, friends and fans he was suffering from cancer. His publicist and longtime friend Henry Bollinger announced, 'René told me he was dying of pancreatic cancer. He never told me anything about a gay lifestyle. He made clear to me before his death that he wanted no autopsy performed on his body and wanted no funeral. He did not want his friends to come together after he had passed.' Death came to Enriquez on 23 March 1990. He was aged 56. The true cause of death became known only when his death certificate was published. Cause of death was given as 'cytomegalovirus enteritis due to Acquired Immune Deficiency Syndrome (AIDS)'. The only people privy to René Enriquez's terrible secret were his two sisters and his 25-year-old Hispanic boyfriend.

American-born actor Douglas Lambert played a ruthless lawyer in ITV's newspaper thriller *Inside Story*. Lambert was a little known actor who made front page news because he kept a diary of his struggle against AIDS that was published in the *Daily Mirror* in November 1986. It was a deeply moving account of how a gentle articulate man coped when his faculties began to desert him and his situation became ever more hopeless. His lover of 16 years David Inches (manager of the trendy Roof Gardens nightclub) stayed constantly by his side in their Crouch End home. On 16 December 1986 Inches left his boy-friend's bedside for an hour to get some fresh air. Shortly before he returned Douglas Lambert died from AIDS.

Acclaimed actor Alec McCowen, CBE, is best known on television for his portrayal of *Mr Palfrey of Westminster*. He was a closet homosexual until 1989 when he was featured on the celebratory programme *This Is Your Life*. The show, which is not by any means a warts and all portrait of celebrities, left out not only the fact of McCowen's homosexuality but also that his gay lover, actor Geoff Burridge of TV's *Foxy Lady*, had died of AIDS on 30 September 1987 aged 39. McCowen refused to allow the programme to be broadcast unless mention was made of Burridge.

Wacky DJ Kenny Everett was sacked from Radio 1 twice and outraged many with his television shows featuring busty Cleo Rocos, Lionel Blair, the sexy dance troupe Hot Gossip and Everett himself in the guise of various revolting characters such as Gizzard Puke, Marcel Wave, Sid Snot the punk and bearded starlet Cupid Stunt who insisted everything was done 'in the best possible taste'. Yet Everett's personal life was conducted in anything but. A homosexual, on 2 June 1969 he married the psychic Audrey Valentine Middleton, known as Lee, but the couple rarely if ever made love. Such a match could not and did not last. The Everetts were divorced in 1983 and gradually Ev began to dip his toe in the waters of public opinion when he revealed in an article that he was bisexual. Eventually the truth came out and, on 6 October 1985, so did Everett. He admitted to living in a ménage à trois with two men, Spanish sculptor Pepé Flores, who worked as a waiter to support himself, and Russian body-builder and ex-Red Army soldier Nikolai Grishanovich. (Grishanovich had been infected with the AIDS virus since 1983 although Everett failed to tell the press that deadly fact.) All was not quite as it seemed. Although the three men did, indeed, live together, they did not all share the same duvet at the same time. Pepé and Nikolai were lovers and Everett and Nikolai were bed partners. Everett and Pepé, by all accounts, never got it together. The handsome Grishanovich was a bisexual who would 'fuck anything that moved' and that included Ev's friend, the pop star Freddie Mercury. In 1986 Everett and Pepé discovered they were both HIV+. All the men had inhabited the twilight world of gay life and all paid the ultimate penalty. A picture shows Everett, Nikolai, Pepé, Mercury and another man on a boys' night out. Every person in that picture is dead, a victim of AIDS. It is believed that Everett, Pepé and Freddie Mercury all contracted AIDS from Nikolai, who died of the disease in 1991 in the Lighthouse Hospice in West London. Freddie Mercury died the same year, one day after admitting to the world he was gay. Kenny Everett succumbed in his two-storey Kensington flat on 4 April 1995. He was just 50 years old. Shortly before he died Kenny, who had been raised a Catholic but had lapsed, asked for a priest.

Actor Raymond Burr, 6´ 2˝, was the epitome of machismo, claiming in his entries in biographical dictionaries that he had married three times. The Mrs Burrs had an unfortunate propensity for dying – or at least that is what he claimed. His first wife, English actress Annette Sutherland, died in the same plane crash that killed Leslie Howard. Their son, Michael, died of leukaemia ten years later aged 12. Burr's second wife, Isabella Ward, he divorced, while the third, Laura Andrine Morgan, died in 1955. In reality the man who played tough wheelchair-bound detective Robert T. Ironside made up his first and third weddings and his son. Emlyn Williams commented, 'He uses the same trick a lot of Latin American actors, singers and writers use – he invents wives and offspring for himself so people will believe him heterosexual.' In fact, Burr lived with his lover of 31 years, twelve years younger Robert

Benevides, whom he 'married' in a gay ceremony in 1963, on a 40-acre ranch in Heraldsburg, northern California. The couple were known as Mr and Mrs Benevides since Burr preferred to be the 'woman' in the relationship. A friend of the couple said that Burr didn't 'like women and preferred not to have them around'. Burr died of cancer at 8.40 p.m. on 12 September 1993. He was 76. The actor left his entire $32 million fortune to the Portuguese-born Robert Benevides.

The squeaky clean children's show *Blue Peter* prides itself on its wholesome image. That image took a severe denting when blond Geordie Michael Sundin joined the team in 1984. Shortly beforehand it was revealed he had taken part in a gay night at London's trendy Hippodrome nightspot. Geordie Sundin never really fitted into the show and left after just a year, claiming it was 'too boring'. He added, 'I wanted to tackle things like warning youngsters of smoking, drinking and drugs.' That same year Sundin had a month-long fling with flamboyant nightclub host Stephen Hayter, self-styled Queen of the Night who ran London's outrageous Embassy Club. The affair ended because of Sundin's promiscuity. In 1984 Hayter had had an affair with Stephen Barry, Prince Charles's valet and a rampant gay. Barry was already HIV+ and he passed the dread disease to Hayter. In turn, Hayter's fling with Sundin condemned the young Geordie to death. Barry died of AIDS on 4 October 1986, exactly three months after his 38th birthday. Hayter succumbed to the same disease in May 1987. Michael Sundin died of AIDS on 24 July 1989 aged 28.

Soap operas are often the most popular programmes among gays. In fact, three of Britain's best loved soaps were the creations of gay men.

Michael Cashman is an articulate advocate of gay rights but when he first appeared as gay designer Colin Russell in *EastEnders* he did not publicly reveal he was gay because he thought it unimportant to the job he was doing.

Cashman's fellow *EastEnder* Pam St Clement is also homosexual. She came out in January 1991 when a gaggle of gays wrote a letter to the newspapers protesting about an article by film maker Derek Jarman criticizing gay actor Ian McKellen for accepting a knighthood from what Jarman saw as a deeply homophobic government. The other signatories – who included Ned Sherrin, Anthony Sher, Alec McCowen, Stephen Fry, John Schlesinger, Simon Callow, Simon Fanshawe and theatre producer Cameron Mackintosh, himself later to accept a similar award – said they 'regard[ed McKellen's] knighthood as a significant landmark in the history of the British Gay Movement'. Pam married Andrew Gordon in 1967 at Hendon Register Office. After two days of married life he went off to sea for nine months. Their nine-year marriage was punctuated by frequent absences – either he was away in the Royal Navy or she was away touring. Eventually, he left the Navy and went to work for Customs and Excise but it was too late to save the marriage and Pam told him she was leaving him – for another woman.

Ronald Allen is one of the few people to have starred in two successful soap operas. In 1962 he was magazine editor Ian Harman in *Compact*, while the following decade brought him renewed fame as David Hunter in *Crossroads*. His matinée idol looks made women swoon but in his private life Allen was devoted to his lover Brian Hankins. When Hankins died of cancer Allen developed a close friendship with his *Crossroads* screen wife Sue Lloyd, much to the surprise of almost everyone who knew him. When Channel 4 launched in 1982 one of the first programmes on air was the Comic Strip spoof of Enid Blyton's famous characters the Famous Five – *Five Go Mad in Dorset*. Allen played Uncle Quentin as a rampant gay. Following his sacking from *Crossroads* in 1985 Allen was wooed by an American film studio but nothing came of it because he was unable to get the necessary documentation. Six weeks before his death, on 18 June 1991, he married Sue Lloyd. They had been together eleven years. Another gay *Crossroads* star was Tony Adams who played womanizer Adam Chance.

Roy Barraclough is once again back among the cobblestones of *Coronation Street* playing Alec Gilroy. In the soap Barraclough's character married man-eating vamp Bet Lynch. In real life Barraclough is a homosexual who has lived with television presenter John Mundy for many years.

Another gay soap star is Dean Sullivan who plays the villainous Jimmy Corkhill in *Brookside*. Like many actors Sullivan has made no secret of his gayness but he hasn't shouted it from the rooftops. It first came to public attention in 1995 when a series of pictures, including one of Sullivan performing oral sex on another man, went missing from his desk when he moved houses.

Brookside bad boy – Dean Sullivan

His brilliant acting made Denholm Elliott a much-sought-after thespian on both sides of the Atlantic. Trained at RADA, he appeared in films such as *A Bridge Too Far*, *The Boys from Brazil*, *Defence of the Realm*, *Maurice* (gay E. M. Forster's novel about homosexuality which was published posthumously), *Trading Places*, *Indiana Jones and the Last Crusade* and the movie version of hit sitcom *Rising Damp*. On television he appeared in *Clayhanger*, *Blade on the Feather*, *Bleak House*, *Hotel du Lac* and many other dramas. In 1980 he won the BAFTA Best Actor award. Through two marriages, Elliott carried on gay affairs that were to result in his death from AIDS on 6 October 1992 at the age of 70.

His dancing won him fans the world over in the early 1980s but today Gene Anthony Ray, Leroy in *Fame*, is sadly dying of AIDS.

Chat show host Russell Harty brought a quaint Northern charm to the television interrogation of the stars – except when crazy singer Grace Jones believed he was ignoring her and walloped him with her handbag before raining down slaps on poor Russell's head. Harty was exposed by a newspaper as a homosexual who used rent boys. The presenter was so terrified his career was over, he accepted every job that was offered to him. His friends believe he died of overwork on 8 June 1988 aged 53. The actual cause of death was a sexually transmitted disease said to be either Hepatitis B or AIDS.

Graham Chapman was a member of the Monty Python team. He was also gay. Born during an air raid on Leicester on 8 January 1941, Chapman decided to become a doctor. Thankfully, showbiz had a greater pull than the medical profession although he did use his medical knowledge to write around thirty episodes of *Doctor at Large* with John Cleese. In the mid-1970s

Chapman, a chronic alcoholic, was close to death but somehow he pulled through and continued to make millions laugh. For twenty years Chapman lived with David Sherlock. On 4 October 1989, the day before the twentieth anniversary of the very first *Monty Python's Flying Circus*, Chapman died of throat cancer.

Robert Reed was wholesomeness personified as Mike Brady, the all-American dad in the 60s sitcom *The Brady Bunch*. On television Reed may have been the father of three sons and stepfather to a similar number of girls but off-screen he was a promiscuous homosexual who trawled gay bars for trade. He kept himself very much apart from the other members of the cast. Reed died of AIDS on 12 May 1992, five months short of his 60th birthday.

Les Dennis's partner Dustin Gee was a homosexual who never fulfilled his true comic potential, dying of a heart attack on 3 January 1986 aged 43.

Also gay is TV weatherman Fred Talbot, known for his bright jumpers and for leaping around on a giant weathermap anchored in Albert Dock on *Good Morning with Richard and Judy* before the show moved to London.

Bluff Jimmy Edwards is probably best known as the conniving headmaster of Chislebury School in the series *Whack-O!* and as Mr Glum in the hit radio sitcom *Take It from Here*. During World War II Edwards was badly burned and grew his mutton-chop whiskers to hide the scars. He married Valerie Seymour in 1947 but it was not to last. His homosexuality kept him from living a normal married life and the couple divorced in 1958. Edwards occupied himself with a succession of young men until his death from bronchial pneumonia on 7 July 1988.

Richard Wattis had a long career in films, theatre and television although he is best remembered by television audiences as the snooty Mr Charles Fulbright Brown, next door neighbour to Eric and Hattie Sykes in the long-running sitcom *Sykes*. He appeared with Marilyn Monroe and Laurence Olivier in *The Prince and the Showgirl*. According to diarist Colin Clark, Marilyn kept her distance from Dicky Wattis because of his homosexuality. Clark goes on to recall that for most of the time he spent with Wattis all the actor 'wanted to do was pick up some gorgeous hunk of a man'.

To millions of TV viewers Nigel Hawthorne is Sir Humphrey Appleby, the garrulous civil servant forever stopping Jim Hacker in *Yes, Minister* (and later *Yes, Prime Minister*) from carrying out a plan that will benefit the country. In 1995 Hawthorne was nominated for a Best Actor Oscar for his rôle as George III in *The Madness of King George*. During an interview with gay magazine *The Advocate* Hawthorne mentioned he was a homosexual and had lived since 1979 with his partner, writer Trevor Bentham. The British press went into a frenzy, which was quite absurd since Hawthorne hadn't 'made a secret of my homosexuality, but I'd never flaunted it. I'd always assumed most people knew.'

Aquiline Jeremy Brett was a deeply troubled man. Unlike Sherlock Holmes, the great detective he played so brilliantly on television, Brett could not solve his own problems. He was tormented by his sexuality. Two marriages seemed only to confuse him further and Brett spent time in a mental institution. He died, a broken man, in 1995.

Stephen Fry has appeared in *Blackadder, Whose Line Is It Anyway?* and his own series, *A Little Bit of Fry and Laurie*, with his heterosexual partner Hugh Laurie. Fry is a celibate homosexual, telling an interviewer, 'It must be ten years since I've rubbed the slimy bits of my body over someone else's.' He is by his own admission a 'pink champagne socialist'. Fry finds it rather odd that he is constantly approached for quotes about homosexuality and appeals for gay causes: 'When I'm actually celibate . . . I seem to be far more out than many fully-fledged, highly practising, not to mention promiscuous gay actors who prefer not to talk.' He adds, 'I have many good friends whom I love dearly and couldn't be without; I just don't want to rub the wet slimy bits of my body all over them. I would have thought I was doing them a favour. I mean, who wants to have their bellies slapping together in a great sea of mucus. It's an awful idea, sex.'

For many years the cookery programmes of Hudson and Halls were compulsive viewing in New Zealand. When the pair came to Britain on 12 October 1987 their BBC-1 show was a great hit. When Peter Hudson became ill with cancer, David Halls, his lover of 25 years' standing, took care of him but to no avail. Hudson died in September 1992 aged 56. In tribute to his

Camp cooking from
Hudson and Halls

boyfriend David changed his name to David Hudson-Halls. However, the grief of being without his lover was too much to bear. On 24 November 1993 Hudson-Halls's body was discovered in his Jermyn Street flat. He had committed suicide with a massive drugs overdose. He was 57.

Many heterosexuals automatically assume that a child raised by a gay couple will turn out to be gay. This is patent nonsense. If the reverse were true there would be no homosexuals in the world. Suave Eton-educated actor Patrick Macnee, star of *The Avengers*, was raised by his mother, Dorothea, and her lesbian lover whom Macnee called 'Uncle Evelyn'. Dorothea Macnee aged 95 appeared on her son's *This Is Your Life* claiming to be 87. Ten weeks later, she died.

There are a number of openly gay comedians on television such as Julian Clary, formerly the Joan Collins Fan Club, and Lily Savage, real name Paul O'Grady. In fact, O'Grady is married and fathered a daughter when he was 16. In 1977 he married Portuguese waitress Teresa Fernandes. The marriage was never consummated but neither was it ever dissolved by divorce.

On the female side is 36D-25-36, 6' 1" supermodel Rachel Williams who graced the cover of *Playboy* and eight pages inside in February 1992. She reeled off a list of the things she likes best and her favourite song was Village People's *YMCA*. In January 1996 she was hired to host *The Girlie Show* for Channel 4 without the station realizing that because green-eyed Rachel is American she could not get a work permit. Still, the tabloid press was more interested in the fact that Rachel, who has her bottom lip pierced, was a lesbian whose lover was former BMX champion Alice Temple, an aspiring pop star, whose name had once bizarrely been linked to Boy George. Rachel spoke out: 'Everybody made such a big deal about [me and Alice]. We didn't exactly press the issue – word got out – but we didn't exactly hide it. Look, for me gender is more of a detail of one's life, like race. When I met Alice I was like, "Wow!" I didn't expect to fall in love with a woman; I fell in love with this person.' Rachel added, 'I have great sex with men and women, so long as I am in love with the person. I have been sexually attracted to women before but never thought I would fall in love with a woman. But then I met Alice and just fell in love with her. We have brilliant sex and I feel very fortunate to be with her.'

Comedian Sandi Toksvig is a regular on the panel game *Whose Line Is It Anyway?*. She has lived with her lesbian lover and her lover's children for some time.

Actress Polly Perkins played Trish Valentine, a fading singer in a bar with a taste for young boys, in the BBC soap *Eldorado*. She had gay affairs, explaining that this was 'because I felt I couldn't trust men'. Her lesbian lover was Sally Becker who was nicknamed the Angel of Mostar for her brave work in Bosnia. Polly's co-star Roland Curram (Freddie) admitted he was gay before he married actress Sheila Gish, straight for the 23 years they were together and 'an extremely well-adjusted bisexual' when she left him for actor Denis Lawson.

In the summer of 1996 superstar Cher finally confirmed longtime rumours that she has had lesbian affairs. She admitted the truth in an interview with her openly homosexual daughter Chastity for gay magazine

It's the person not the sex that counts with Cher

The Advocate. 'I had relationships with women. I can't say whom I'm going to be attracted to in my life. I think it has to do with the person not the sex.' Cher did take time to dispel age-old canards that she'd had flings with Liza Minnelli and *Charlie's Angels'* Kate Jackson.

Known to millions of National Lottery viewers, Mystic Meg (real name Margaret Lake) used to write sexy stories for the men's magazine *Club International.* She also had a three-month affair with the then editor David Jones. The editor claimed that Mystic Meg told him she was bisexual and showed him a picture of herself naked that she said was taken by a girlfriend.

American sitcoms are not the most liberal of places. The openly gay Amanda Bearse (she lived with Sandra Bernhard for two and a half years) of *Married . . . with Children* plays a man-eater on the show. Ellen DeGeneres caused a national sensation in the States when her character Ellen Morgan became prime time's first gay lead character on 30 April 1997. Can America recover?

Samantha Janus

Sexy Samantha Janus, now the girl interest in *Game On*, first came to public attention when she represented the United Kingdom in the 1991 Eurovision Song Contest with a ditty called *A Message to Your Heart.* She finished 10th. 'I was packaged as this young, blonde girl with a short skirt and high heels – singing a song about starving children!' The illegitimate daughter of folk singer Noel Janus and niece of Angie Best, 5´ 9˝ actress-singer Sam left home at 15 to live in a bedsit.

She lost her virginity the following year to an Italian called Rafaello: 'There is great eroticism in having sex for the first time when you don't know someone.'

Sam has always been outspoken on the subject of sex. 'Promiscuity is acceptable if you're single, honest and not hurting anybody. I've had a one-night stand and I felt quite strange afterwards because it was quite obvious that neither of us wanted it to lead anywhere. It was great while it lasted, but it probably wasn't really worth it.'

Sam, who admits to 'about nine' lovers, has also experimented with hard drugs: 'I've been through the wars a bit but we're talking about things that happened when

Game on for savvy Samantha Janus

I was 16 or 17.' In an interview with *FHM* Sam declared, 'If I initiate [sex], then I probably think I'd give myself a ten. I am very good in bed if I'm in the mood. I'm probably more a seven if someone else initiates it. Or a two when I have to simulate orgasm.'

Doug Harwood, a former boyfriend of the 36C actress when she worked as a barmaid at the Camden Palace, revealed amongst other things in a *News of the World* interview, 'She was very adventurous sexually.' Following her split with Harwood she dated male stripper Mauro Manero who is still her boyfriend.

Till Fame Us Do Part

Comedy actor Paul Shane has said, 'One thing I've never been able to understand is how guys who suddenly become successful trade in their wives for new models. It's unbelievable how women can go through thick and thin with a man through the bad years and then when he makes it a dolly bird flashes her eyes at him and he's off. Of course there are temptations in this business and I've had women come on to me. I always say, "I'm quite happily married, thank you." Unfortunately, a lot of guys don't.' Here are some of those guys.

In September 1996 Eamonn Holmes admitted that his marriage to childhood sweetheart Gabrielle had been over for a year and he was reportedly close to TV presenter Ruth Langsford.

The Bill's Andrew Mackintosh (DS Greig) left his wife, Lucy, and three young daughters in May 1995 for former pop singer Kathy Dooley. The couple met while appearing in the pantomime *Beauty and the Beast* – he was the Beast and she was Beauty. Amazingly, Kathy Dooley moved into the family home in King's Walden, Hertfordshire, while Lucy Mackintosh and the three girls moved into the couple's other home. Said the actor, 'I am not an unkind person. I have done the right thing in the long term.'

TV smoothie Michael Aspel seemed very happy with third wife Lizzie Power who as Christine Hewitt entranced Arthur Fowler in *EastEnders*. It came as a shock to the public when Michael left her in 1994 for Irene Clark, a production assistant on his *This Is Your Life* show.

Ralph Fiennes left his actress wife Alex Kingston, whom he married in 1993 after eight years together, for much older TV beauty Francesca Annis in 1995. 'My relationship with Ralph did not end because of *Schindler's List* or his fame. My problem was that I put my career second to nurture Ralph's, so my career didn't do as well as it might have. I turned down TV work to travel and be with Ralph. I'm not saying they were huge parts but I put Ralph first.'

SOAPS IN BABYLON

The most popular programmes in Britain today are undoubtedly soap operas. Millions tune in every day of the week to see what is happening in Weatherfield, Brookside Close, Albert Square, Beckindale and the numerous other fictional places that pass for reality in the minds of many people. So let's visit them, starting with Merseyside . . .

The Beasts of *Brookside*

Channel 4's first soap was the brainchild of former quantity surveyor Phil Redmond who had devised *Grange Hill* and *County Hall* for the BBC. When Jeremy Isaacs was appointed chief executive of the fledgling Channel 4 Redmond approached him with an idea for a soap set in his home town of Liverpool. Redmond pointed out potential cost savings by buying six houses which would form the set rather than the continual process of demolishing and rebuilding new sets. Encouraged by Isaacs's response Brookside Close was built. Redmond ordered a bungalow, a four-bedroomed house, four three-bedroomed houses and another three for office space. The houses cost around £25,000 each and Redmond says it is the best investment he ever made.

The first visit by the television audience to the Close was on 2 November 1982 and viewers were introduced to the Grants, the Corkhills, the Collinses and grumpy old Harry Cross and his gnomes. At first *Brookside* was roundly criticized in the press – mainly for its swearing. The clean-up-TV campaign swung into action and the *Daily Express* called for the resignation of Jeremy Isaacs. Phil Redmond changed tack and *Brookside* began to flourish. For years *Brookside* was seen as the poor relation to its big brothers *Coronation Street* and *EastEnders*. The audiences and tabloid coverage concentrated on the big two. Yet *Brookside* was steadily building an audience with gritty story lines and social realism, covering topics the big two shied away from.

It was in the early 1990s that *Brookside* began to veer towards what might be termed sensationalist story lines rather than gritty dramas. On 4 October 1991 Sue Sullivan and her young son Danny were killed by being pushed off a scaffold by Barry Grant, the best friend of her husband, Terry. In October 1992 Peter Harrison was accused of the rape of Diana Corkhill during a party and although he was acquitted many residents on the Close never believed in his innocence. Eventually he was forced to move to Oxford to get a new life away from the jibes. In 1993 Anna Wolska, who was working as the Farnhams' nanny, was discovered to be an illegal immigrant and lost her job. She moved in with Peter Harrison and fell in love with him although her feelings were not reciprocated. She was forced to become a nude model then a prostitute to make ends meet. When Terry Sullivan fell in love with her, his bezzy mate (best friend) Barry Grant intervened and paid her to have a baby for him. When he discovered she was secretly taking the pill he sent her away.

Meanwhile, the Jordaches had moved to the Close in March 1993. They were Mandy, a battered mother, and Beth and Rachel, her two teenage daughters. The elder of the daughters, university student Beth, had been sexually abused by her father but fell for Peter Harrison. When she discovered his rape acquittal she finished with him. It was the story lines surrounding the Jordaches that really gripped the country for the first time in *Brookside*'s history. This was mainly due to the sensational nature of the stories and the beauty of Anna Friel who so eloquently played Beth. The Jordaches were placed in a safe house to escape their violent father and husband, Trevor. When he discovered their whereabouts he came to see them, hoping for a reconciliation and trying to persuade Mandy that he had changed. At first Mandy was unsure but then the old violent ways returned and Mandy and Beth decided enough was enough. Their only salvation would be to get rid of terrible Trevor for ever. They tried to poison him but when he discovered their plan he attacked them. Mandy pulled a kitchen knife and stabbed him to death on 7 May 1993. (When the omnibus edition of the soap was shown on Saturday afternoon, before the 9 p.m. watershed after which children are no longer supposed to be watching, the stabbing had been edited out. *Brookside* actually goes out at 8.30 p.m., before the watershed anyway.) With the help of Sinbad, the friendly neighbourhood window cleaner, they buried the body in the garden and built a patio on top of it. Mandy and Sinbad grew closer while Beth, after her involvement with Peter Harrison, began to turn her sexual feelings towards women in general and her friend Margaret Clemence in particular. Margaret's previous romantic entanglement, in 1991, had been with a Catholic priest! At first Margaret was revolted by her friend's feelings but gradually softened and the two girls slept together. It was this, the sexual involvement of two attractive young women, that caused a frenzy in the tabloid press. Gay groups adopted Beth as their mascot. The episode in which the two actresses kissed was one of the highest rated and one of the most criticized in the soap's history. (Again, the kiss was excised from the Saturday omnibus edition.) The lesbian adventures of Beth did not end there for Anna Friel was also required to kiss her 30-year-old lecturer Chris and, rather more passionately, fellow student Viv. When Mandy discovered Beth was dating Chris she approached the lecturer and told her to leave her daughter alone or she would inform the university dean.

A flood in the back garden of their neighbours the Bankses revealed the Jordaches' darkest secret and the family and the ever faithful Sinbad went on the run. It was the first time

Brookside had been screened five nights in a row. The runaways were eventually captured by the Garda in the Irish Republic. At the trial, another five-nighter, Mandy and Beth were both sentenced to prison. Having been a symbol for gay liberation, Beth and her mother became the hope for battered women everywhere. By this time Anna Friel had tired of playing Beth and wanted out. Beth was discovered to have a heart condition and died the night before the two women were freed. It was a cop-out from the producers and angered many gay groups as well as Friel's growing army of fans.

Brookie's Lipstick Lesbian –
Anna Friel

In 1993 *Brookside* also covered drugs when character Jimmy Corkhill became a heroin addict, stealing and lying to pay for his fixes. His wife Jackie was almost forced away by his behaviour but loyally stood by him. While out of his head on drugs Jimmy ran down and killed 14-year-old Tony Dixon. As the boy lay in a coma in hospital Jimmy became the chief fundraiser for his medical appeal but it was too late. Tony's dad was horrified when Jimmy did not end up in prison after admitting his rôle in the accident. Realizing it was a mug's game, Jimmy got himself off smack and instead became a drug pusher, enlisting the help of his son-in-law Gary. It was the drug-related death of an Australian soap star boyfriend of Jacqui Dixon that brought Jimmy to his senses and he forswore drugs. Meanwhile, in a Romeo and Juliet twist, Gary's wife Lindsey had left him for Mike Dixon. The young lovers, with

Lindsey's daughter Kylie, decided to start a new life together in Australia. Afraid this would mean he would never see his daughter again, Gary planted heroin in the child's cuddly toy. Mike and Lindsey were arrested in Thailand and imprisoned. The feuding Dixons and Corkhills at first worked together to ensure their children's freedom but Lindsey was released first and the feud resumed once more. With both kids eventually home things seemed to revert to normal or as normal as they ever can be in Brookside Close, until the arrival of Little Jimmy Corkhill who turned out, like his father, to be a heroin addict. Another five-parter in November 1996 saw Little Jimmy murdered by the drug barons to whom he owed money. Yet another murder came to light at the same time when Jack Sullivan, Terry's errant dad, admitted to killing a man accidentally during a fight over Terry's mum.

Having covered marital abuse, rape, drug addiction, racism, loan sharks, cancer (Patricia Farnham underwent a mastectomy in 1993), religious cults (Katie Rogers and Terry Sullivan were sucked into an organization run by Simon Howe, who later contracted AIDS but died as a result of suicide), it seemed as if no subject was taboo to the producers. Then the dysfunctional Simpson family moved into the Close. Outwardly a model family, inner turmoil raged in Ollie Simpson's house. His wife Bel had been sacked from her job for sexual misconduct while the elder two children, the beautiful blonde Georgia and the darkly handsome Nat, were having an eight-year-long incestuous affair. It was this story line that caused most criticism of *Brookside*. The governing body of independent television, the ITC, made the soap apologize to viewers for a scene in which Nat and Georgia appeared seemingly naked in bed together having just had sex. Viewers wrote in with the inane complaint that *Brookside* was condoning incest because Nat and Georgia were both very attractive people.

One thing is for sure: *Brookside* has never been a cosy soap like *Coronation Street* or a depressing one like *EastEnders* and while it continues to run exciting, gritty and controversial story lines it will gain momentum and, more importantly, viewers.

The Curse of *Coronation Street*

Coronation Street began at 7 p.m. on Friday 9 December 1960, the creation of Tony Warren, a former child actor who was then writing at Granada. Having written some episodes of a series called *Shadow Squad*, Warren was given a job in Granada's promotions department. Others already installed there were Jack Rosenthal and Geoffrey Lancashire (the father of Sarah Lancashire, the *Street*'s Raquel Watts). Warren's assignment was to write the show *Biggles* which he hated. He hated it so much he climbed on top of a filing cabinet and screamed at his boss, 'Let me write what I know about!' Warren was coaxed down and given twenty-four hours to write what he knew about. What he knew about was a six-part serial called *Coronation Street* that took Britain by storm . . .

Fort Knox

Barbara Knox first appeared in *Coronation Street* in November 1964 as Rita, an exotic dancer friend of Dennis Tanner. She returned in 1972 to become a regular as the live-in lover of Harry Bates. Her love affair with Len Fairclough both ended her relationship with Bates and endeared her to the nation. On 20 April 1977 Rita and Len married. The couple had their ups and downs but Rita was shocked to discover after his car crash death on Bonfire Night 1983 that Len had a secret mistress.

Off-screen life was just as eventful. Barbara Knox was born Barbara Brothwood on 30 September 1933 in Oldham, Lancashire. She was illegitimate. Her father was known as 'Tommy Two Homes' and he didn't marry her mother, Emma, until 16 February 1946 after his divorce came through. She married Denis Mullaney in 1954 and had one daughter, Maxine, born in 1959. The marriage ended in divorce in 1977, the year she married businessman John Knox. It is remarkable for an actress to change her professional name in mid-career but that is just what Barbara Mullaney did, becoming Barbara Knox both personally and professionally. Less than two years after they married, John Knox was sent to prison for fifteen months for fraud. Loyally, Barbara stood by him. He was to serve two further terms and still Barbara stayed. It was only in 1994 that the couple finally divorced.

Beautiful Bev

Beverley Callard first appeared in *Coronation Street* in May 1984 playing June Dewhurst, a friend of Gail Tilsley. It was five years later in 1989 that she became a regular as army wife Liz McDonald. Beverley Callard has at least one thing in common with Liz McDonald – they both married young. Liz gave birth to the twins when she was 17. Bev was only a year or so older when she had her daughter, Rebecca, on 2 June 1975, having married aged 16 on 19 January 1974. Her husband was painter and decorator Paul Atkinson. That marriage didn't last and 5′ 6″ Bev married rock musician David Sowden, a man until recently thought to be her first husband. Again that marriage was doomed to failure although neither will explain why. Beverley was so distraught over the break-up that even now she cannot bring herself to mention his name. He insists that neither of them had an affair. In 1989 she married Steve Callard who is nine years her junior. 'I'm not a promiscuous person. After all I don't just shag them, I marry them.'

In 1993 Bev's third husband, Steve, had an affair with Elaine Ramsden, a girl who worked in a shop in Chorlton, South

Manchester. The couple separated in July 1993. When Ramsden's boyfriend found out about the affair he punched Steve. Bev demanded a divorce and consulted a lawyer. Business turned to romance as Bev started a close friendship with the brief. However, that did not last and the Callards reunited. That didn't last either.

Good-time Charlie

Charles Lawson started work in the *Street* as tough ex-army sergeant Jim McDonald on 17 September 1989 – his 30th birthday – on a salary of £70,000 a year. From the off, it looked as if the actor was determined to emulate his hard-drinking screen character.

Thanks to a combination of Irish whiskey and cocaine the actor has no recollections of his first four years with Britain's most successful TV show. 'I was permanently pissed, drinking up to a bottle and a half of whiskey a night and snorting cocaine to get a buzz and to keep drinking. I was a complete mess.' Lawson first took cocaine when he was 17 and occasionally took Ecstasy. He often went out drinking with *Street* colleague Philip Middlemiss.

In the summer of 1994 he went public with the affair he had been conducting clandestinely. While his wife of nine years, Susie, looked after Laura, their 7-year-old daughter, Lawson, whose real name is Quentin Devenish, was secretly seeing *Street* make-up artist Ellie Bond, 40.

'The first time I saw Ellie was [March 1994] when I came back to the *Street* after a long break. I have to say I fancied her as soon as I saw her. We talked and talked and at first things progressed pretty slowly. But then it took off like a bat out of hell and the next thing I knew was that I had quite simply fallen in love with her.'

One of the people who fell out with Lawson over his affair was his longtime *Street* friend and drinking partner, Lynne Perrie. Lawson had saved her life after she collapsed and when she returned to work she went to thank him. While doing so, she made some flippant remark about his rumoured affair, little knowing it was true.

When Susie Lawson got to put across her side of the story, she admitted she was still in love with her wandering husband. She claimed he was nothing like his violent, hard-drinking *Street* alter-ego. 'Jim McDonald is a brute but Charlie is just a pussycat really. Charlie's always loved women's company and liked the attention that fame brought him but he was never the type to have an affair. I always thought that if anything could break up our marriage it would be his drinking.'

At a function Beverley Callard, who plays Liz McDonald, played a mean trick on her. She told her not to dress up so Susie put on a business suit, only to find the entire cast dolled up in their Sunday finest.

Two years on there has been no reconciliation. Charlie is still with Ellie Bond and Susie is facing up to 'the fact that [she] may never find another man'.

Curvy Chloe

Chloe Newsome joined *Coronation Street* as the spoiled rich girl Vicky Arden in 1990. After the death of her parents in a car crash the following year, Vicky went to live with her grandfather Alec and his wife Bet Gilroy. She soon set her cap at wastrel Steve McDonald and what Vicky wanted, Vicky got – even though it was obvious to everyone but her that Steve only wanted her for her money.

Off-screen there was chemistry too as the pair became

lovers. In August 1995 Chloe was discovered to be in possession of the drug Ecstasy at Sheffield's Leadmill Club. That same month she went through a phase of flashing her knickers in public. A year later, she was repentant. 'Taking Ecstasy was a stupid mistake and I bitterly regret doing it. After I told my family my dad couldn't speak to me for three days.' Like many before her, Chloe has found that life after the *Street* is no bed of roses.

Eve of Destruction

Eve Steele auditioned for the rôle of hairdresser Maxine in *Coronation Street*, the part that went to Tracy Shaw. 'Tracy's right for the rôle. I didn't really look the part of a hairdresser at the time. Maxine should be gorgeous with loads of beautiful hair.' She said, 'I know [the producers] were right to reject me – I wasn't physically right for the part. Okay, I could have played Maxine, but I don't think I would have been as glamorous as Tracy – and I couldn't have made Maxine as tarty as Tracy does. There's no way I could have worn those hotpants. It just wasn't me. I'm not a proper girl . . . I'm not. If I'm in a dress with high heels I feel like I'm in drag. I'm more comfortable in clothes I can run away in, you know, if you get into trouble.'

The *Street* was a far cry from 5′ 2¾″ Eve Steele's early years when as Emma Steele (her real name) she was a punk. 'I used to have my head shaved at the sides. I suppose that started when I was eleven years old . . . Siouxsie and the Banshees was my favourite band. Then I sold out for a couple of years when I liked Paul Young. But eventually I got back into punk again. I even played drums in a punk band called Digestive System for a while. My mum used to shrug and say, 'Oh well, she'll grow out of it,' and I used to insist I wouldn't. I'm still prone to be wild.'

It was the wild streak that surfaced in Eve when she was at drama school. Drugs were freely available and she became addicted to heroin for eighteen months. Eve battled to keep her drug problem a secret but the rings around her eyes and weight loss quickly gave the game away. The habit spiralled ever upward and, at one stage, Eve was reputedly paying dealers £200 a week.

It was the love of Sue Steele, Eve's mum, that finally persuaded the young would-be actress that she was on a fast train to nowhere. In 1994 she checked into a detoxification unit in Manchester and stayed for two and a half weeks battling the drug demons. Prescribed the heroin substitute methadone she gradually weaned herself off the killer drug. Eve has been clean ever since and as a result of impressing the producers with her audition for the rôle of Maxine in early 1996 she was chosen to play the part of strait-laced Anne Malone in the *Street*.

Gail Force Problems

Gail Potter Tilsley Platt has suffered. Born illegitimate on 18 April 1950, she married lunk head Brian Tilsley on 28 November 1979, had an affair with his Australian cousin in 1986 and divorced Brian, remarried him on 24 February 1988, had a son by her toyboy on Christmas Day 1990, married him the following year on 27 September, suffered his infidelity on Christmas Day 1994, discovered an unknown half-brother and has to serve tea cakes to misery guts Percy Sugden.

Off-screen, like many of her *Street* colleagues Helen Worth is a very private person who tends not to give press interviews. Born on 7 January 1951 in Leeds, Helen was raised in Morecambe. Aged 12 she won a part in *The Sound of Music*. She joined the cast in 1975. In 1979 Helen moved in with actor

Michael Angelis, best-known as the rabbit-loving Lucien in the sitcom *The Liver Birds*. They married in 1991. It appeared the couple were happy together until May 1995 when Angelis was photographed holding hands with the married Jennifer Khalastchi who lived in the same block as the acting couple. He denied any romance but Angelis and his lady friend were seen regularly together.

She Ain't Heavey, She's Anorexic

Stunningly beautiful 23-year-old Tracy Shaw joined the cast of the *Street* in April 1995 as flirty hairdresser Maxine Heavey at a reported salary of £70,000 a year. It wasn't long before Maxine made her mark. Dressed in the bare minimum of clothing for cold Weatherfield, she bedded bookie Des Barnes, toyed with the affections of studious good guy Andy McDonald and even romped with Curly Watts after a drunken night out.

Off-screen, it seemed as if she lived a happy life with her publican parents, Ann and Karl, and brother, also called Karl. 'I'm not as forward as Maxine is – in fact, I'm very shy when it comes to men. Girls like Maxine don't think twice about going over to a man and chatting him up . . . If it was someone I really fancied like Brad Pitt for instance, I like to think I might make the first move, but, in reality, I wouldn't dare.' On 21 May 1996 she was crowned female 'Rear of the Year'. It was at this time that the real story of Tracy Shaw began to emerge. On 13 May she had been stopped leaving her local Safeway in Belper, Derbyshire, without paying for a 99p punnet of strawberries. It was said she had been daydreaming about her boyfriend, Glenn Williams, 27, who, by all accounts, was actually seeing former *Gladiators* cheerleader Joanna Mitchell, 20. Tracy was not charged with theft but was banned from the supermarket. It soon became clear that this was not an isolated incident. She had been shoplifting regularly but the thefts were blamed on an illness – anorexia nervosa.

'Anorexia is like total madness. It's like another voice in your head telling you not to eat,' she said. Vegetarian Tracy's weight plummeted to six stone and she became more and more depressed, during which time she regularly stole from shops. Tracy's illness began in 1993 when she was a dancer at the Arden School of Theatre, a stage school, and determined to keep her weight down. The anorexia led to shoplifting and she was caught three times but admitted many more thieving sprees. Just before Christmas 1994 she was admitted to a psychiatric ward. It was a dreadful experience. 'The patients were all severely mentally ill. It got to the stage that I thought if I stayed there any longer, I would turn that way.' One of her fellow patients was a nutter who wanted to murder someone and didn't particularly care who. 'I can't tell you how terrifying it was.' Tracy was released from her own personal hell just in time for the festive season and she gorged herself silly on food.

In June 1996 it was revealed that Tracy had attended a showbiz party for the Manchester launch of the musical *Grease* at the Hacienda Club where she had snogged Glenn Williams. They left the party and returned to the Victoria and Albert Hotel where Tracy was staying. The actress went to the toilet where she snorted cocaine. After more kissing she decided to go to bed and Williams followed her. Two hours later, he returned but Tracy stayed in her room. Said a witness, 'Glenn didn't brag about having sex with her but it was pretty obvious what had gone on.' Williams at first denied the romp, fearing it could wreck his relationship with his girlfriend. He was apparently annoyed that Tracy had described them as an item. Maintaining her dignity, Tracy refused to comment. Fortunately, Williams was around when Tracy accidentally bumped into a girl in a Manchester nightclub. The girl became abusive and even threatened to have Tracy shot!

In October 1996 Tracy received a two-month driving ban after being caught speeding. The ban was originally six months but was reduced because of her need to be near her parents who are crucial in her fight against anorexia. Since early 1997 Tracy has been squired about town by *You Bet* presenter Darren Day, whose previous girlfriends have included beautiful blonde Andrea Bourdman and soap star Anna Friel.

Oh, Julie!

Julie Goodyear had an ignominious start in life. Born as Julie Kemp on 29 March 1942 in Bury Infirmary, Lancashire, she took the name of her mother's second husband, builder Bill Goodyear. (By a coincidence Julie's mother's maiden name was Duckworth.) Julie became pregnant aged 17 and married the father, draughtsman Ray Sutcliffe, on 26 September 1959 at the Saint Church, Heywood, Lancashire. Their son, Gary, was born on 28 April 1960 at Fairfield General Hospital, Bury, weighing 9lb 12oz. According to Sutcliffe, Julie did not take to being a housewife and mother and often went out with other men. He said one night he saw their Hillman Minx car half a mile away from their home. When Julie returned the next day she told him she had spent the night with a friend in Blackpool. When Ray decided to lay down some ground rules, she left him taking Gary although Sutcliffe claims he babysat the infant. A year after their marriage Julie instigated divorce proceedings. The decree absolute was granted in 1963. Ray emigrated to Australia where he still lives. Julie remained in Heywood – and still does.

In July 1965 Julie won a beauty title, Miss Britvic, and lied about her age to the local paper, the *Heywood Advertiser*. It started her on a modelling career. Three years after her divorce, in May 1966, Julie made her first appearance in *Coronation Street*, the series that would bring her fame, fortune – reputedly she was paid £200,000 a year when she left – and an awful lot of press coverage, not always favourable. Asked why she had let so many stories pass she said, 'Oh, I'll do my autobiography one day; it'll happen all right. But it won't be unkind. I don't hurt. I don't do kiss'n'tell. I think it's rude, bad-mannered.'

Julie's first appearances in Weatherfield were not a roaring success. After six episodes she was let go. Pat Phoenix (Elsie Tanner) told her to learn her trade, advice that Julie took to heart, landing a rôle in *A Family at War* before returning to the *Street* on 18 May 1970.

In 1971 Julie became engaged to cabaret artist Jack Diamond but it was destined not to end in a trip to the altar. In his case it ended with a journey to a hospital after a drugs overdose. (Jack is now married to the brunette in the Roly Polys.) By the end of the following year Julie was seeing Tony Rudman, a businessman 12 years her senior. This time marriage was on the cards and the two tied the knot on 19 February 1973 at Bury Register Office. Two months later, the marriage was blessed in Bury Parish Church. The reception did not go according to plan and bride and groom had a massive argument. The marriage ended before it had started. A year later, the match was annulled on the grounds of non-consummation.

On Valentine's Day 1980, a leap year, Julie took advantage of female prerogative and proposed to restaurant manager Andrew McAllister whom she had met on holiday in Tunisia. Again, the relationship did not last. On 22 October that year Julie was the Guest of Honour on *This Is Your Life*. McAllister sat by her side even though they had split up. When she told him it was all over, he threw a glass at the wall. The police were called and he was removed by force.

In 1981 Julie met American Richard Skrob who was destined to become husband number three. Despite his proposals and constant transatlantic telephone calls Julie announced in December 1983 that she was marrying Bill Gilmour, *Coronation Street*'s Scottish director. The affair had been going on for twelve months but was kept a secret from the cast. Anne Kirkbride (Deirdre Barlow) guessed as did Neil Phillips, Bet's current flame Des Foster. Richard Skrob knew nothing of the affair. The lovebirds planned to marry on 5 January 1984. On 22 December 1983 the wedding was called off. Gilmour told a close friend that Julie had dumped him and he believed the only reason their affair had occurred was because Julie was jealous of press attention given to Pat Phoenix. Suddenly Richard Skrob was back in favour and he and Julie were married in the Caribbean on New Year's Day, 1985. It was to be a strange marriage. He spent most of his time in America while she continued to live in her old house in Heywood.

In June 1986 a report appeared in the *Sun* claiming that Julie had 'stolen' another woman's husband. According to reports she lived with cabbie Duncan Ford when her husband was in the States and threw him out when Richard Skrob came to visit. Yet more bizarre stories were to come. Apparently, Julie had met Ford three years earlier when he brought her home from Granada TV Studios. She invited him in and began kissing him. Suddenly she stopped and told him, 'You can either fuck off home or get up those fucking stairs.' Ford went home after Julie whacked him one. Eventually he succumbed but when they were in the bath Julie allegedly told him, 'I'm a lesbian.' Her Scottish personal assistant, Janet Ross, 34, was also her gay lover. It was a strange situation – a man and a lesbian fighting over the soap star. Two former friends, gay lovers themselves, came out of the woodwork to reveal that Julie had a string of lesbian partners including Janet Ross's sister, Joanne. Apparently, Julie was a regular visitor to gay clubs where she picked up women. Janet Ross denied she and her boss were ever lovers when she left her employ. However, that was not the story told by former *Street* actor Fred Feast who played fat barman Fred Gee. He revealed that Julie and Janet would stay in bed for days at a time making love. According to the garrulous Duncan Ford, Julie's third marriage, like her second, was never consummated. Many have suggested that it was a 'lavender marriage' – a match made by two homosexuals to conceal their true sexual inclination from the public. (Lavender marriages, such as those of Charles Laughton and Elsa Lanchester, are well known in Hollywood. Lesbian Barbara Stanwyck married two gays, Frank Fay and Robert Taylor, and at least two current Hollywood leading men have married lesbians.) Richard Skrob flew from America to be at his wife's side to show his support. It did not matter – the marriage was over. Another romantic failure. Richard Skrob married again. He died of leukaemia in December 1988 aged 47. Julie did not attend the funeral. In September 1989 Julie began an affair with Tony Sipes, a short, incredibly vain kissagram twenty-five years her junior, who billed himself as 'Toy Boy Tony', had his initials sewn on his clothes and spent his spare time walking around shopping centres in the forlorn hope someone would recognize him! After two months the affair became public knowledge and Julie finished it. Her young lover was devastated and, in 1990, committed suicide. Another of Julie's boyfriends was a transvestite who had deserted his wife and kids and wanted a sex change operation. He was apparently proud of his 36" breasts.

In October 1991 newspapers 'discovered' Julie's real father, George Kemp, who lived very near her. A story appeared and she rang to berate him for selling stories. He protested, truthfully, that he had never done so. [This author approached Mr Kemp with a view to writing a biography of the actress. Loyally, Mr Kemp said he would be happy to talk to me *if* Julie approved. I wrote to her but received a reply from her solicitors saying she did not wish a book to be written about her.] Her father died of cancer in February 1994 aged 76. Julie did not attend his funeral or send a wreath.

In December 1992 *Coronation Street* celebrated its 32nd birthday and Julie's date was Justin Fashanu, the gay black footballer who claimed to have had homosexual affairs with two Cabinet ministers. The relationship fizzled out inevitably.

In August 1994 Julie hosted a pilot for *The Julie Goodyear Talk Show*. By all accounts it was dreadful and a series was never commissioned.

In recognition of her long service to the *Street* Julie was awarded the MBE in the 1995 New Year's Honours List. On 25 May that year she announced she was leaving Weatherfield to try her hand at something new – what that something new is her fans are still waiting to find out. The chat show isn't going ahead. *Bet's Bar*, the supposed *Corrie* spin-off, seems to be a figment of a journalist's fevered imagination and, in January 1997, when Julie intimated she would like to come back to the Rovers Return she was told she wasn't wanted. Julie has not been the first and will surely not be the last person to walk down the cobbles of *Coronation Street*, become rich, successful and confident they can live outside the cloistered walls of Weatherfield and find it harder than they thought. Pat Phoenix (Elsie Tanner). Mark Eden (Alan Bradley). Madge Hindle (Renee Roberts). Ken Morley (Reg Holdsworth). Lynne Perrie (Ivy Tilsley). Stephen Hancock (Ernie Bishop). Julie Goodyear (Bet Gilroy). Life after soap? There isn't any!

Poison Ivy

After a long career in Northern clubs where she entertained the patrons by singing and telling jokes, Lynne Perrie joined *Coronation Street* full time as the God-fearing Ivy Tilsley in 1978. With her hen-pecked husband Bert (Peter Dudley – by coincidence Lynne Perrie's real name is Jean Dudley) and gormless son Brian (Christopher Quentin) she quickly established herself as a *Street* busybody nonpareil.

When Bert died and Brian married Gail Potter, Ivy was alone but soon busied herself interfering in her son's married life more than his wife would have wanted. Chris Quentin also tired of the *Street* and married American TV hostess Leeza Gibbons. He emigrated to America hoping for international film stardom. It never came and he returned to Britain with his tail very firmly between his legs. Meanwhile back in Weatherfield 'R Brian' was stabbed to death in a fight outside a nightclub. Ivy flung herself even more into the lives of her grandson Nicky and granddaughter Sarah Louise.

Although on-screen she played the devoted wife, off-screen 4′ 11½″ Lynne Perrie's life was very different. She had married Derrick Barksby in Rotherham Town Hall on 14 October 1950 when three months pregnant with their son, Stephen. Barksby was by his own admission bone idle and did not like spending money even when he hadn't earned it. According to Lynne Perrie's autobiography, he refuses to buy newspapers and goes to the bookmakers every day to read them.

Theirs was not a match made in heaven and Perrie's private life was full of extramarital affairs. She gleefully admitted to a penchant for toyboys and copious amounts of alcohol. The couple lived separate lives but still remained married. From the time she hit 50 Perrie admitted to bedding more than twenty toyboys. She also hinted that she had had an affair with a member of the *Street* cast although she refused to name him.

In December 1979 Lynne appeared in court on a charge of drink driving after 38-year-old salesman Dave Birch spiked her vodka in an attempt to get her into bed. It failed but Lynne drove off and fell asleep at a roundabout on the M1. She awoke with a broken rib and head injuries to find a blond policeman tending her wounds. At her trial she was banned for driving for three years and fined £150.

In October 1983 Lynne suffered a heart attack while alone at her two-bedroomed Manchester flat. Barksby was at their Rotherham cottage. While she lay in bed recuperating in Salford Royal Hospital, Peter Dudley died in a nearby ward. The following year she underwent an operation to correct a defective heart valve. Four years later there was more trouble as Lynne admitted to blowing £200,000 on gambling.

In 1991 it was revealed that Lynne had been undergoing psychiatric treatment in a bid to beat her emotional demons. The bill was footed by Granada TV.

On 7 June 1993 Lynne collapsed on the set of *Coronation*

Street and it was only the quick thinking of actor Charles Lawson (Jim McDonald) that saved her life. He rolled her on to her side and cleared her airway, allowing her to breathe. Doctors later said that Lynne was just half an hour away from death. From that moment Lynne decided to give up the booze that had earned her the nickname 'Champagne Perrie'.

In early 1994 Perrie spent £2,800 undergoing cosmetic surgery, twenty years after her first face-lift. A few weeks afterwards she returned to the clinic to have some fat from her thighs inserted in her mouth. Her lips swelled up and did not go down for some time, during which period she foolishly returned to work and the harsh television cameras. Unfortunately, rather than looking like a glamorous actress she looked as if she had undergone ten rounds with Mike Tyson. It all became too much for Granada TV and on 7 March 1994 Lynne was told that her contract was not being renewed. In her book she relates how she felt a tremendous weight had been lifted from her shoulders when executive producer Carolyn Reynolds told her the news. Then in a fit of pique Perrie decided she never wanted to return to Stage 1 and bluntly told Granada, after over 1,200 shows, they could despatch Ivy in her absence. Ivy was sent off to a nunnery where she later died, unmourned, of a heart attack.

In December 1994 Lynne was booked to appear on *The Word* singing 'I Will Survive' but she failed to show. When the chauffeur sent to pick her up arrived at her home, he found the doors open and the lights on. Lynne admitted to being 'unwell' although the tone of reports at the time suggested she was tired and emotional.

In an interview in February 1995 she claimed that the way she slurred her words was down to bad dental work. 'A while ago I lost a lot of weight. I thought I looked great but my husband told me I looked like a Martian so I went to my dentist and asked him to widen my back teeth to fill my cheeks out. He thickened the teeth from the inside. Now I don't have enough room in my mouth for my tongue. So when I get excited I can't talk properly and all my words get slurred.'

At midnight on 15 June 1996 Perrie appeared as a special guest on a satellite and cable porn TV station. When a male stripper called Predator appeared wearing a pair of see-through briefs Perrie's mouth dropped open and she declared, 'You don't get many of those to the pound.' Worse was to come when she beckoned the stripper over, pulled down his trunks and licked his penis, much to the consternation of the producer not to mention the stripper. The pictures were published in a pornographic magazine that boasts its content is too rude to allow it to be sold in W.H. Smith's or John Menzies.

The Murder of Ernie Bishop

Almost from the very beginning of *Coronation Street* Emily Nugent was unlucky in love and seemed destined to remain a spinster in Weatherfield. Her luck seemed to change when she fell for the pompous Leonard Swindley but it was not to be and she jilted him at the altar in July 1964. In 1968 she had a brief fling with Hungarian Miklos Zadic but dropped him when it became obvious he was only interested in a resident's permit. Then, in June 1969, she met photographer Ernie Bishop. She began to work for him in his photography shop and they fell in love and became engaged in August 1971, much to the disapproval of Emily's friend Mavis Riley, who accused Emily of 'flaunting herself. Like a latter-day Rita Hayworth!' A month after the engagement Ernie went to Spain to photograph some models and was arrested for shooting an orgy. Emily flew out to plead on his behalf while Rovers' landlady Annie Walker protested to the Spanish Embassy. Despite Mavis's objections and this unfortunate incident Emily and Ernie were married on Easter Monday 1972 at Mawdsley Street Congregational Church. Unable to have a family, in November 1974 they fostered two black children while their father was hospitalized. Owing to economic misfortune Ernie went bankrupt and the photography shop had to be sold. Ernie then got himself a job as wages clerk at Mike Baldwin's factory. On 11 January 1978 a wages snatch at the factory went terribly wrong and Ernie was blasted to death with a shotgun.* Once again Emily was alone.

That was the fictional story but events behind the scenes were almost as dramatic. For years rumours have flown that Ernie Bishop left *Coronation Street* in a row over money – that actor Stephen Hancock† was unhappy with the salary he was being paid.

This isn't true. Hancock was unhappy but his gripe was with his contract, not the salary. Granada TV, the makers of *Coronation Street*, had a system whereby actors were guaranteed appearances in at least 52 episodes. In effect this meant an assurance of 26 weeks of work each year. Certain senior actors such as Doris Speed, Peter Adamson and Pat Phoenix were paid for every episode made in a year – then 104 in all – even though they did not appear in every episode. This meant that their pay packets were slightly larger. Hancock believed this was grossly unfair and insisted on a meeting with producer Bill Podmore. At the meeting Podmore sympathized with Hancock but informed him the system would not and could not be altered for one actor. Hancock threatened to resign if the matter was not settled. Podmore told him to go away and think things over very carefully. Many actors would give their right arms for a regular rôle in *Coronation Street* and here was Hancock throwing away job security and a not inconsiderable salary on a point of principle.

* One of the actors playing the robbers was Tony McHale, later to write many episodes of *EastEnders*. He said that shortly after the shooting episode was shown he was accosted by an old woman in Manchester market who hit him with her handbag and shouted 'Murderer!' McHale was also one of the regular 'repertory' actors playing tricks on people in *Beadle's About!*

† Another coincidence. Stephen Hancock's brother, Christopher, played Charlie Cotton, Dot's errant husband in *EastEnders*.

Over the next few days Hancock mulled over his future but when he returned to see Podmore his mind was made up. He was adamant that he was being treated unfairly. He could not stay with the show. This presented Podmore with a seemingly insoluble dilemma. Emily and Ernie Bishop were one of the show's happiest married couples. For Ernie to go off without Emily was unthinkable but Eileen Derbyshire who played Emily did not want to leave. The problem of what to do with Ernie was discussed at script conferences for many weeks.

Eventually, writer John Stevenson came up with the solution – Ernie had to die. Bill Podmore decided to give Stephen Hancock the bad news personally rather than in writing or over the telephone. However, before he had the opportunity he was approached by two tabloid journalists who had heard the news via a mole at Granada. Podmore refused to deny or confirm the story but it was too late and Hancock was furious that he had heard the news of his departure from a newspaper rather than his employers.

Bill Podmore called Hancock to Manchester and told him there really was no alternative: Ernie Bishop must die. No one was prepared for the public outcry at the demise of one of the *Street*'s best-loved characters. It was even the subject of a documentary, *Death on the 'Street'*. Oddly enough, Stephen Hancock attended his own funeral. He hid behind some trees in the background as Ernie was laid to rest.

Simple Simon

Street bad boy Steve McDonald gets more fan mail than any other member of the cast. Whether this is due to the acting ability of Simon Gregson or his boyish good looks is a matter of debate. It is not unusual for a pair of knickers to appear in the post with a request to wear them and return them to the smitten owner.

At first, policeman's son Gregson and his mates thought this was a laugh, but he soon became accustomed to the adulation and now he revels in it. A number of girls have come forward to kiss'n'tell about the young actor. His first real love was blonde Wendy Kingston who went to school – Kingsway High in Gatley, Manchester – with the then Simon Gregory. He changed his name when he joined Equity as there was already a Simon Gregory. The couple dated for two months before going their separate ways. In that time Simon met Gloria Hickson, nine years his senior, and lost his virginity to her. She said, 'He was so shy and awkward. It didn't last long but he was only a boy and I could see he had great potential as a lover.' At 17 he and Wendy got back together but 'it was clear three years of *Coronation Street* had really screwed him up'. Despite that they dated and even went on a Loch Ness monster hunt. They spent more time making love than monster hunting. 'Sex with Simon was always great. We were very touchy-feely, we couldn't keep our hands off each other. Simon's a very passionate and adventurous lover – and he bought me lots of sexy satin underwear.' Passion can only last so long and they split up again after just six months. Not long afterwards Gregson found himself in all sorts of trouble. In 1994 he was pictured smoking a cannabis joint on holiday. He spent £13,000 on a white Suzuki jeep and then lost his licence for a year as a result of drink driving. In May 1995 he also admitted to having a £300-a-week cocaine habit.

Another lover was his *Street* co-star Chloe Newsome who played his wife Vicky, although the fling came to nothing.

Although he burps regularly through interviews, Gregson is still the object of a thousand pre-pubescent fantasies. Trying to sound self-deprecating, the actor admits he has 'big feet, a concave chest, big ears and I'm too skinny'. As well as smoking 40 fags a day he confesses to other dirty habits: 'I pick my nose, I bite my nails and pick my feet – in that order. I have nice rough edges to pick with.'

Charming!

The Ill-fated Hunt for the Show of Gold

For many years television soap operas were considered de trop by the BBC. The independent sector had no such qualms. Two of the most famous soaps, *Coronation Street* (1960–?) and *Crossroads* (1964–88), were created by Granada and ATV (later Central) respectively. For the most part, however, the BBC shied away from this form of entertainment. *United!*, about a football team, and *Compact*, about a women's magazine, were perfunctory attempts at a BBC soap but it wasn't until 1985 that the corporation put all its resources behind a soap opera. Ignoring the success of *Coronation Street* was no longer feasible or, for that matter, particularly sensible. On 19 February of that year *EastEnders* was launched, created by Julia Smith and Tony Holland who had worked together on *Z Cars*, *Angels* and *District Nurse*.

EastEnders caught the public imagination like no BBC soap had done before. For months on end no day went by without the tabloids running a (usually) far-fetched story about the programme or its stars. Gold was discovered by the hacks when it was revealed that a surprisingly large number of the cast had criminal records. One young actor, David Scarboro, who played Mark Fowler before Todd Carty took over, became clinically depressed and later committed suicide. He was 20 years old.

The public lapped up the on-screen trials and tribulations of Albert Square and its inhabitants. For a while, *EastEnders* even knocked *Coronation Street* off its number one slot in the viewing figures charts.

Flush with the success of *EastEnders*, BBC chiefs began to think in terms of another soap. This time they wanted a soap that would be glamorous, in direct contrast to the dreariness of Albert Square. In November 1991, three senior BBC executives

– Jonathan Powell, Mark Shivas (who had been responsible for another much-maligned BBC show, *The Cleopatras*) and Peter Cregeen – sat down to discuss a programme to replace the ailing *Wogan* chat show. It was a difficult decision to make. *Wogan* represented 156 cheap shows (just £25,000 each) per year. However, since it was so settled in its slot (Mondays, Wednesdays and Fridays at 7 p.m.) it was a sitting duck for the ITV schedulers. They constantly tried out their new programmes against *Wogan*, seeing what was successful and what wasn't. As a result *Wogan*'s share of the audience began to drop. The big three were presented with three soap operas and chose one – *Little England*, about British expatriates living in Marbella – as the potential replacement. It was the brainchild of John Dark, a producer whose credits included work on *Casino Royale* and *Shirley Valentine*, in conjunction with Cinema Verity run by former Thames producer Verity Lambert who was responsible for, among others, *Minder* and *Rumpole of the Bailey*.

The BBC liked the idea but wanted Julia Smith and Tony Holland to oversee its production. The name of the show was changed to *Eldorado* ('the gilded') after Mark Shivas pointed out that the original title would not go down well in Scotland, Wales or Northern Ireland. Work began in earnest in January 1992. A set was specially built in Spain and the producers began assembling a cast. Experienced comedy actress Patricia Brake was cast as Gwen Lockhead. Brake had appeared in numerous sitcoms including a stint as Ronnie Barker's daughter in *Going Straight*, the follow-up to *Porridge*. She had also played Eth in the television version of *The Glums*. Handsome Jesse Birdsall played evil Marcus Tandy and lesbian Polly Perkins was Trish Valentine, a middle-aged woman with a taste for toyboys. Other cast members included Roger Walker, previously known for his appearances on the children's show *Rainbow*.

The original launch date of the show of 'sun, sea, sangria and, of course . . . sex' was to be that September. In the spring of 1992 Jonathan Powell declared that *Eldorado* would begin instead in July. He claimed that the senior figures involved always knew the programme was aiming for a July launch and the September date was a piece of misinformation designed to mislead ITV.

Eldorado first hit the screens on 6 July 1992. It was immediately lashed by the critics who likened it to the halcyon days of *Crossroads* when the acting was more wooden than the sets. *Today* opined the show was 'like a sugary pink chunk of Spanish seaside rock' while veteran critic Nancy Banks-Smith of the *Guardian* wrote, '*Eldorado* goes straight for the young, drunk vote with a directness that leaves you winded.'

The audience for the first show began at 7.3 million but dropped 800,000 viewers within minutes as ITV's rival *Take Your Pick* soared from 7.8 million to 9.4 million. *Eldorado*'s figures continued to drop steadily. Six weeks into the project just 2.8 million tuned in for the Friday episode. On that same day producer Julia Smith went on an extended leave of absence while inexperienced young actress Kathy Pitkin, in her first acting job, was sacked from her rôle as Fizz.

The show became the brunt of jokes. One hæmorrhoid ointment company claimed their preparation made sitting through an episode of *Eldorado* bearable. A recycled toilet paper manufacturer's product bore the legend 'In my previous life I was an *Eldorado* script.' It was also claimed that the residents of Eldorado Close in Studley, Warwickshire, petitioned the council to change their street name because it was making them a laughing stock.

Departures continued apace. Kai Maurer, Trish's toyboy Dieter, left on 9 December 1992 (on the day that *Coronation Street* celebrated its 32nd birthday). He went to drama school to learn how to act. Twelve days later, Jon Morrey (who played Allan Hindle) was fired. He subsequently sold stories of his love life on the show to tabloid newspapers. In the same month Jonathan Powell left the BBC to become Director of Drama at Carlton TV. On 12 February 1993 Iker Ibanez (Javier Fernandez, one of the Spanish contingent) was booted out. He went into rep in Madrid. On 24 February Patch Connolly

(Snowy) left. Incongruously, he went from a failed soap to appearing in Chekhov's *The Cherry Orchard*. Nine days later Roger Walker, who had played Kathy Pitkin's husband on the show, was sacked. A week later, on 12 March, new BBC-1 Controller Alan Yentob decided not to extend the show beyond its first-year run. In April Mark Shivas became head of BBC Films. On 14 June, the last of the original triumvirate, Peter Cregeen, resigned as head of BBC Drama Series.

Eldorado had cost the BBC £10 million. It ended at 7.30 p.m. on 9 July 1993.

Emmerdale

Emmerdale began life as *Emmerdale Farm* on 16 October 1972. Unlike the other soaps, *Emmerdale Farm* started out as a series rather than a serial and did not become a regular part of the TV landscape until 1984. The show was not networked until 1978. Created by Kevin Laffan, it concentrated on the Sugden family. The first episode showed elder son Jack Sugden (Andrew Burt) returning to Beckindale, the fictional setting for the show, to claim his inheritance, Emmerdale Farm, on the death of his father, Jacob. Younger brother Joe (Fraser Hines) had his nose put out of joint by the return of the prodigal. Their elder sister Peggy Skilbeck (Jo Kendall) was annoyed he hadn't left the farm to her. Thus the scene was set.

Emmerdale Farm has changed considerably over the years. In 1989 its name was shortened. In 1985 creator Laffan left the show saying there was too much 'sex, sin and sensationalism'. Even Mary Whitehouse got in on the act, labelling the programme 'a den of vice'. Unlike *Crossroads*, *Emmerdale* has never been the butt of jokes about wooden sets and cardboard acting although some comedians have noted, 'If it wasn't for watching *Emmerdale Farm* I'd get no fresh air at all.' In 1993 the show's makers, Yorkshire TV, revamped it by bringing in *Brookside* creator Phil Redmond. It was Redmond who engineered the famous Christmas plane crash on Beckindale that brought the criticism from some quarters that the show was cashing in on the Lockerbie disaster. Yorkshire TV also placed in 1992 a series of advertisements featuring younger members of the cast scantily clad and in suggestive poses. And sexy Zoe Tate had a steamy lesbian affair. Jacob Sugden would be turning over in his grave.

Some of the story lines in *Emmerdale* have been sensational – but not quite as enthralling as the off-screen lives of some of its stars.

Sheila Mercier (Annie Sugden) is the older sister of farceur Lord Rix. She was raped on 31 December 1939, the night before her 21st birthday, and became pregnant. She gave birth to a daughter, Monica Janet, but her parents forced her to give the baby up for adoption.

Christopher Chittell (Eric Pollard) appeared in a porn film when he was a young, struggling actor.

Ian Sharrock (Jackie Merrick) slept with co-star Malandra Burrows when they flew to Tunisia to film scenes for the show. His wife was pregnant with their second child at the time. 'Having Malandra gave me a real kick. It was all about sex,' said the actor. 'Malandra was a very passive lover, she

Malandra Burrows – *Emmerdale*'s resident sex symbol

liked sex to be straightforward. We never did anything kinky or adventurous. She's seen as a sex symbol, but it was really an anti-climax.' For a fortnight after their return from location Sharrock was faithful to his wife but he was soon bonking Malandra in lunchtime romps. Their affair came to a halt when William Ian Sharrock was born in May 1988 and Malandra didn't speak to her lover for three months. After that it was bed business as usual. In June 1989 Sharrock left Beckindale and his £50,000-a-year salary for the comparative safety of Chelmsford in Essex. In 1993 he had an affair with a member of the crew while appearing in a play in York. When his wife, Pam, found out she attacked the woman. At this time she was didn't know about her husband's fling with his co-star. Terrified by what would happen if she found out, Sharrock tried to kill himself. He survived and the family went on holiday to start afresh. However, when they returned Pam Sharrock opened a letter from a woman who had had a one-night stand with Ian. Again there were arguments and again Pam showed her character by forgiving her errant husband. Worse was to come. In September 1993 she received an anonymous phone call from a woman who told her all about Malandra Burrows. Pam rang Malandra and left a message on her answering machine calling her a bitch and a slut and threatening to kill her if she ever saw her again. Amazingly, Pam and Ian Sharrock are still married.

Jacqueline Pirie (Tina Dingle) had a fling with a convicted, tattooed thug who boasted he was 'the hardest man in Birmingham'. Their affair began in July 1996 and the thug, who has already fathered seven children by four different women, took her to see a boxing match in Blackpool. 'We cracked open a bottle of champagne. We'd booked separate hotel rooms but got on so well I ended up in his bed.' The brief fling resulted in the impressionable 5′ 1″ actress becoming pregnant. The villain, who has 'Triumph' tattooed on his bottom lip, tried to sell his story to the *News of the World* for £20,000. He proudly told a reporter, 'I'm a hardened, known criminal and have been in jail five times for violence. I have been on an attempted murder charge, have been involved in protection rackets, intimidation of witnesses, shootings and gang warfare.' The thug claimed that Jacqueline knew of his reputation and had hired him as her bodyguard. 'I'm a top villain and I know all the gang leaders. Jacqueline knows all about me and what I'm up to.' The *News of the World* sensibly declined the offer.

Curvy Claire King plays the sexy, scheming Kim Tate who loathes her disabled step-son, Chris. In real life Claire is married to the actor who plays Chris, Peter Amory. Claire was once offered a million pounds by one of her admirers who wanted to spend the night with her.

Malandra Burrows (Kathy Tate) cancelled her wedding on 1 August 1996 because she had a record, 'Summer Night Love', coming out. Her fiancé Jonathan Armstead not surprisingly walked out on her although the couple have been reconciled. The record did not set the charts alight. It was the second time Burrows had cancelled a wedding. She had previously been engaged to children's TV presenter Mark Granger.

The Enigma of *EastEnders*

In 1983 TV producer Julia Smith and writer Tony Holland were summoned to the BBC where they were informed that the corporation wanted a successful bi-weekly serial. The show they created would become compulsive viewing for millions of Britons. Set in a fictional East London square, the serial would follow the lives of a variety of characters and the situations, often desperate, in which they found themselves. A name had to be found for Smith and Holland's new baby. They flirted with *E8*, *Square Dance*, *Round the Square*, *Round the Houses*, *East 8* and *London Pride* but all were discarded. Characters were formed as actors arrived for casting sessions. Eventually, the show went on air on 19 February 1985 under the title *EastEnders*. The cast included just one 'name' – Wendy Richard – although soon they would all be household faces. The public warmed to irascible Lou, Dirty Den, good old Ange, dotty Ethel, spotty Michelle, wimpy Ian, moaning Mary, sulky Sue, podgy Sharon and the rest. The cast's experience of TV had been mostly in bit-parts. For instance, Bill Treacher (Arthur Fowler) had played a regular soldier in an episode of *Dad's Army*.

David Scarboro – Deadender

One member of the cast found he could not handle the recognition that came with being in a successful TV programme. David Scarboro was born on 3 February 1968 and became an actor when he was 12. After appearing in a small rôle in *Grange Hill*, the starting place for numerous child actors, Scarboro landed the prized part of mixed-up Mark Fowler in the soap. However, the young man was not cut out for soap stardom and he was sacked after not turning up for a vital day's filming. His excuse was that he had made a mistake because the date was not printed clearly on the script. The story line had to be rewritten to accommodate Scarboro's absence so Mark Fowler was made to run away two months after the show began. By public demand, he returned to the soap on 2 January 1986 when the Fowlers tracked down their errant son to Southend-on-Sea. However, the comeback was not to last and once again the actor found himself on the unemployment register.

It was too much for Scarboro to cope with and he began drinking heavily. In March 1986 he was fined by magistrates at Reigate, Surrey, for insulting three young girls. In October of the following year he suffered a mental collapse and admitted himself to the psychiatric wing of Farnborough Hospital. In January 1988 he attempted suicide with an overdose of anti-depressants while drunk. Three months later, he went to a girlfriend's house and left a ring and some records on her doorstep. When she discovered them the girl rang Scarboro's home in Tatsfield, Surrey, but his parents were away and she spoke to Simon, Scarboro's 17-year-old brother. Police were alerted and at 6.30 a.m. on 27 April Scarboro's Ford Cortina was discovered abandoned in Eastbourne, East Sussex. The coastguard was asked to check the shoreline at Beachy Head, Britain's most notorious suicide spot. Scarboro's broken body was discovered on the rocks at around 8.30 a.m.

French with Tears

To millions of *EastEnders*' female fans David Wicks, the randy car dealer played by Michael French, is their ideal man.

In February 1996 Philip Chard, the husband of *EastEnders* star Lindsey Coulson, announced he had split from his wife and named Michael French in the divorce. It was claimed that the two actors had become 'close' and had shared 'late night meetings'. French would often be invited to the Chards' for dinner. Philip would go to bed around midnight leaving his wife alone drinking and chatting with the actor. It all became too much for Chard who once chased French out of the marital home with a knife. Chard believed there was more than just friendship between his wife and the bachelor actor.

The following month the *Sunday Mirror* revealed that French was, in fact, gay. Apparently, he had begun dating fellow *EastEnders* actor Bryan Lawrence in the late summer of 1995. The two men had first met in 1983 when they were both auditioning for a play and Lawrence had caught French's eye. It was only when they were reunited on the set at Albert Square that they became romantically involved. For a time French had worked as an airline steward – a trolley dolly in aeroplane vernacular – and, according to former colleagues, had a number of one-night stands with male colleagues. In September 1995 the two men holidayed together in Corsica and when they returned went house-hunting, although they never did find their lovenest. They decided to cool things towards the end of that year when they believed the press were snooping around. Too late – the *Sunday Mirror* already had the scoop and emblazoned the story on its front page.

French left *EastEnders* in September 1996. Two months later, more details emerged. Philip Chard had apparently written a roman à clef detailing his wife's affair with French. Apparently, French had seduced Lindsey after his homosexual advances had been spurned by Chard. The two men had been friends in the early 1980s and had often gone cycling together. As with Bryan Lawrence, French had lost contact with Chard and *EastEnders* brought them together. It was to the Chards that French had unburdened himself when he thought his gay secret was about to be revealed. The actor and Chard enjoyed long evenings smoking joints and drinking. By all accounts Lindsey Coulson kept off the dope. Chard believed that French had set out to wreck his family because he was jealous. Both French and Coulson have refused to comment. French has subsequently appeared as Slade, a maverick policeman, in the BBC series *Crime Traveller*.

The Ballad of Spotty Gaffney

Dean Gaffney is a gawky-looking, greasy-haired, spotty-faced adolescent with, if one ex-girlfriend is to be believed, long, dirty toenails as well. Yet women fall at his apparently unclean feet. Why? Solely because Gaffney has played Robbie Jackson in the top-rated *EastEnders* on BBC-1 since 1993.

Robbie Jackson is a loser in love in Albert Square. His attempts at chatting up girls are regularly rebuffed and the only time he did manage to bed a girl she developed a nasty rash. Nature has not been kind to him.

It's a different story with 19-year-old Dean Gaffney although he does share the greasy hair and seemingly terminal acne with Robbie. In May 1995 he began dating a very pretty, very busty student called Sarah Burge whom he had met at Options nightclub in Kingston-upon-Thames. One night as they made love a condom burst but neither of them thought anything more about it. In November of the same year the couple decided to go their separate ways. 'Things got a bit boring,' remembered Sarah. A week later, Sarah found out she was pregnant. Despite the impending baby the couple did not decide to make a go of things. 'I suppose it would have been nice if Dean had said, "Okay, let's get married," but I always knew that was never really likely,' said Sarah. 'I guess it would be wrong to get back together just for the sake of the baby.'

Sarah rang Gaffney on the set of *EastEnders* to tell him the news. He went round to see her but was too scared to go into her house and so she had to sit in his car outside discussing the future. Sarah refused to have an abortion and says Dean seemed surprised when she stuck to her decision.

Further shocks were in store for Sarah and her family. Numerous other girls came out of the woodwork telling of their passionate flings with Gaffney.

Busty blonde insurance broker Julia Edwards, 18, took Sarah's place in Gaffney's affections but not, it would appear, in his bed. She claimed they dated for two months after meeting in a nightclub in Chelmsford, Essex, and did not have sex. He apparently told her he would wait ten years if necessary before sleeping with her. She described him as 'a gentleman' as she posed in the *Sun* showing her knickers to the world.

Gaffney could afford to be a gentleman. There were other women more than willing to take Julia's place in his bed. Blonde Lucy Allen, 19, was one. She ended up there after they met in a club. 'He was okay in bed,' she remembered. 'Let's put it this way – I'm not going to cry my eyes out if he never phones me again.'

Another girl to fall for Gaffney was 16-year-old Nicola Reid from Newark, Nottinghamshire, and although they ended up in her single bed with her sleeping father in the next room, the couple did not have sex. Gaffney insisted on keeping his shirt on. 'He must have been trying to hide his scrawny body. He looks a real weakling.'

Blonde model Stephanie Hudson, 16, of Malvern, Worcestershire, also played tonsil tennis with Gaffney but refused to have sex with him. 'I'll only sleep with someone if I've known them a few months.' She passed Gaffney's home telephone number on to her friends who all rang the star until he changed it. She was not to be the last of Gaffney's conquests.

In the summer of 1996 he and actor friend Omer Hibbert-Williams met blondes Simone Cameron and Tara Leers, both 20, in Henley-on-Thames. They invited the girls back to Gaffney's Hounslow home. Gaffney and Hibbert-Williams rushed upstairs as soon as they got in and called Tara to the bedroom. The girl walked into the darkened room and was grabbed by the two actors. She screamed and turned on the light to find the pair naked and ready for action. She refused their kind offer and went back downstairs to join her friend. Later, when Hibbert-Williams and Tara were asleep, Gaffney tried it on with Simone and the former nanny to Steve Wright succumbed. 'The next morning we went out for the day and when we got back to his place we made love in nearly every room in the house,' she recalled, before Gaffney got out his scrapbook of cuttings about himself. Simone asked about Sarah Burge. 'She's history,' was the thoughtful reply. Simone asked if Gaffney ever indulged in group sex. 'Yeah, I love threesomes but I'm game for more if it's on offer.'

Gaffney's 'history' gave birth to twin daughters, Chloe and Charlotte, on 17 July 1996. Compassionate as ever, Gaffney said, 'She'd suffered an uncomfortable nine months and been through a traumatic worrying birth – all on her own while I tried to distance myself from everything. I thought at one stage I ought not to visit the babies. I debated whether to have anything to do with their upbringing apart from financial support.' Thankfully – or perhaps not, depending on your viewpoint – Gaffney came to his senses and visited his daughters in hospital.

To add to his woes, on 22 November 1996 Gaffney was fined £40 for speeding on the M4.

Gilly, the A1 Lay-by & the Thug

Gillian Taylforth comes from a large loving family, which makes her choice of boyfriend all the more puzzling. Since 1988 Taylforth has been dating Geoff Knights, the man who when asked in court to list his previous convictions said, 'What? All of them?' On one occasion he beat her up so badly Taylforth was left with a black eye and a broken nose.

Gillian Taylforth was born in London on 14 August 1955, the second of four daughters of master printer Ron and Margaret Taylforth. The family grew up in a four-bedroom flat in Islington. Gillian shared a bed with her sister until she was 17 and didn't leave home until she was 27. At 19 Gillian was a Sunday School teacher. She trained as a go-go dancer but never worked as one in deference to her father. After appearing in the remake of the popular sitcom *The Rag Trade*, she got her big break as Kathy Beale in *EastEnders* in February 1985. During filming she fell in love with co-star Nick Berry who played her stepson. The relationship was destined not to last and Taylforth met Knights, whose previous lovers included ex-page 3 girl Tracy Kirby.

In 1991 when she was pregnant with their daughter, Jessica, the home of boyfriend Knights was raided by the drug squad. Gillian feared she would lose her baby.

In January 1994 Taylforth sued the *Sun* at the Old Bailey after the newspaper ran a story saying she had fellated Knights in a Range Rover in a lay-by on the A1. The pair claimed that Knights suffered from pancreatitis and Taylforth was rubbing his stomach. At the police station, Knights signed a caution admitting outraging public decency. The court was shown a video of Gillian miming oral sex with a sausage. The couple became the first to lose a libel suit against the *Sun* for many years. Following the verdict, Taylforth mysteriously collapsed and was driven away in an ambulance. Her sister Janice memorably yelled at bemused journalists, 'You've killed her! You've killed her!' The case cost her £250,000. She tried to claim back the VAT on her legal expenses but, in December 1994, Customs and Excise refused her application.

Gillian's hardships were not over. In October 1994 Knights was arrested after assaulting a police officer. On 25 November 1994 Knights appeared at Hendon Magistrates Court. (On 15 March 1995 he was fined £2,000 for the assault and ordered to pay £250 compensation.) On 23 January 1995 Taylforth was arrested for drink driving when, after a night out with *EastEnders* colleagues, she crashed her BMW316i at 7.08 p.m., wrote off two parked cars and hit a garden wall. The smash occurred 50 yards from the BBC's Elstree studios as Taylforth set off home. Her daughter was in the back of the car.

In March 1995 Taylforth was found guilty of drink driving. She lost her licence for 23 months and was fined £480. Her alcohol level had been measured at more than twice the legal limit.

On Easter Sunday that year Geoff Knights beat up taxi driver Martin Davies, a friend of Gillian's. Both the cabbie and the
actress ended up in hospital and the boyfriend was again
arrested. Knights claimed the driver got what he deserved and
pleaded self-defence. The cabbie told a different story.
'Knights was smashing my head against the side of the house.
He was screaming, "You're fucking my girlfriend. You're
going to die." Then he started choking me. I managed to break
free then he jabbed two fingers into my eyeballs. The pain was
unbearable. When I was lying on the floor he started repeat-
edly kicking me in the head.' Knights was released on bail on
condition he did not contact Gillian. In August he was seen
with her on the *EastEnders* set. For contempt of court Knights
spent a weekend in Wormwood Scrubs. Gillian claimed that a
mix-up over care for their daughter resulted in the meeting,
yet newspapers at the time reported that the couple had met
not just once but three times. Judge Myrella Cohen, freeing
Knights, warned the pair that if they met again she would lock
up Knights. In the end his assault case did not go to court
because the judge said press coverage of Knights's record
would preclude a fair trial.

In November 1996 Gillian miscarried what would have been
her second baby. As of now, the odd couple are still together.

Having Your Phil

Balding Steve McFadden first appeared in Albert Square as
one-half of the notorious Mitchell Brothers – Phil and Grant –
in February 1990. McFadden could not have been more suited
for the rôle of Phil. Leaving home at 17, he moved into a cat-
ridden squat in Bethnal Green. With some bizarrely named
mates, McFadden spent his time smoking marijuana, getting
drunk and going to see bands. McFadden fell into a life of

crime. When he was 15 his father, John, was arrested in connection with a £1,000,000 robbery. He was eventually acquitted at the Old Bailey but the pressure he was under made him become an alcoholic.

By the time Steve McFadden was 16 he was a delinquent running around with a gang who stole cars. On the way home from a concert he was arrested and charged with assaulting a police officer. The next six years were spent getting into various kinds of trouble. In 1977, aged 18, McFadden and some friends stole some canoes. He received a fine and was bound over to keep the peace for two years. That same year also saw the future EastEnder done for possession of cannabis.

In 1979 he was arrested for running away from a cab without paying the fare. In 1980 McFadden was involved in a pub brawl and more trouble with the law. Smoking a joint at an England–West Indies Test match saw him arrested and convicted yet again. McFadden decided to go on holiday rather than attending court and so was done for jumping bail. In 1982 he was charged with assault and threatening behaviour. The Crown Court gave him a suspended two-year sentence. When he finally decided to go straight McFadden went through a series of mundane jobs. One of his less wholesome ones was working in a sex shop called the Love Tunnel but that was too much even for his palate and he left after three months.

In 1986 McFadden fathered a son, Matt, by childhood sweetheart Sue Marshall. The boy lives with his mother, seeing the soap star whenever possible.

One of the by-products of fame is that women suddenly find you irresistibly attractive where previously they would not have given you a second glance. McFadden certainly made the most of this. A stream of women came forward to claim that they had been bedded by him.

First off was 29-year-old divorced barmaid Sarah Player, the mother of a two-year-old daughter, whom he met in Ritzy's nightclub in Bristol. He asked her if she was wearing knickers and when she said yes, he told her to take them off. She refused. Later she sent him a picture taken of the pair of them and 'said if no pants were his thing [she'd] drop them for him'. McFadden rang her and asked her to send him her knickers. The barmaid did as she was told. 'They were my best ones too – the white g-string type with lace and pearls in them.' He told her to meet him at the Severn View service station on the M4 and to wear a mini-skirt. They got into his messy camper van and had sex before having a meal at the service station. Then it was back to the van for another session. 'It was better this time and lasted a lot longer. I remember his kisses because they were all lovely and moist. I felt he thought I was some-thing special. It seemed that he desperately wanted me and was doing everything possible so that I'd be satisfied. He was certainly a very experienced lover. I'd give him more than ten out of ten . . . he went off the scale really and he was very good at giving oral sex.' The romp lasted nearly three hours. McFadden refused to let Sarah give him a blowjob. She gave him another g-string as a souvenir. The fling ended in August 1994.

McFadden was doing a personal appearance at a nightclub in Neath, South Wales, when single mum-of-two Emma Trick, 24, rushed up and snogged him. As McFadden signed auto-graphs his driver shouted that the first girl to take her bra off would get a signed T-shirt. Barmaid Emma removed hers dou-ble quick and threw it at the EastEnder. An assistant asked if she wanted to go back to London with McFadden and Emma agreed. They 'started mucking about' in the back of the car but she refused to go any further while the driver was watching. The couple were dropped off at McFadden's dressing room on the *EastEnders* set and they bonked in the shower. 'Steve's got a gentle touch and we did it standing up. He's very well-endowed and quite proud of his manhood. He certainly reached parts of me that others have never reached.' After the shower, they had sex on the sofa bed. 'Steve kept going on about what a lovely bum I've got and after the moment came for him he gave me oral sex, which was brilliant. He wasn't a selfish lover.' McFadden was twice called for make-up and while he was away Emma busied herself reading his fan mail.

'I felt really chuffed that these girls were writing for a picture and I was shagging him in his dressing room.' After a third session McFadden filmed a scene for the show before taking Emma back to his North London home. Once inside, he took his trousers off saying he preferred to walk around in his pants. After feeding her a curry, McFadden told the impressionable barmaid, 'I really enjoy your company and you turn me on like fuck.' Then he took her to his bedroom: 'We had the most incredible sex, the best. He was so experienced and big. I really got him going. We were doing things all over the bed and it was getting really frenzied. It must have lasted an hour and we did it twice, I think. At the end we were both exhausted and sweating like pigs.' Later, when she sold her story to a newspaper, Emma said, 'I think he's a rat of course because he only wanted me for one thing. But it did take two to tango and I really enjoyed it. He wined me, dined me, sixty-nined me and then dumped me. I'd do it all again any day.'

Next up was chubby brunette Katrina Taylor on a nightclub chair. McFadden met the mother of four at the Coliseum nightclub in Luton. 'I ran straight over, threw my arms around his neck and gave him a great big smacker. It was a big Frenchie kiss and lasted about ten seconds. He was a fantastic kisser.' The actor disappeared into a private room with the woman who was five months pregnant at the time. 'I sat on his lap. I told him I was pregnant but I just thought I'd go for it. To be honest I was a bit disappointed because he hadn't risen to the occasion properly. I was expecting the full ticket but certainly didn't get it. Still I'll remember the moment for the rest of my life.'

Then came blonde Vikki Marlowe from Leicester. Again they met in a nightclub and the persistent girl went back to the actor's hotel where 'we made love six times in every possible position. Steve was sensational. He's got an incredibly high sex drive. After that we dozed off but when we woke up we did it twice more. He likes to be slapped and scratched a lot. He's weird about things like that. He liked me to bite him all over his neck, shoulders and body and he especially enjoyed being slapped on the arse. He told me his fantasy was to watch me make love to five men at the same time. Afterwards he wanted my g-string but I refused. I didn't want him showing it around like a trophy.' The relationship continued and the couple apparently had sex in a public park in London. Finally, black divorced mum-of-three Leah Armstrong came forward to say McFadden had had her in a railway station.

Perhaps McFadden's Lothario-like behaviour had upset someone because at 2 a.m. on 24 September 1994 he was attacked by a gang of dossers as he walked by Waterloo Station with two friends. The trio were singing and the tramps took umbrage, claiming they couldn't sleep because of the noise. McFadden's left hand was badly slashed between his thumb and forefinger by a machete-like weapon. Trying to escape, McFadden fell down a set of stairs and injured his shoulder. The frenzied attack continued unabated. At one point the 5´ 10˝ skinhead attacker screamed, 'Who do you think you are? Fucking Phil Mitchell?' McFadden was taken to St Thomas's Hospital where his wounds were attended to.

On 15 March 1996 McFadden attended a magazine launch party at Drones nightspot in London's swanky Pont Street. On his way home to Kentish Town in his Rolls-Royce the actor was stopped by police on Waterloo Bridge and breathalyzed. He was discovered to be 3½ times over the limit and arrested. On 16 May he pleaded guilty to drink driving.

The Punk & the Café Owner

Linda Davidson was born in Toronto, Canada, on 18 June 1964. Her real first name is Lynda but she simplified the spelling. Her major break came as punk single mum Mary Smith in Albert Square. Circumstances forced Mary to become a stripper and then go on the game at Nick Cotton's insistence. Most actors have fond memories of their big opportunity. Not Linda.

During the first few days on set Linda fell for Nejdet Salih who played Turkish café owner Ali Osman. She claimed that his picture on an *EastEnders* poster sent her weak at the knees. Whatever attraction Mr Salih had for Linda remained a mystery for most of the rest of the population who regarded him as possibly one of the worst actors ever to disgrace the screen. His delivery of lines made the shop dummies in *Are You Being Served?* seem animated.

One day while rehearsing a scene in the Albert Square laundrette Salih punched Linda in the face. It was a typical episode. Violence would erupt and no one on the set went to Linda's defence. She began to suffer the typical battered woman syndrome – believing she deserved to be hit. The first time was when the couple were out with friends and Linda wanted to go home to learn her lines. Without warning, in the taxi he punched her. '[The violence] carried on every few months and I kept it a secret because I blamed myself. I was such a mess I thought I deserved it. I never had a black eye. Nej was far too clever for that. I don't believe anyone knew he was hitting me until the day he lost his cool with me on the set.'

A month later, the couple went on holiday to Rome and the constant bickering got to Linda. After a comment about her mother she slapped her boyfriend in the mouth. He retaliated by putting her in hospital with a cracked rib. When he visited her, Linda gathered the strength to tell the thug that it was over.

In April 1989 Linda began dating *EastEnders* floor manager Robin Greene, brother of TV presenter Sarah and weathergirl Laura. The pressures on the set became too much for Linda and she tearfully split from Robin.

In August 1994 Linda declared, 'I don't care what people think of me any more. I've got the confidence to do what I please. And I still hope one day after all this, I'll learn to love again.'

The Pop Star & the Actress

Both are vertically challenged. He was best known for his bum
fluff goatee and ridiculous outfits which included a baseball
cap worn back to front and oversize shorts. The words 'looking like a complete prat' did not do him justice. She was
notorious for her wild lifestyle. They seemed perfectly suited.
It saved two other people from having to go out with either
of them.

He was the appalling Brian Harvey, a former plumber's
mate and now one of the singers in teen band East 17, so called
because the group hails from Walthamstow, London, E17.
She was the dreadful Danniella Westbrook, Sam from
EastEnders. For two years this delightful duo dated and even
got engaged. Their relationship was punctuated with drug use
and violence.

In an interview when she supposedly came clean about her
drug abuse Westbrook claimed she had first used cocaine on
New Year's Eve 1992 in a London club. 'I was terrified. I felt
pressured into doing it,' she snivelled. (In a later interview she
admitted she had been doing the drug since she was 15.) Three
months later she took another line and another a few more
months after that. Soon rarely a weekend went by without her
taking the drug. She would spend around £150 a weekend on
three grammes of cocaine but as her tolerance grew so did her
need for more and more charlie.

At 2 p.m. on 6 October 1994, Westbrook tried to commit suicide by overdosing on sleeping pills and paracetamols. She
wrote a farewell note to her parents and Harvey. The pop star
came home from tour a day early and found her, rushing
her to Whipps Cross Hospital in East London. Westbrook
ignored doctors' advice to seek psychiatric help and dis-
charged herself.

An argument in January 1995 resulted in Westbrook climb-
ing on to the roof of the home she shared with Harvey in

Buckhurst Hill, Essex, clad only in her silk pyjamas. Harvey had had enough and was leaving in a taxi when he spotted her half-in and half-out of a skylight window. 'What the fuck is she doing now?' he asked the cabbie rhetorically. He then spent fifteen minutes coaxing the temperamental actress inside.

In January 1995 she left the pantomime *Babes in the Wood* where she had been playing Maid Marion after telling the producers she was too sick to work. This was despite the fact that she had been seen raving it up in Browns nightclub on New Year's Eve. 'I was relaxing. I wasn't going mental or anything,' she claims. Westbrook claims to have been hurt in a scuffle with photographers. She also says that she received weird telephone calls from someone whose voice she recognized but couldn't place. 'I hadn't wanted to tell anyone because I didn't want to worry them. I didn't tell the police because I didn't want the fuss.' One of the side-effects of cocaine is paranoia. At the same time her mother persuaded her to go to the doctor's where she was diagnosed as depressed and given tranquillizers.

Later the same month the couple announced that they would be prepared to sell their wedding pictures exclusively to the highest bidder. They would also move the day to accommodate whoever was paying. Said their lawyer, Paul Rodwell, 'They're very flexible. Of course they're in love and all that crap but they want to make the most out of it.' Rodwell added that Westbrook was looking for someone to pay for her wedding dress as well. The happy couple were looking for £150,000 or thereabouts for the ceremony which was due to take place in April or May when Westbrook was scheduled to return to her £40,000-a-year job in Albert Square. Amazingly, there were no takers.

The following month she came clean about her rampant drug use, admitting having wasted £100,000 on cocaine in the previous two years. 'Cocaine ruined my life,' she wailed.

In February 1995 Westbrook fell down the stairs and broke her wrist. Harvey took her to the Princess Alexandra Hospital in Harlow, Essex, where he insisted Danniella was seen quickly and in private to avoid hassle from autograph hunters. Among the angry patients left outside was a sick Down's Syndrome baby. The hospital accommodated Harvey's request. Perhaps they didn't realize that Westbrook would be unable to sign autographs with a broken wrist.

The happy couple split in April 1995. Harvey described Westbrook as a 'nightmare woman' in October of that year. 'She fleeced me to feed her drug habit – she's just a nasty liar and a money grabber. She's barking mad, off her trolley and I can't understand why I stayed with her for so long.' A year later Harvey was still narked by his ex-fiancée. In an interview in November 1996 he did not mince his words: 'I hate Danniella. She was saying I had got her into [using] cocaine and she knew damn well that she was using it before I met her. I tried to help her stop but it got completely turned round and I was made out to be the bad one, and I wasn't. She's just a fucking idiot.'

What does the lady think of her ex-partner? 'He's got beautiful eyes, a nice smile and not a bad little butt. He's like a cute Oompa-Loompa. You sort of wanted to keep him in your pocket. He's got a lovely voice and he was generous and kind, a nice bloke. He just had a bad temper. I'd say the worst thing about him was talking like a homeboy, which was really fucking annoying and embarrassing at the time. I'd pick up words and be using them every now and then, like, "Yeah man, yeah man" and "sweet" and all that rubbish.'

In November 1993 Harvey was arrested at 5.30 a.m. for possession of cannabis while on the way home from a party. After the split with Westbrook he began to date East 17 backing singer Natasha 'Tash' Carnegie and in April 1996 he married her.

Westbrook went out with professional footballer Ian Walker for a while. She also dated another footballer, Jamie Moralee. '[He] was really good in bed. Everything he done was good. Brian wasn't that bad, but Jamie was the guvnor. He was a giver not a receiver, most blokes are receivers not givers. He also had a big dick.

'I like a bit of rough, builders, roofers, footballers, blokes who are always getting banged up. I stood a surety for one of my boyfriends when he got nicked for drugs. Then we split up and I handed in the bail notice and he got nicked. It's the rugged character I like.'

Westbrook also revealed she had had sex with Harvey in some very strange places. 'We had to do it in more than one place because Brian never lasted very long.'

In September 1995 she began dating car dealer Robert Fernandez. It was another tempestuous relationship. Fernandez told of an incident where she punched him on the nose as he was driving. 'Sometimes I had to restrain her when she came at me. I've had to grab her arms so she can't hit me. Once when I pinned her down she spat in my face.' That didn't stop him getting involved. 'Sex with Danniella was always amazing. She'd do anything in bed. She's good at everything and she'll do anything you want to do. She really loves sex and talks very dirty when you're on the job. She liked me to talk dirty back. When there was no one else there she used to scream out loud.' Fernandez recalled a time when Westbrook tried to have sex while he was driving but he wouldn't let her so she settled for giving him a blowjob instead.

In January 1996 Westbrook's name was linked to Jake Stevens who worked in the City. Other boyfriends were said to be roofer Mark Biggs and male model Mark Baron. The following month it was revealed that dopey Danniella was having an affair with a drugs baron who used his weekend passes to bed the actress. Keith Brooks, 30, told a newspaper, 'I've been seeing her for quite a while now – it's sexual. I've told her I can't have a relationship because I've got a missus and a kid.'

That same month Westbrook found herself pregnant and newspapers took great delight in publishing a list of possible candidates for fatherhood. Was it the footballer or the car dealer? Westbrook even went to the extent of posing naked and very pregnant in a magazine à la Demi Moore. Baby Kai – named after the spiritual healer (yes, really) who attended Westbrook and her mother – was born in Whipps Cross Hospital on 23 November 1996. Two months later Westbrook put an end to the controversy by naming the father as Fernandez.

Murder of a Taxi Driver

When *EastEnders* began, little could the BBC know just how many of the cast had criminal records. One of the more serious belonged to Leslie Grantham who played the evil Dennis Watts, a man who thought nothing of cheating on his wife, working for the local mob, making his daughter's best friend pregnant and getting up to all sorts of other villainy.

The story of Leslie Grantham broke three days after the soap went on the air. Born at 12 Flodden Road, Camberwell, London SE5 on 30 April 1947, Grantham left school aged 15 with a distinct lack of qualifications. Like many in a similar situation, he joined the army. On 3 December 1966, while serving in Albertstrasse, Osnabruck, West Germany, 6´ 1˝ Lance Corporal Grantham of the Royal Fusiliers robbed and shot dead, with a .22 Walther, 5´ 5˝ taxi driver Felix Reese. Nine days later Grantham was arrested. On 17 April 1967, the fifth day of his trial, Grantham was found guilty, dismissed from the service and sentenced to life imprisonment. He served the first four years of his sentence in Wormwood Scrubs. While inside he took an interest in drama and with the help of actress Louise Jameson auditioned for the Webber Douglas Academy on his release in 1978. It was there he met Julia Smith who cast him as Dirty Den and Australian-born Jane Laurie whom he would marry on 29 December 1981. (Jane has a little secret of her own. Grantham is actually her second husband.)

In between acting parts Grantham did menial jobs such as painting the VD clinic at St Thomas's Hospital, working in a pub and selling suits. *EastEnders* made him a star and exposed another skeleton in his closet. Grantham had been estranged from his family for some time. On 7 October 1986 his gay younger brother, Philip, died of AIDS aged 35. Neither Grantham nor his wife attended the funeral. Unlike most of the people who have left Albert Square, Grantham has had a measure of success in breaking away from his character. However, there are some who believe Leslie Grantham should not be earning a comfortable living as an actor but should still be behind bars.

STUPIDITY IN BABYLON

Living in Babylon is no guarantee of brains or exemption from foolish behaviour, as this section amply demonstrates . . .

Unlucky Number

Phillip Schofield made a name for himself as the highly popular presenter of children's TV for the BBC. Hoping to transfer to the world of adult entertainment, he looked for shows to host. One show he did present (with Emma Forbes, for independent London station Carlton Television) was called *Talking Telephone Numbers*. The idea was that viewers rang in to compete for a £10,000 jackpot if the last five digits of their telephone number matched five numbers chosen at random on the show. On 18 January 1995 three callers rang in and answered the questions wrongly. Schofield spoke to a fourth and asked, 'How many winks in a nap? How many legs does a spider have? And how many children in the Von Trapp family?' The contestant answered, 'Forty winks, six legs and seven children.' Schofield yelled excitedly down the phone, 'Fantastic! You've won £10,000!' The show's adjudicators then pointed out that the contestant had got the second answer wrong. Realizing his gaffe, Schofield put the phone down on the unfortunate player. Said a spokesman for the TV station, 'There were literally seconds to go before the show was due to end and Phillip was just trying to fit everything in. It's live and these things happen.' Small consolation for the ordinary player that the highly paid TV star can't listen properly.

Gun Law

Police were not impressed when actor Rik Mayall threatened a couple in a London street with a fake gun. They promptly arrested him.

Ken Tynan & That Word

Kenneth Tynan was one of the finest drama critics of the twentieth century as well as being responsible for *Oh! Calcutta!* and a host of other fine writing. A close friend of Laurence Olivier, on 13 November 1965 Tynan, then literary manager of the National Theatre, was booked to appear on the live satirical television show *BBC3*. The host of the programme was the erudite Robert Robinson who asked Tynan if he would allow sexual intercourse to be portrayed on stage. Tynan did not hesitate. 'Oh I think so, certainly. I think there are very many rational people in this world to whom the word "fuck" is particularly diabolical or revolting or totally forbidden. I think that anything that can be printed or said can also be seen.' The BBC was inundated with complaints. Producer Ned Sherrin and Huw Weldon, in charge of programming, both defended Tynan but Robinson said, 'I think he was up the pole to use that word.' *Daily Express* political correspondent William Barkley described Tynan's speech as 'the bloodiest outrage I have ever known'. Mary Whitehouse said Tynan needed his bottom smacked and that there must be no more filth on TV. She also announced she was writing to the Queen in protest. In the House of Commons four motions were put down by 133 Labour and Tory backbenchers condemning Tynan. The first of the motions called upon the Home Secretary to refer Tynan to the Director of Public Prosecutions on the grounds that Tynan had used obscene language in public. Others called for the sacking of the BBC's Director-General Sir Hugh Greene, the setting up of a body to protect the public from 'filth' and for Tynan to be sacked from his job at the NT. Then Prime Minister Harold Wilson promised not to use four-letter words in any of *his* speeches. Oddly, Tynan received just 38 letters on the subject, many supporting him.

Bill Grundy & the Sex Pistols

Bill Grundy was born on 18 May 1923 and by 1976 was working on Thames Television's teatime magazine show *Today*. On 1 December he had a rather fine lunch courtesy of *Punch* magazine and when he returned to Thames's Middlesex studio Grundy was feeling no pain.

That evening he was due to interview an up-and-coming band called the Sex Pistols. They had brought along a rather frightening-looking entourage which included a girl called Siouxsie Sioux, later to become a punk pop icon herself as leader of Siouxsie and the Banshees. The band were known for their torn clothes, outlandish hairstyles and the violence at their concerts which culminated in a girl being glassed and blinded by future Pistol and all-round loser Sid Vicious.

Grundy clearly was not impressed by the motley crew assembled before him and made his contempt known. He goaded Pistol Glen Matlock into saying 'fuck' and when one of the female entourage said she'd always wanted to meet

Grundy, he said they could meet afterwards. This resulted in Grundy being labelled 'a dirty old bastard' by a Pistol.

With the floor manager desperately signalling for the anchorman to wind up the 'interview', Grundy attempted one last folly. He informed a Pistol, 'You've got five seconds to say something outrageous.' The youth obliged and Grundy, amid catcalling, ended the show and, virtually, his career. Thames's switchboard was flooded with complaints from viewers claiming Grundy was drunk and that the group should be banned.

The viewers got their wish. The Sex Pistols were dropped by their record label EMI and Grundy was suspended for a fortnight. Some months later, the *Today* show was canned for good.

Grundy went on to become a columnist for the *Sunday Express* but never really got over being the man who encouraged the Sex Pistols to swear on live television. When he died on 9 February 1993 his obituaries focused mainly on his teatime folly.

VANITY IN BABYLON

Age

If there is one thing guaranteed to get the good citizens of TV Babylon up in arms it is asking how old they are. It seems they would rather tell you the age they lost their virginity or details of their father's criminal record than reveal the year they were born. The Scott Inquiry probably garnered more truthful information than the innocent scribe asking a celebrity's age.

If you believe the press handouts all male celebrities are six feet tall, handsome, have full heads of hair and are of indeterminate age. Most female celebrities have yet to reach the big four-o. This is simply not good enough. We want to know how old our favourite stars are. Thanks to the voluminous books on display at St Catherine's House we can clear up many a mystery regarding just how old celebrities really are.

✗ To many viewers Noele Gordon was *Crossroads*. Meg Mortimer or Richardson epitomized the motel that was either loved or laughed at. When newspapers reported Noele's death from stomach cancer on 14 April 1985 they gave her age as 61. Noele Gordon was actually born on Christmas Day 1919, making her 65 when she finally went to the great motel in the sky.

✗ The stars of *Coronation Street* have been known to be less than honest when it comes to their real ages. For years Doris Speed, formidable landlady Annie Walker, refused to reveal when she was born. A year of 1914 was suggested and accepted. Imagine the shock when it was revealed that she was actually born on 3 February 1899 and was already a pensioner when the series began in 1960. In all interviews Pat Phoenix (Elsie Tanner) claimed to have been born in Portumna, Galway in 1924. In *All My Burning Bridges*, her first volume of autobiography, she revealed she had really been born in St Mary's Hospital, Manchester on 26 November 1923 'but if you were to ask me I would *still* say I was Irish and born in Portumna'. Thelma Barlow (Mavis Riley Wilton) first appeared in the *Street* as Emily Bishop's friend in 1971. Most books list her birthday as 19 June 1937. In fact she was born in 1929. Barbara Knox (Rita Sullivan) is one of the *Street*'s most private stars, rarely if ever giving interviews. If she has the choice she opts not to go into *Who's Who on TV*. Most journalists have estimated her year of birth as 1938. In fact she was born five years earlier, on 30 September 1933. Violet Carson (Ena Sharples) gave her year of birth as 1905 in most directories. In fact she was born on 1 September 1898.

The Collins sisters have been in Babylon for many, many years. We have watched Joan in episodes of *Starsky and Hutch* and in numerous old films as well as in the rôle of the evil Alexis on *Dynasty*. For many years her age was a mystery. In the 1988 edition of *Who's Who on TV* she claimed to have been born in 1936 yet when she married fourth husband Peter Holm in November 1985 her year of birth mysteriously changed to 1938. A slip or two of the pen surely because Joan Henrietta Collins was born in Bayswater at 7 a.m. on 23 May 1933. Sister Jackie has had us all enthralled with her sexy sagas made into films and mini-series. Jackie really is forgetful about when she was born. In *Hollywood Sisters,* their dual biography of the Collinses, authors Susan Crimp and Patricia Burstein quote Jackie as saying, 'I'm eight years younger than whatever age Joan is telling the magazines she is that week.' This would give Jackie a birthdate of 1941. Shurely shome mishtake? In his autobiography their father tells us when Joan was born but carelessly omits Jackie's birthday. However, he does reveal that she was evacuated when World War II broke out. Evacuating a daughter two years before she was born seem cautious in the extreme. Jackie was being economical with the truth. She is, in fact, four, not eight years younger than her big sister and was born on 4 October 1937.

X Another celebrity who has done nothing to correct scribes when they get her age wrong is Nanette Newman. Each year on 29 May the birthday columns lay claim to the 'fact' that Nanette was born in 1939. No, no, Nanette. Mrs Bryan Forbes, that scourge of grease on plates and stirring advocate of a particular brand of washing-up liquid, was born in Northampton in 1934.

X Comedienne Janet Brown was born in Rutherglen, Glasgow. She has been careful never to reveal how old she is or when her birthday is. Her star sign is Sagittarius which probably places her birthday in December. Guesses as to the year range from 1922 to 1927. A letter to her asking for her birthday was met with a very polite refusal. 'You won't find any dates [in my autobiography] because I don't give any but I certainly don't mind you asking.' If anyone does have proof of Janet Brown's age, I'd love to know.

X Jaclyn Smith was one of the original *Charlie's Angels* and the only one to stay with the show from beginning to end. She has always given her birthday as 26 October 1947 except in the very first press releases for the show when a flack slipped up and revealed her real year of birth as 1945.

X Marina Sirtis was born in London and appeared topless in the Michael Winner remake of the Margaret Lockwood classic *The Wicked Lady* before moving to Hollywood to seek fame and fortune. That came in the shape of *Star Trek: The Next Generation* where she plays Counselor Deanna Troi. Most references say Marina was born on 29 March 1960 although one book is exceptionally generous, giving the year of birth as 1964. A quick check at St Catherine's House proves Marina was born in 1955.

X Helen Mirren won accolades for her portrayal of the tough Jane Tennison in the five *Prime Suspect* mini-series. If you look in most reference books you will see Helen was born in Southend in 1946. Actually, she wasn't. According to her birth certificate Helen was born in Hammersmith on 26 July 1945, the day Clement Attlee became the first post-war Labour Prime Minister – a fact that no doubt pleases socialist Helen immensely.

X Sarah Greene is quite open in letting everyone know her birthday is 24 October. She is surprisingly cagey about the year, which is 1958. Perhaps she imagines children will think of her as Great-Aunt Sarah rather than Auntie Sarah if they know how old she really is.

X Paula Hamilton was the divorced woman in the famous Volkswagen advert. In December 1991 Paula appeared in court on a drink-driving charge and gave her age as 33. When she published her autobiography, *Instructions Not Included*, in 1995 she claimed to be 34. Paula was born on 23 January 1958.

X American actress Kirstie Alley starred in *Cheers* and, according to her press biographies, was born in Wichita, Kansas on 12 January 1955. Actually she was born four years earlier, in 1951.

✗ Penelope Keith also keeps her year of birth quiet. She was born as Penelope Hatfield on 2 April 1940.

✗ Sally Farmiloe played the bitch Dawn in the sailing soap *Howard's Way*. She tells interviewers including, on one occasion, the author of this book that she was born in 1954. Her mum tells the truth. Sal was born in 1948.

Cheers says Scientologist Kirstie Alley

✗ *Dallas*'s Victoria Principal was born in Fukuoka, Japan. Of that there is no dispute. She claims the date was 3 January 1950. She also claims to have been the first American baby born in Japan *after* World War II. Others claim the real year is 1945. The war with Japan did not end until August 1945 so is it likely an American baby would have been born on Japanese soil seven months before the end of hostilities? The more plausible date is 3 January 1946.

It's not just women who are not always 100 per cent accurate when it comes to their ages. Men can be just as bad.

✗ Old Jimmy Young, as Terry Wogan calls him, seems to have been in Babylon for ever. Between 1953 and 1964 he had a dozen hit pop records including two number ones – *Unchained Melody* and *The Man from Laramie*. According to most sources Jimmy was born in September 1923 or possibly 1927. Jimmy's autobiography is no more helpful, casually omitting the year. Leslie Ronald Young (his real name) first saw the light of day on 21 September 1921 which makes him a sprightly 75.

X Another DJ who conveniently forgets old how he is is Mike Read. Mancunian-born Mike makes no secret of the day – 1 March – but the year? He'll have you believe the all-important year is 1951 or possibly 1952. In fact Mike, one of the original authors of *The Guinness Book of British Hit Singles*, made his (astrological) chart début in 1947 which makes him five years older than the pop charts he used to write about.

X For many years Larry Grayson gave his birthday in *Who's Who on TV* as 31 August 1930. Generous to say the truth. He was born illegitimate as William White in 1923.

X Comedians Frankie Howerd and Benny Hill were also less than truthful in their lifetimes about their ages. Benny Hill knocked just a year off, claiming Alfred Hawthorne Hill was born in Southampton on 21 January 1925 instead of the real 1924. When quizzed he replied, 'Maybe I decided to be a year younger and maybe I didn't.' Frankie Howerd was more blatant and took five years off his 6 March 1917 birthdate. Norman Wisdom, yet another comic, also fibbed about his age for years. His birthday was reported as 4 February 1920 or even 1925 in reference books. It was only when he published the first volume of his autobiography, *Don't Laugh at Me*, that he came clean. The real date was 4 February 1915.

X Nicholas Parsons has been a straight man to many comedians – Arthur Haynes and Benny Hill to name but two. He was born in Grantham, Lincolnshire in the 1920s (as was Margaret Thatcher) and boy, was he upset when journalist Peter Tory asked him how old he was. 'I have not worked it out. A person is as old as he bloody feels. Anything between forty and sixty.' Look in *Who's Who on TV* and you will see Parsons was born on 10 October. The year is wrong. Old Nick was born not in 1928 but five years earlier in 1923.

X Handsome Nigel Havers took the opposite route.
Directories give his birthday as 6 November 1949 yet he
was actually born in 1951.

X Lionel Blair was born in Canada which makes it difficult
to check his real age. In the 1970 edition of *Who's Who on
TV* he gives his year of birth as 1931. By the 1982 edition
he claimed to have been born on 12 December 1932.
Three years later he was claiming 12 December 1934. In
his autobiography, *Stagestruck,* he again claims 12
December 1932 and says his sister Joyce was born on 4
November 1934. Yet on Tommy Boyd's show on LBC
Joyce said she was born on 4 November 1932. Stranger
and stranger.

X Reg Varney celebrates his birthday on 11 July, say all the
reference books. They plump for 1922 as the birth
year. In his autobiography, *The Little Clown*, Reg comes
clean. He was born in 1916.

X You would have thought the last person to be vain about
his age would be Les Dawson. Yet for years Les claimed
to have been born in 1933 and occasionally 1934. His first
wife, Meg, let the cat out of the bag and finally Les
confirmed he was actually born on 2 February 1931,
making him 62 when he died, not 59.

X 'Can I have a Y please, Bob.' 'What Y is the year that quiz-
master Bob Holness was born?' Well, okay, perhaps you'll
never hear that on *Blockbusters* but the answer is 1927.

X In the 1988 edition of *Who's Who on TV* Chris Quentin
gives his birthday as 12 July 1959. Naughty, naughty,
you were born two years earlier than that, in 1957.

X He's been around the world numerous times and must
have run out of quite a few passports. Perhaps that is

where the confusion arises as to Alan Whicker's real age. He wasn't born on 2 August 1925 but four years earlier, in Cairo.

X GMTV weather forecaster Simon Biagi celebrated his 31st birthday on the show on 18 September 1994. This came as a bit of a surprise to his ex-wife who knew he should have been celebrating his 33rd.

. . . & Beauty in Babylon

In Babylon perfection is a virtual necessity for success. Celebrities live glamorous lives and this is reflected in their appearance – or so the denizens of Babylon would have us believe. Image is everything. Age, wrinkles, grey hair, no hair and paunches are the natural enemies of the glamorous celeb. How many bald men not called Clive can you regularly recall seeing on television? The inhabitants of Babylon go to all sorts of lengths to maintain the image and here we look at a few.

Plastic surgery is a popular and increasingly inexpensive way to right nature's wrongs. Since her days as a hat-check girl in the Cavern, Cilla Black has had a nose job.

Next time you're at the check-out and you hear the beep – think of the fun you could be having . . . reading *TV Babylon*

Camp TV host Dale Winton had a rhinoplasty – to give it its posh name – in March 1977. Dale went to the same plastic surgeon as Cilla.

✂ Former *Coronation Street* actress Lynne Perrie had a face-lift in 1984 and had her lips enlarged in 1994.

✂ Beautiful actress Elizabeth Hurley has had her lips cosmetically enlarged.

✂ Host Nicholas Parsons has had at least one face-lift.

✂ *Golden Girl* Bea Arthur has had two face-lifts. Betty White had the puffiness removed from her eyes.

✂ Richard Chamberlain has had surgery on his eyes.

✂ Michael Douglas has had his chin lifted.

✂ Former *Charlie's Angel* Cheryl Ladd has had her teeth fixed, a nose job and surgery around her eyes.

✂ Michael Landon of *Little House on the Prairie* and *Highway to Heaven* and his wife Cindy had face-lifts on the same day.

✂ *Knots Landing* star Michele Lee has had a nose job.

✂ TV's *Saint* Roger Moore has had a face-lift and eye tucks.

✂ *Hart to Hart's* Stefanie Powers has had a nose job.

✂ *Dallas's* Victoria Principal is married to the eminent Beverly Hills plastic surgeon Dr Harry Glassman, yet she denies having any surgery.

Breasts seem to be an obsession all over the world and not just in Babylon. At least two members of the cast of *Beverly Hills 90210* – Tori Spelling and Shannen Doherty – have enlarged their breasts. Other women who have had surgery include:

✄ *Baywatch* babes Pamela Anderson (twice) and 5′ 10″ Gena Lee Nolin who said, 'People just love big boobs. I got mine done before I was ever in the business. I got them done just for me, because I was obviously very small chested and I wanted to enhance myself.' She now measures 35C-22-34. Nicole Eggert had her breasts enlarged and then had the implants removed. Donna D'Errico seems to have a Dannii Minogue attitude to her breasts and became quite agitated when questioned on the subject during an interview with *loaded*.

Pamela Anderson avoiding radiators

✄ Gladiator Scorpio, 5′ 9″, who boosted her breasts from 34AA to 38C and her former colleague Sharron Davies who paid £3,000 in 1995 to put back what nature took away after breastfeeding her son, Elliott. *Dr Quinn, Medicine Woman* star Jane Seymour had her breasts enlarged in October 1990 for the same reason.

✄ Soap star Morgan Fairchild.

✂ Charlie's former angels Farrah Fawcett and Tanya Roberts.

✂ Former child star Dana Plato of *Diff'rent Strokes*.

✂ Ex-groupie Paula Yates in June 1995 at a reputed cost of £2,000. Her size went from 34B to 34C.

✂ Emma Noble, 5′ 10″ hostess on *Bruce's Price is Right*, had her breasts enlarged at a hospital in Bromsgrove, Worcestershire, from 34B to 34C on 11 June 1995 at a cost of £4,000 and then dumped her boyfriend of eighteen months.

Hair is often a problem in Babylon and many male celebrities and the occasional female one (Joan Collins springs immediately to mind) take to wearing wigs to hide their crowning glory or lack thereof. Frankie Howerd would never be seen in public without his wig. When Wogan was solely on Radio 2 he regularly referred to his thinning thatch. When he started his thrice-weekly chat show he stopped mentioning his hair. Many columnists referred to Wogan wearing an Irish.

✂ When he played Detective Bobby Crocker on *Kojak*, Kevin Dobson had a sparse patch of hair yet when he played good guy Mack McKenzie on *Knots Landing* he sported a full head of curly hair, thanks to a new wig.

✂ After his stint as Captain Kirk in *Star Trek* William Shatner began losing his hair, but when he reappeared as T. J. Hooker in the programme of the same name his bonce was bountifully covered.

✂ Larry Hagman wore a wig throughout the entire run of *Dallas*. Pop superstar Michael Jackson is rarely seen in public without a wig these days.

Even having hair isn't always enough. Comedian Leslie Crowther dyed his hair when it first showed signs of going grey. His secret only came to light when on holiday other tourists noticed his chest hair was snowy white. Leslie admitted that he had tried dyeing his chest hair to complete the effect but was left with a matted mess.

Phillip Schofield dyed his hair for many years and then, in the mid-90s, decided to let the natural grey show through. He obviously did not like what he saw because he immediately started dyeing it again.

Not all the inhabitants of Babylon are vain and narcissistic. Jane Seymour said, 'I ordered long legs but they never came. And both eyes are peculiar. One's brown and one's green. My smile's crooked and I have a ski-jump nose. I certainly would not win any prizes in a beauty contest.'

Dynasty star Heather Locklear complained, 'When I look in the mirror I see the girl I was when growing up: braces, crooked teeth, a baby face and skinny body. My legs are still too thin. And I'm knock-kneed – my knees can look at each other and have a conversation. I have to walk on the edges of my feet so my knees can be a little straighter.'

Judging by the number of exercise videos on the market, that seems a good way for celebrities to keep young and beautiful. Two who are fitness fanatics are *Coronation Street*'s Beverley Callard (Liz McDonald) and *Birds of a Feather*'s Lesley Joseph. Beverley smokes 20 cigarettes a day and says that people in the gym are amazed when she lights up after a strenuous work-out. 'I even smoked in hospital after my hysterectomy,' she reveals. Lesley became an exercise junkie after she put on weight as a teenager.

EPILOGUE

Guess Who? Don't Sue . . .

In the course of the research for this book I have come across numerous stories that are just too juicy to tell but also too enticing to leave out. I have decided to finish this book with some of those stories. The names have been omitted to protect the guilty. Can you guess who they are?

On television this actor plays a doctor but he recently called a prostitute to a hotel where he registered under his character's name. When the call girl arrived the actor was dressed in whites complete with a stethoscope around his neck. He ordered her to strip off before he examined her. His diagnosis? She needed a good seeing to! After sex they shared some drugs of the kind you normally can't get over the counter in Boots.

This hell-raising former soap actress often worked in cahoots with photographers, letting them know where she would be and in what state – usually off her face on drink and drugs. She then split any money – fifty-fifty – that the snapper happened to make.

She is a celebrity who is famous for being famous. He is an unusual looking rocker. At a party she slid seductively on to his lap expecting to be carried to his boudoir. He stood up and she fell to the floor. 'She's too old,' he complained, 'and she smells of Bisto.'

Mr Heart-throb looks the picture of health. Not quite – he's addicted to speed and prescription drugs. His young wife is trying to help him by taking as many drugs as he does. Not only that but he is a sex addict and he and his wife spend their time in nightclubs and gay bars looking for group sex.

This supermodel is lusted after by millions of men all over the world. Little do they know, despite her failed marriage, she is a total dyke who hits on almost every female in sight.

This comedian claims he is in favour of family values. He only appears in 'nice' shows and is always bragging about how happily married he is. However, during a recent trip to New York he hired a call girl and explored his S&M fantasies complete with chains, ropes and black rubber sheets.

Little Miss Beauty has surely got it made – she's sexy, her career is going great guns and she's got a hunky other half. Only, she doesn't believe she's good enough for him – too fat, or so she thinks. So, after every meal, it's off to stick her fingers down her throat.

He's a television heart-throb who is forever squiring a gorgeous blonde around town. However, she is only at his side to prevent the truth about his sexuality becoming public knowledge. Lately he has become careless and has been seen regularly at gay bars. His numerous female fans would be heartbroken to know that he has tied the knot – with another man! Not only that but his 'girlfriend' was his bridesmaid!

Blonde and beautiful, she has appeared in hit television shows in the 60s, 70s and 80s. She has married once but has spent the last twenty-five years living with her female secretary in a cosy arrangement that hasn't stopped her 'dating' gay actors.

This diminutive television star has since moved on to greater stardom in films. However, his career almost ended before it had started because of his rampant homosexuality. It was said it was amazing he ever got off his knees long enough to make a film. Eventually his studio forced him to marry but the old flames are still there.

Missy Sex Symbol was the envy of girls throughout the world who copied her fashionable image and she was lusted after by boys. Missy Sports Star was a beautiful practitioner of her sport. The two ladies had a brief but passionate fling in the 70s. Missy Sex Symbol divorced her hunky husband and lives in unmarried bliss with an ex-soap star although Missy Sport has made it up the aisle a couple of times.

This television comic met his girlfriend at the strip club where she works. She also hooks on the side. Mr Comic got her a cushy job but, unbeknownst to him, she still works as a prostitute. She tells friends she does it for the money and because his bedroom performance makes her laugh louder than his routines.

Mr Hunk has millions of women swooning but he's not the type to settle for Miss Homely. His preference is hookers and he's notorious for cruising red-light areas checking out the toms. He was recently seen in a well-known hooking area with a barefoot streetwalker sticking her head through his car window and we don't think it was because he had lost his *A–Z*!

He is well known for being a party animal and squiring numerous beautiful women around town. He has married two sex symbol wives but once he's got 'em, he beats 'em up. Why do they stay? Because he gets them high on drink or drugs (his personal favourite is heroin) and then takes sexually explicit videos of them starring himself or other women. If they threaten to leave he blackmails them into staying with his video nasties.

At one time this man was so sexually active that many thought he was a sex addict. Then he met the girl of his dreams and settled down – or so she thinks. Little does she know that he has a harem of three women in three separate hotels and visits them all in the afternoon before returning home to play happy families.

They are one of showbiz's most high profile couples but she went ballistic when she found out he had slept with a waitress. She went back to one of her old boyfriends and jogged horizontally with him. Then she went back to hubby and told him all about it – in great detail.

Mr Tough Guy is a womanizer of the first order. However, his girlfriends are treated to a bizarre show. Once in his bedroom he jumps around naked demonstrating what he believes is his machismo. The girls have difficulty trying not to laugh at his antics.

 If you know any true stories of TV stars then please write to me c/o the publishers with all the juicy details. Alternatively, you can e-mail me – paul@uk.com

DID I REALLY SAY THAT?

We all say silly things sometimes, usually after imbibing too frequently and too deeply, but many celebrities seem to make a habit of engaging mouth before brain is in gear. Here is a selection – some ill-advised, some hopelessly optimistic and some just plain dumb.

? 'Our marriage is now stronger than ever. The bottom line is that, if you can get through something like this, you can get through most things. We're much more aware of each other's needs now. We know we're together because we want to be together.'

>ULRIKA JONSSON on her reconciliation with her husband after she'd had an affair, February 1995. She split from her husband eight months later.

? 'TV-am is bloody rubbish, shabby, unprofessional and garbage. I can't work there any more.'

>MICHAEL PARKINSON, 20 April 1983 (morning)

? 'I am glad to be staying on. I was very happy with what Timothy Aitken had to say and I would like to be part of that progress.'

>MICHAEL PARKINSON, 20 April 1983 (afternoon)

? 'It was our own affirmation of our love and how we will never leave each other – ever.'

> PAMELA ANDERSON on her marriage to Tommy Lee, February 1995. They left each other, for a time, in November 1996.

? 'I would rather die than watch an episode of *Dynasty*.'

> JOAN COLLINS, May 1984

? 'I wouldn't act again. Not for anything. I don't want to be looked upon as a pretty, brainless idiot any more.'

> VICTORIA PRINCIPAL, 1976, two years before she took on the rôle of pretty, brainless idiot Pamela Barnes Ewing in *Dallas*.

? 'I've got ten pairs of training shoes, one for every day of the week.'

> SAMANTHA FOX

? 'In some ways I'm a lot like Vince. I like to flirt with women. Like Vince I value my freedom.'

> Actor PAUL NICHOLAS playing Vince Pinner in the successful BBC sitcom *Just Good Friends*, 1984.

? 'I know I've said that in some ways I'm a lot like Vince, but the truth is I can't think of one similarity.'

> Actor PAUL NICHOLAS playing Vince Pinner in the successful BBC sitcom *Just Good Friends*, 1985.

? 'Pam's just a cupcake in frosting.'

> GENA LEE NOLIN's considered opinion of
> *Baywatch* castmate Pamela Anderson, May 1996.

? 'I honestly prefer chocolate to sex.'

> DALE WINTON, June 1995

ACKNOWLEDGEMENTS

This book was not written without the help of many people. However, because of the very nature of the book I am unable to acknowledge here most of my sources for the information – writers, publicists, make-up artists and often the celebrities themselves. You know who you are. However, I will say a tremendous thank you to the staffs of the following newspapers and magazines, some of them sadly no longer extant, who provided me with leads, stories and endless entertainment: the *Advocate, Arena, Celebrity Sleuth, Daily Express, Daily Mail, Daily Mirror, Daily Star, Daily Telegraph, FHM, GQ, Hello!, Here!, Hollywood Star*, the *Independent*, the *Independent on Sunday, loaded, National Enquirer, New York Daily News, News of the World, Out, People, The People, Private Eye, Q, Revue, Scallywag, Spiked, Star*, the *Sun, Sunday Mirror*, the *Sunday Times, The Times, Today, US, Vanity Fair* plus all my 'confidential' sources . . .

The following books were also helpful: *All My Burning Bridges*, Pat Phoenix (London: Star Books 1976); *The Bare Facts Video Guide*, Craig Hosoda (Santa Clara: The Bare Facts 1995); *Beverly Hills 90210 Factfile*, Janet Macoska (London: Boxtree 1991); *Blind in One Ear*, Patrick Macnee and Marie Cameron (London: Headline 1989); *The Boxtree A–Z of TV Stars*, Anthony Hayward (London: Boxtree 1992); *Britain's Top 100 Eligible Bachelors*, Nesta Wyn Ellis (London: Blake 1994); *The Complete Book of Dallas*, Suzy Kalter (New York: Harry N. Abrams 1986); *The Complete Directory to Prime Time Network and Cable TV Shows 1946–present*, Tim Brooks and Earle Marsh (New York: Ballantine 1995); *Coronation Street*, Jack Tinker (London: Octopus Books 1985); *Coronation Street: Celebrating 30 Years*,

Graeme Kay (London: Boxtree 1990); *The Coronation Street Story*, Daran Little (London: Boxtree 1995); *Coronation Street: 25 Years*, Graham Nown (London: Ward Lock 1985); *Dallas*, Laura Van Wormer (London: Comet 1985); *Diana Confidential*, Chris Hutchins and Peter Thompson (London: Pocket Books 1994); *Doctor Who: The Completely Useless Encylopedia*, Chris Howarth and Steve Lyons (London: Virgin 1996) *Doctor Who: The Key to Time*, Peter Haining (London: W.H. Allen 1984); *Dod's Parliamentary Companion 1994* (London: D.P.C. 1994); *Donnelley's Dirt Dossier*, Paul Donnelley (Unpublished ms.); *Dynasty: The Authorized Biography of the Carringtons* (London: Comet 1984); *Early Reagan*, Anne Edwards (London: Hodder & Stoughton 1987); *Emmerdale Farm: The Official Companion*, James Ferguson (London: Weidenfeld & Nicolson 1988); *Exposed*, Gerry Brown (London: Virgin 1995); *Famous Mugs* (New York: Cader Books 1996); *The Full Monty*, Jim Davidson (London: Little, Brown 1993); *Fuzzy Monsters, Fear and Loathing at the BBC*, Chris Horrie and Steve Clarke (London: Heinemann 1994); *The Guinness Book of British Hit Singles*, Tim Rice, Paul Gambaccini and Jonathan Rice (Enfield: Guinness 1995); *The Guinness Book of Classic British TV*, Paul Cornell, Martin Day and Keith Topping (Enfield: Guinness 1993 and 1996); *The Guinness Book of Sitcoms*, Rod Taylor (Enfield: Guinness 1994); *The Guinness Television Encyclopedia*, Jeff Evans (Enfield: Guinness 1995); *The Guinness Who's Who of Soap Operas*, Anthony Hayward (Enfield: Guinness 1991); *Halliwell's Filmgoer's Companion* (10th edn), John Walker (London: HarperCollins 1993); *Halliwell's Television Companion*, Leslie Halliwell with Philip Purser (London: Granada 1982); *The Hollywood Death Book*, James Robert Parish (Las Vegas: Pioneer Books 1992); *Hollywood Kryptonite: The Bulldog, The Lady and The Death of Superman*, Sam Kashner and Nancy Schoenberger (New York: St Martin's Press 1996); *Hollywood Sisters*, Susan Crimp and Patricia Burstein (London: Robson Books 1989); *Honeytrap: The Secret Worlds of Stephen Ward*, Anthony Summers and Stephen Dorrill (London: Weidenfeld & Nicolson 1987); *Idol – Rock Hudson: The True Story of an*

American Film Hero, Jerry Oppenheimer and Jack Vitek (New York: Villard Books 1986); *'If You Don't Have Anything Nice to Say . . . Come Sit Next to Me'*, Coral Amende (New York: Macmillan 1994); *I'll Tell the Jokes, Arthur*, Arthur Edwards (London: Blake 1993); *In for a Penny: The Unauthorized Biography of Jeffrey Archer*, Jonathan Mantle (London: Hamish Hamilton 1988); *The International Murderers' Who's Who*, Robin Odell (London: Headline 1996); *Jay Robert Nash's Crime Chronology*, Jay Robert Nash (New York: Facts on File 1984); *Kelsey Grammer: The True Story*, Jeff Rovin with Kathleen Tracy and David Perrell (New York: HarperPaperbacks 1995); *Let's Get Through Wednesday*, Reginald Bosanquet with Wallace Reyburn (London: New English Library 1981); *The Life of Python*, George Perry (London: Pavilion 1994); *Love Is an Uphill Thing*, Jimmy Savile, OBE (London: Coronet 1976); *Mugshots*, George Seminara (New York: St Martin's Griffin 1996); *The New and Revised Guinness Who's Who of Soap Operas*, Anthony Hayward (Enfield: Guinness 1995); *Oh, Yus, It's Arthur Mullard*, Arthur Mullard (London: Everest Books 1977); *Patrick Duffy: The Man Behind Bobby Ewing*, Lee Riley (London: W.H. Allen 1987); *Phil Redmond's Brookside: The First Ten Years*, Geoff Tibballs (London: Boxtree 1992); *Phil Redmond's Brookside: Life in the Close*, Geoff Tibballs (London: Boxtree 1995); *Phil Redmond's Brookside: The Official Companion* (London: Weidenfeld Paperbacks 1987); *Philip Lynott the Rocker*, Mark Putterford (London: Castle Communications 1994); *The Q Encyclopedia of Rock Stars*, Dafydd Rees and Luke Crampton (London: Dorling Kindersley 1996); *Queen of the Street*, Sally Beck (London: Blake 1995); *Queer in America*, Michelangelo Signorile (New York: Random House 1993); *René and Me*, Gorden Kaye with Hilary Bonner (London: Pan 1990); *The Richard and Judy Story*, Carole Malone (London: Virgin 1996); *Rock Hudson: His Story*, Rock Hudson and Sara Davidson (London: Bantam 1987); *Rock Hudson Public and Private*, Mark Bego (New York: Signet 1986); *Rupert Murdoch*, William Shawcross (London: Chatto & Windus 1992); *Secret Lives*, John Sachs and Piers Morgan (London: Blake 1991); *Secrets of the*

Street: My Life as Ivy Tilsley, Lynne Perrie with Charles Yates and Clare Morrisroe (London: Blake 1994); *Soap Box*, Hilary Kingsley (London: Papermac 1988); *The Soap Opera Book of Lists*, Gerard J. Waggett (New York: HarperPaperbacks 1996); *Star Stalkers*, George Mair (New York: Pinnacle 1995); *Stick It Up Your Punter: The Rise and Fall of the Sun*, Peter Chippindale and Chris Horrie (London: Heinemann 1990); *Television's Greatest Hits*, Paul Gambaccini and Rod Taylor (London: Network Books 1993); *This Is My Life*, Malcolm Morris (London: Virgin 1996); *This Is Their Life*, Jonathan Meades (London: Salamander Books 1979); *This Is Your Life*, Roy Bottomley (London: Thames Methuen 1993); *TV Rock*, Mark Bego (Toronto: Paperjacks 1988); *TV Unforgettables*, Anthony and Deborah Hayward (Enfield: Guinness 1993); *Video Movie Guide 1997*, Mick Martin and Marsha Porter (New York: Ballantine Books 1996); *Who's Who on Television* (various edns); *The X-Rated Videotape Star Index*, Patrick Riley (New York: Prometheus Books 1994).

SOURCES

Bad Boys and Girls in Babylon

Nick Nick – Jim Davidson: *Sun* 28.5.83, 9.5.85, 19.2.94, 9.1.95, 5.8.96; *News of the World* 20.11.83, 5.5.85, 10.1.88, 26.9.93, 3.10.93, 10.10.93; *Sunday Mirror* 12.8.84, 2.7.89, 26.09.93; *Sunday Sport* 5.10.86; *Who's Really Who* (3rd Edn.), Compton Miller (London: Sphere 1987); *The Mail on Sunday You Magazine* 11.12.88; *Sport* 16.1.91; *Today* 27.10.93; *Q* January 1994; *The Full Monty*, Jim Davidson (London: Little, Brown 1993); *Daily Mirror*, 6.1.96. **The Chris Evans Story**: 'Heart Attack Tragedy of Chris Evans' Secret Love', *Daily Mirror*, 11.11.96; 'Is Ginger Losing His Charm?', *Daily Telegraph*, 2.8.96; 'Rachel's Just a Numbskull', *Sunday Mirror*, 11.9.94; 'Chris, Me and the Big Break-Up', *Daily Mail Weekend*, 28.12.96; 'Hands Up If You Think I've Lost It', *loaded*, October 1996; 'Cruel Chris Made Suzi Dress Like a Tart', *Daily Mirror*, 12.11.96; 'Return of the Cereal Killer', *Daily Mail Weekend*, 22.4.95. **Bad Grammar**: *Kelsey Grammer: The True Story*, Jeff Rovin with Kathleen Tracy and David Perrell (New York: HarperPaperbacks 1995); *Famous Mugs* (New York: Cader Books 1996); 'Cheers Shrink Parties Instead of Going to Rehab', *Star*, 22.5.90; 'Kelsey Grammer's Pregnant Wife Tries to Kill Herself', *National Enquirer*, 29.6.93; 'Kelsey Grammer Fights to Get Ex Thrown Out of U.S.', *National Enquirer*, 12.10.93; 'No Jury Indictment Against "Frasier" Star', *New York Daily News*, 25.2.95; 'My Nightmare Life with Cheating Frasier Star Kelsey', *National Enquirer*, 2.7.96; 'Kelsey Grammer's Bizarre Sex Life', *National Enquirer*, 3.12.96; 'Frasier Show in Jeopardy as Kelsey Grammer Acts Up in Rehab', *Star*, 29.10.96; 'Kelsey's Back – Alive and Kissing', *Star*, 5.11.96. **Rascally Ross**: 'My Hideous Affair with Telly Rat Ross', *News of the World*, 26.2.95; 'Life from Weetabix to *The Word*', *OK! Weekly*, 28.7.96; 'Brekkie Star's Secret Blonde', *Sun*, 13.2.95; 'Paul's Grovelling . . . But I'm Keeping the House Whatever Happens!', *Sun*, 14.2.95. **The Pop Star and the Groupie**: *Paula Yates: The Autobiography*, Paula Yates (London: HarperCollins 1995); 'Paula You're A Fibber', *Sunday Mirror*, 29.10.95; 'The Girl Can't Help It', *FHM*, July 1995; 'Hutch Cheated on Me with Paula 7 Years Ago', *News of the World*, 26.3.95; 'Paula Took Fertility Drugs to Ensnare Hutchence', *Daily Mail*, 26.10.96; 'Cheating Nights in Michael's Suite', *News of the World*, 12.2.95; 'I Had That Paula Yates Bonking in the Back of My Cab', *News of the World*, 12.2.95; 'How the Helena Could You

Hutch!', *Sun*, 25.3.95; 'Appalling Yates', *Sun*, 23.11.95; 'The Phoney War', *Daily Mirror*, 8.1.96; 'I'll Love You Forever', *Sun*, 13.6.96; 'Geldof Goes to Court for His Kids', *Sun*, 27.9.96; 'I Saw Paula Buy That Opium', *News of the World*, 29.9.96.

Booze & Drugs in Babylon

Uncle Frank & the Cocaine Orgies: *News of the World*, 29.5.88, 5.6.88; *Daily Mirror*, 6.6.88, 3.12.88, 31.8.92, 2.9.92; *Sunday Mirror*, 30.8.92; *Exposed!*, Gerry Brown (London: Virgin 1995). **Cheggers Drinks Pop**: 'Cheggers Drinks Pop', *loaded*, December 1995; **Out of the Shadows of Gladiators**: *Sunday Mirror*, 29.1.95; 'Shadow Beat Me Senseless', *Sunday Mirror*, 5.2.95; *News of the World*, 5.2.95; 'Shadow in Strip Sleaze', *Daily Mirror*, 19.1.96. **Awight? No! The Story of a Tormented Genius**: 'Cheryl's Uncle Was on the Show . . . He Had to Pretend He Didn't Know Michael', *Sunday Mirror*, 20.8.95; 'End This Evil Barry-War', *Sun*, 13.4.95; 'You're All Invited Back to My Place for a Party', *News of the World*, 20.8.95; 'Barrymore Threw Off His Wedding Ring Then Crooned: "Start spreadin' the news, I'm g-a-a-y today!"', *Sun*, 21.8.95; 'Barrymore Axed', *News of the World*, 19.1.97. **Making an Impression – Mike Yarwood**: 'The Girls Who Saved Mike Yarwood's Life', *Daily Mail*, 10.1.94; 'Every Day I Yearn for My Ex-Wife', *Sun*, 7.1.91; 'The Fight to Save Mike, by Ex-Wife', *Daily Express*, 23.3.89; 'TV Yarwood in New Health Drama', *Daily Mirror*, 21.5.90; 'Heart-Attack Mike Won't Get Wife Back', *Daily Mirror*, 11.7.90. **Oprah's Drug Confession**: 'Oprah Admits: I Smoked Cocaine', *Daily Express*, 14.1.95; 'Oprah Drug Nightmare', *Star*, 31.1.95. **Devine Intervention**: 'I Was Saved from Drugs Hell by BBC', *Today*, 29.3.93.

Crime in Babylon

'Allo, 'Allo, 'Allo – Good Morning with Richard and Judy: 'Squalid Quiz That OJ Wasn't Allowed to Answer', *Daily Express*, 14.5.96; *The Richard and Judy Story*, Carole Malone (London: Virgin 1996); 'Richard and Rudy Show', *Sun*, 11.2.95; **The Fear of Stalkers**: 'In Fear of the *Street* Stalker', *OK! Magazine*, December 1995; 'My Thug Girl Hell by *Street* Star Maxine', *Daily Star*, 28.6.96; 'Game Girl', *For Him Magazine*, July 1996; 'Gender Bender Stalks EastEnder', *News of the World*, 10.12.95; *Famous Mugs* (New York: Cader Books 1996); *Dynasty* Star Secretly Weds Gal Who Helped Him Survive Stalking Charges', *National Enquirer*, 27.9.94; 'TV Beauty Trapped Stalker Who Made Her Life Hell', *News of the World*, 13.10.95; '"This Stalker Has Caused Me 5 Years of Misery," by Helena Bonham Carter', *Today*, 19.2.93; 'Terrorized By a Pervert', *Daily Mirror*, 4.12.96. **Fry's Porridge**: *Mostly Men*, Lynne Barber (London: Viking 1991); 'If You're Going to Be Smug, Why Not Go All the Way', *Sunday Times*, 2.10.94. **In the Drink**: 'Swim Star Sharron Nicked for Driving Con', *Sun*,

17.1.95. **Woody or Woodyn't He?**: 'Woody Harrelson Vows: I'm Gonna Free My Murder-Rap Dad', *National Enquirer*, 27.9.94; 'Screen Killer Had Me Scared', *News of the World Sunday Magazine*, 13.11.94; *Mug Shots*, George Seminara (New York: St Martin's Griffin 1996).

Sir Jimmy Savile, OBE, KCSG

'His Mother Died 23 Years Ago but He Still Cleans Her Clothes and Says She's at Home', *Daily Mail*, 2.11.96; 'My Violent World, by the Godfather', *Sun*, 11.4.83; 'Who the Hell Does Sir Jimmy Savile Think He Is?', *Q*, November 1990; *Mostly Men*, Lynne Barber (London: Viking 1991); Don't Care', *Daily Mail* 8.1.94; *I'll Tell the Jokes, Arthur*, Arthur Edwards (London: Blake 1993); *This Is Their Life*, Jonathan Meades (London: Salamander 1979).

Feuds in Babylon

Holmes v. Turner: 'I Told the TV Chiefs It Was Her or Me . . . They Chose Me', *Sunday Mirror*, 29.12.96; 'Holmes Carpeted over Anthea', *Daily Mail*, 2.1.97; 'I Watched Eamonn Making Anthea's Life Hell', *Sun*, 2.1.97. **Motormouth v. the Mancunian**: 'Mark Is Having the Last Word', *Daily Mail*, 23.4.93; 'How Terry Had the Last Laugh with Motormouth Mark', *Daily Mirror*, 1.12.94; 'I Was the Most Hated Host on TV', *Sunday Mirror*, 22.12.96; 'My Girlfriend Thinks I'm a Pain in the A***', *News of the World*, 15.1.95. **The Big Brek-feud**: 'My Big Break', *Sun*, 4.10.95; 'Why Zoë Is Having a Ball', *Daily Mail Weekend*, 16.11.96. **Kelvin MacFrenzy v. Jahnet Street-Pawta**: *Stick It Up Your Punter*, Peter Chippindale and Chris Horrie (London: William Heinemann 1990); *Rupert Murdoch*, William Shawcross (London: Chatto & Windus 1992); *Daily Mail*, 13.9.95; 'Street-Porter Moves', *The Times*, 22.9.94; *The Times*, 26.8.95.

Money in Babylon

Ken Dodd v. the Inland Revenue: 'Tax Probe Doddy's Stage Tears', *Sun*, 8.6.88; 'Comic Doddy "Fiddled His Tax for 15 Years"', *Daily Mirror*, 9.6.88; 'Doddy's Passport Seized', *Daily Mail*, 11.8.88; 'Sick Doddy May Never Star in a Show Again', *Sun*, 7.6.89; '"Diddy Doddy's £700,000 Diddling"', *Daily Mirror*, 20.6.89; 'Millionaire Doddy's Life on the Cheap', *Daily Mirror*, 21.6.89; '"Ruthless Doddy Told Me To Diddle The Taxman"', *Daily Mirror*, 5.7.89; 'Why I Kept £300,000 in the Loft, by Doddy', *Daily Mirror*, 8.7.89; 'Agony of Doddy's Fight to be a Dad', *Daily Mirror*, 11.7.89.

Sex in Babylon

Pammy & Tommy: 'The Budding Pamela', *Sun*, 17.6.95; 'Pam Tied a Napkin on Her Head and Led Us Dancing around the Room', *Today*, 6.6.95; 'Compared to Some of the Girls I Know . . . I'm a SAINT!' *Sun*, 13.2.95; 'There Are Many Nights I Go to Bed Alone and Wish I Had a Guy to Hold Me', *Sun*, 14.2.95; 'Pamela Used Me as Her Sex Toy', *News of the World*, 4.6.95; *The Guinness Book of Rock Stars*, Dafydd Rees and Luke Crampton (Enfield: Guinness Publishing 1994); *The Q Encyclopedia of Rock Stars*, Dafydd Rees and Luke Crampton (London: Dorling Kindersley 1996); 'Pam Stole My Looks, My Body and My Tommy', *News of the World*, 26.2.95; 'We Made Our Home into the Palace of Love', *Sun*, 2.5.95; 'Pamela Outraged as Private Sex Pictures Are Passed Round Hollywood', *Today*, 30.4.95; 'Diary of Love on the Rocks', *Daily Mirror*, 21.11.96; 'I'm Desperate to Have Tommy's Babies . . . I've Picked the Names', *Sun*, 4.5.95; Private information; 'Tommy Beat Me Up and Made Me His Sex Toy', *Daily Mirror*, 21.11.96; 'Spend Spend Spend Pam Will Make Tightwad Tommy Pay', *Daily Star*, 25.11.96; *The X-Rated Videotape Star Index*, Patrick Riley (New York: Prometheus Books 1994); 'We Made Love on Pam's Piano', *News of the World*, 24.11.96. **Ulrika, the Cameraman and the Gladiator**: 'One of the Boys', *Night and Day*, 2.6.96; 'Ulrika in Split on Baby's 1st Birthday', *Sun*, 19.10.95; 'I Married to Stick My Tattered Life Together', *Daily Mirror*, 26.10.93; 'Ulrika Has Ditched Me and Now I'm Devastated', *Daily Express*, 25.10.93; 'I Was Attracted to Another Man. Nobody Put a gun to My Head . . . When I Told John His Life Fell Apart', *Daily Mirror*, 25.10.93; 'Why It's Happy Ever After for Ulrika Jonsson', *OK! Magazine*, February 1995; 'Ulrika's "Warm" Love for Hunter', *Here!*, 15.7.96; 'Divorce for TV's Ulrika', *News of the World*, 5.5.96; 'My Gladiator Muscled In on Love', *News of the World Sunday Magazine*, 13.3.94; 'My Lust for Telly Ulrika', *Sun*, 2.12.95; 'We Know Where You've Just Bin to Get That BIG Grin!', *Sun*, 28.12.95; 'Why I Told Hunter to Jet Out of My Life', *News of the World Sunday Magazine*, 7.7.96; 'Eureka! Ulrika's Found the Best of Both Worlds', *Daily Mail*, 4.11.96; 'Absolut Ulrika', *FHM*, February 1996; 'Funny Side Up', *The Express Saturday*, 5–11.10.96; 'I Wept The Day Mum Walked Away', *News of the World Sunday Magazine*, 29.3.92. **The Truth Is Here – The Se-X File**: 'Jailed and Treated Like an Alien Just for Being a Punk', *Daily Mirror*, 20.5.96; '10 Things That Give Scully X Appeal', *Sun*, 7.9.96; 'I Cheated on the World's Sexiest Woman', *Daily Mirror*, 9.9.96. **The Downfall of Jason King**: 'King Jason Rules Again', *Daily Star*, 19.11.83; *Sun* 18.10.75. **The Weathergirl & the Cad**: 'Telly Sally Had "Dirty Weekend with Di's Brother"', *News of the World*, 19.12.93; *The Times*, 17.10.88; *Dod's Parliamentary Companion* 1994 (London: D.P.C. 1994); *In for a Penny: The Unauthorised Biography of Jeffrey Archer*, Jonathan Mantle (London: Hamish Hamilton 1988); *Britain's Top 100 Eligible Bachelors*, Nesta Wyn Ellis (London: Blake 1994); 'MP Names Hewitt as He Divorces TV Girl Sally', *Daily Mail*, 17.5.96; *Diana Confidential*, Chris

Hutchins and Peter Thompson (London: Pocket Books 1994); 'Eclipse of the Moone?', *Daily Mail*, 15.7.92; 'The Eye for Di', *Daily Star*, 26.7.96; 'Operation Send-up', *Daily Mail*, 26.7.96. **Gorden & the Rent Boys**: 'My Life without Women', *Sunday People*, 3.11.85; 'My Rent Boy Secrets', *Daily Mirror*, 21.1.89; 'Tormented Tragic Life of René', *Daily Mirror*, 21.1.89. **Mariella Frostrup – the Voice**: 'Room of My Own', *Observer Magazine*, 28.3.93; *News of the World*, 24.10.93; 'Mariella Dumps Men', *Today*, 24.9.94. *Blind Date*, **the Porn Star & the Vicar**: 'Cilla's Porn Date', *Sunday Mirror*, 29.10.95; 'My Blind Date Vicar Was Too Font of Hymnself', *Sun*, 2.2.95; 'A Lamb to the Slaughter', *Daily Mail*, 4.2.95. **A Fair Cop!**: 'I Grew Up in Mum's Wardrobe', *Sunday Mirror*, 4.12.94; 'He Has Corrupted Her', *Sunday Mirror*, 18.2.96; '*Bill* Star In Secret Sex and Drugs Shame', *News of the World*, 11.2.96. **It's a Gay Old World**: 'This Is My Gay Life', *Daily Mirror*, 13.10.89; 'EastEnder Pat Comes Out of Closet', *Sun*, 10.1.91; 'EastEnd Pam Left Me for Another Woman', *News of the World*, 1.10.95; 'Bet Lynch's Hubby Is Gay', *People*, 2.4.89; '*Brookside* Jim in Gay Snaps Scandal', *News of the World*, 30.7.95; 'The 1995 Out 100', *Out*, December 1995/January 1996; 'If You're Going to Be Smug, Why Not Go All the Way', *Sunday Times*, 2.10.94; *Mostly Men*, Lynne Barber (London: Viking 1991); 'Cher's Lesbian Secrets', *Star*, 30.7.96; 'Kinky Sex Fantasies of Mystic Meg', *Daily Star*, 12.11.96. **Samantha Janus**: 'Sam: I'm Not As Easy As I Look', *Daily Mirror TV Weekly*, 25.2–3.3.95; 'Broke Sam Sold Her Dog for 50p', *Sun TV SuperGuide*, 4.5.91; 'Game Girl', *FHM*, July 1996. **Till Fame Us Do Part**: 'Be Happy With Your New Love, Says Eamonn's Wife', *Here!*, 4.11.96; '*Bill* Star Ditches Wife and Three Babies', *Sunday Mirror*, 28.5.95; 'He Left Lizzie for Another Woman but Now Michael is Home Alone', *Sunday Mirror*, 30.10.94; 'Hollywood Wrecked My Marriage', *Daily Express*, 16.2.96.

Soaps in Babylon

Fort Knox: 'Born on the Wrong Side of the Street', *Sunday Mirror*, 9.5.93; 'Sad Rita in Split from Hubby', *Sun*, 21.1.95. **Beautiful Bev**: '*Street* Liz's Love Split', *Daily Mirror*, 22.7.93; 'They Kissed and Cuddled Like a Couple of Lovebirds', *Sunday Mirror*, 26.2.95. **Good-time Charlie**: 'My Cocaine and Booze Shame', *Daily Mirror*, 4.11.96; 'Meet the Mistress', *Sunday Mirror*, 21.8.94; *Secrets of the Street*, Lynne Perrie with Charles Yates and Clare Morrisroe (London: Blake 1994); 'I'm About to Divorce the Man I Love', *Sun*, 2.3.96; 'It's Agony, but I Can't Give Up Watching My Love Cheat Husband in the *Street*', *Sunday Mirror*, 23.4.95. **Curvy Chloe**: 'Coronation Cheek', *Sun*, 17.8.95; 'Ecstasy Shame of *Street* Star Vicky', *News of the World*, 6.8.95; 'Hollywood? No Thanks, They'd Want to Rearrange My Body', *News of the World Sunday Magazine*, 12.5.96. **Eve of Destruction**: 'All About Eve', *OK! Weekly*, 18.8.96; '*Street* Fighter', *Sky Magazine*, February 1997; 'The Secret Heroin Hell of New *Street* Star Eve',

Sunday Mirror, 5.5.96. **She Ain't Heavey, She's Anorexic**: 'In Fear of the *Street* Stalker', *OK! Magazine*, December 1995; 'My Secret Life as a Shoplifter', *People*, 26.5.96; 'Max Power', *Daily Star*, 26.11.96; '*Street* Star Tracy's Cocaine Romp with Hunk', *News of the World*, 2.6.96; 'Jealousy-Crazed Girl's Threat to Shoot Me', *Daily Mirror*, 26.11.86. **Oh, Julie!**: 'I Was Left Holding Baby As She Dated Other Men', *Sunday Mirror*, 28.5.95; *Queen of the Street*, Sally Beck (London: Blake 1995); 'Why It's Been 25 Good Years for Julie', *OK! Magazine*, August 1995; *Soapbox*, Hilary Kingsley (Papermac 1988); 'TV Bet Told Me She Was Gay, Says Fred Feast', *Sun*, 2.10.86; 'Julie's Long-Range Love Is a Flop', *Daily Mirror*, 2.5.86; 'Julie's Ex Took His Bitterness to the Grave', *Sunday Mirror*, 13.5.90; 'Oh Julie, These Lovely Pictures Broke Your Old Dad's Heart', *Sunday Mirror*, 26.6.94. **Poison Ivy**: *Secrets of the* Street: *My Life As Ivy Tilsley*, Lynne Perrie with Charles Yates and Clare Morrisroe (London: Blake 1994); 'I'd Go for Any Fella Who Was a Bit Younger. I Wasn't Fussy . . . Just Horny All of the Time', *Sun*, 23.8.94; 'We're All Quaking Says "Poison" Ivy', *Revue*, 16.7.83; '*Street* Star Ivy Finds Love in Paradise', *Sun*, 9.11.83; 'I Blew £200,000 in Casinos', *Daily Mirror*, 12.1.88; 'Secret Turmoil of *Street*'s Ivy', *Sunday Mirror*, 11.8.91; 'I Wanted to Go On TV to Sing "I Will Survive" but I Just Felt Under Too Much Pressure to Sing', *Sunday Mirror*, 4.12.94; 'Perrie's Too Merry', *News of the World*, 4.12.94; 'I'm No Drunk and the *Street* Didn't Fire Me', *Daily Express*, 3.2.95. **Simple Simon**: 'Dear Steve, Please Wear My Knickers', *Sunday Mirror Magazine*, 17.4.94; 'My Monster Nights of Lust in *Street* Star's Loch Ness Love Nest', *News of the World*, 24.11.96. *Emmerdale*: 'Animal Lust made *Farm* Star a Cheating Pig', *News of the World*, 19.3.95; 'I Won't Let Mad Axeman Play Mummies and Baddies', *News of the World*, 15.12.96; 'Emmerdale Tina is Having Mad Axeman's Baby', *News of the World*, 13.10.96. **French with Tears**: 'Romeo EastEnder French Named in Co-Star Divorce', *Sunday Mirror*, 25.2.96; 'Soap Hunk's Gay Secret', *Sunday Mirror*, 24.3.96; 'How Dirty David Took Drugs Till He Dropped, Groped Me and Then Had Sex with My Wife', *Sunday Mirror*, 24.11.95. **The Ballad of Spotty Gaffney**: *Sunday Mirror*, 31.12.95; 'I'm So Proud of My Little Albert Pair', *News of the World*, 21.7.96; 'My Dean Says He'll Wait 10 Years to Get His Ender Away With Me!', *Sun* 2.1.96; *Sun*, 4.1.96; 'Naked EastEnder Wanted 5-in-Bed Bender', *News of the World*, 7.7.96. **Gilly, the A1 Lay-by & the Thug**: 'As Long As They Need Her . . .', *Evening Standard*, 1.2.95; '*EastEnders* Star No. 3 in Drink-Drive Shame', *Sun*, 17.5.96; 'That Bloody Cabbie Got What He Deserved', *News of the World*, 8.10.95; 'Gillian's Big Knights Out', *Daily Mirror*, 22.8.95. **Having Your Phil**: 'Deadender to EastEnder', *News of the World*, 12.5.96; 'EastEnd Phil's Secret Life of Crime', *News of the World*, 5.5.96; 'I Perched on Window Ledge in My Pants as Police Hunted Me', *News of the World*, 5.5.96; 'EastEnder Serviced Me in His Pokey Passion Wagon', *News of the World*, 4.9.94; 'EastEnder Phil Had Wicked Way with Me, Too!', *News of the World*, 11.9.94; 'We've All Been Serviced by the *EastEnders* Mechanic Too!', *News of the World*, 18.9.94; 'Thug Was Out to

Kill Me', *News of the World*, 25.9.94; '*EastEnders* Star No. 3 in Drink-Drive Shame', *Sun*, 17.5.96. **The Punk & the Café Owner**: '*EastEnders* Stars Watched in Silence as Nejdet Punched Me', *Sun*, 4.8.94. **The Pop Star & the Actress**: *loaded*, May 1996; 'I Tried to Kill Myself', *Sunday Mirror*, 26.2.95; 'Dangley-Ella Hangs Out of Window in 2 a.m. Love Bust-up', *Sun*, 19.1.95; 'Don't Call Me a Wild Child', *Sunday Mirror*, 8.1.95; 'The Newly-Wads', *News of the World*, 8.1.95; 'TV Daniella (*sic*) "Jumped 999 Docs' Queue"', *Daily Mirror*, 20.2.95; '*EastEnders* Danniella Fleeced Me to Feed Her Drug Habit', *Sun*, 27.10.95; 'To Think I Almost Married Danniella Westbrook', *Here!*, 11.11.96; *The Q Encyclopedia of Rock Stars*, Dafydd Rees & Luke Crampton (London: Dorling Kindersley 1996); 'There's No Ender Madness with Bad Girl Danniella', *News of the World*, 11.2.96; 'It's Danniella's Bottom Line', *Sunday Mirror*, 14.1.96; 'Soap Vixen's Sex Romps with Jailed Mr Big', *News of the World*, 25.2.96. **Murder of a Taxi Driver**: *The Leslie Grantham Story*, Jean Ritchie (London: Angus & Robertson 1989).

Stupidity in Babylon

Bill Grundy & the Sex Pistols: 'A Bit Strong for Tea', *Sunday Times Magazine*, 1.3.87.